"What I love about this book is the
early Christian forebears in the sec(
missing them as theological children   ...orld have
done—he takes them seriously as c   partners about that most
vital of subjects: How should we live God-glorifying lives in an increasingly
pagan culture? His answers, though drawn from the riches of our Christian
past, are not at all escapist or antiquarian but take into consideration the
contours of the present. No easy task to relate that far-off world of late antiquity to our so-called postmodern West, but Presley does it with scholarly
depth and literary verve."

—Michael A. G. Azad Haykin
The Southern Baptist Theological Seminary

"Stephen Presley offers us a wonderfully profound and broad sketch of how
Christians of the first centuries, living before Christendom, comported themselves
within the world: one that was neither flight nor fight, as are often assumed to
be the only alternatives available in today's post-Christendom world, but one of
cultural sanctification, pilgrims transforming the world in which they lived, for the
better. The rich resources of this period of Christian history are drawn upon not as
an exercise in archaeology but as one that has much to offer us as we continue the
task today, so that we can do so, as the last chapter concludes, with hope."

—John Behr
University of Aberdeen

"Engulfed by an increasingly paganized culture, Christians often perceive a
desperate choice between fight and flight. Should Christians struggle to recap-
ture politics and culture, or rather retreat to the catacombs? In *Cultural Sanctification*, Stephen O. Presley presents a compelling and practical alternative
to the extreme options by looking closely at how Christians in late antiquity
lived within the pagan world of their own times—namely, through faithful engagement with that world. Erudite but clearly and engagingly written, *Cultural
Sanctification* is informative, insightful, even inspiring, and it culminates in the
Christian virtue so desperately needed today—hope."

—Steven Smith
University of San Diego

"Christians anxious about an increasingly pagan culture have many reasons to be encouraged. One of them is that Christ's church has already experienced such a trial and has left us extensive evidence of how it responded. Stephen Presley has done honorable service for contemporary Christians by presenting the early church's wisdom in confronting and engaging its own pagan culture. Presley helps us see an attractive, godly, and productive way forward that provides a strong remedy for the bitterness and discouragement many Christians feel today as they survey their cultural landscape."

—**David VanDrunen**
Westminster Seminary California

CULTURAL SANCTIFICATION

Engaging the World like the Early Church

Stephen O. Presley

WILLIAM B. EERDMANS PUBLISHING COMPANY

GRAND RAPIDS, MICHIGAN

Wm. B. Eerdmans Publishing Co.
4035 Park East Court SE, Grand Rapids, Michigan 49546
www.eerdmans.com

Book design by Lydia Hall

Printed in the United States of America

30 29 28 27 26 25 24   1 2 3 4 5 6 7

ISBN 978-0-8028-7854-0

Library of Congress Cataloging-in-Publication Data

A catalog record for this book is available from the Library of Congress.

Contents

Abbreviations

1 Apol.	Justin, *First Apology*
2 Apol.	Justin, *Second Apology*
1 Clem.	1 Clement
2 Clem.	2 Clement
Adv. nat.	Arnobius, *Case against the Pagans*
Ann.	Tacitus, *Annals*
Apol.	Aristides, *Apology*; Tertullian, *Apology*
Autol.	Theophilus, *To Autolycus*
Bapt.	Tertullian, *Baptism*
Barn.	Epistle of Barnabas
Catech.	Augustine, *Catechizing the Uninstructed*
Cels.	Origen, *Against Celsus*
Civ.	Augustine, *City of God*
Comm. cant.	Origen, *Commentary on Song of Songs*
Comm. Dan.	Hippolytus, *Commentary on Daniel*
Comm. Rom.	Origen, *Commentary on Romans*
Conf.	Augustine, *Confessions*
Cor.	Tertullian, *The Crown*
Dial.	Justin, *Dialogue with Trypho*
Did.	Didache
Diogn.	Epistle to Diognetus

Disp.	Archelaus, *Acts of the Disputation with Manes*
Doctr. chr.	Augustine, *Christian Instruction*
Don.	Cyprian, *To Donatus*
Ep. Greg.	Origen, *Letter to Gregory the Wonderworker*
Epid.	Irenaeus, *Demonstration of the Apostolic Preaching*
Exh. cast.	Tertullian, *Exhortation to Chastity*
Fug.	Tertullian, *Flight in Persecution*
Haer.	Irenaeus, *Against Heresies*
Herm. Vis.	Shepherd of Hermas, Vision(s)
Hist. eccl.	Eusebius, *Ecclesiastical History*
Hom. Ps.	Origen, *Homilies on the Psalms*
Idol.	Tertullian, *Idolatry*
Inst.	Lactantius, *The Divine Institutes*
Jejun.	Tertullian, *On Fasting, against the Psychics*
Leg.	Athenagoras, *Embassy for the Christians*
Marc.	Tertullian, *Against Marcion*
Mart. Pol.	Martyrdom of Polycarp
Med.	Marcus Aurelius, *Meditations*
Mon.	Tertullian, *Monogamy*
Oct.	Minucius Felix, *Octavius*
Or.	Tertullian, *Prayer*
Orat. paneg.	Gregory the Wonderworker, *Address of Gratitude to Origen*
Paed.	Clement of Alexandria, *Christ the Educator*
Pan.	Epiphanius, *Refutation of All Heresies*
Pat.	Cyprian, *The Advantage of Patience*; Origen, *The Advantage of Patience*; Tertullian, *Patience*
Peregr.	Lucian, *The Passing of Peregrinus*
Philoc.	Origen, *Philocalia*
Poet.	Aristotle, *Poetics*
Pol. *Phil.*	Polycarp, *To the Philippians*
Praescr.	Tertullian, *Prescription against Heretics*
Prax.	Tertullian, *Against Praxeas*
Princ.	Origen, *First Principles*
Protr.	Clement of Alexandria, *Exhortation to the Greeks*
Pud.	Tertullian, *Modesty*

Res.	Athenagoras, *On the Resurrection*
Spec.	Tertullian, *The Shows*
Strom.	Clement of Alexandria, *Miscellanies*
Trad. ap.	Hippolytus, *The Apostolic Tradition*
Ux.	Tertullian, *To His Wife*
Virg.	Tertullian, *The Veiling of Virgins*
Vit. Const.	Eusebius, *Life of Constantine*

INTRODUCTION

The Lateran Baptistery

The eager taxi driver met us at the front door of the hotel and ushered us into his car. My friend and I explained that we were headed to the Archbasilica of Saint John Lateran. He whisked around the circle drive and began weaving through the old Roman streets like an experienced race-car driver. While the scenery whizzed by, we exchanged pleasantries. I told the driver that we were professors of early Christianity and in town to visit a few historic sites. The driver smiled and began gesturing at the important buildings we passed, while offering some lively commentary. Rome, the ancient imperial city, is filled with many wonderful vestiges of its Christian past.

The church of Saint John Lateran, located on Caelian Hill just inside the ancient Aurelian Walls, is built on the site of an old fort established by the Roman emperor Septimius Severus (193–211) in 193.[1] Many years later, much of the garrison was destroyed during the emperor Constantine's rise to power. After he defeated Maxentius at the Battle of the Milvian Bridge (312), Constantine donated the property to Silvester, the bishop of Rome (314–335), for the construction of a basilica, palace, and baptistery.[2] This gift was not only one of the first Christian building projects funded by Constantine, it was also strategic; it simultaneously fulfilled the pledge he made to God just before his military victory and positioned the Christian community on the outskirts of the city, away from the pagan political powers.[3] In this place, the church began taking some initial steps toward building Christendom.

1

The church itself was not our primary destination, however; we were headed to an ancient building adjacent to it: the Lateran Baptistery.[4] Here one of the oldest baptismal fonts in the world stands tucked away behind the imposing basilica. It was built in a unique octagonal shape by Sixtus III (432–440) upon the foundation of a similar structure that dates back much earlier, perhaps even upon the baths of a private *domus* that may have some connection with the home of the bishop of Rome.[5] When Sixtus became bishop in the years following the sack of Rome in 410, he initiated a prolific restoration campaign throughout the city to resurrect the image and power of imperial Rome. In the budding age of Christendom, the church was flooded with many new converts and needed buildings like this to facilitate their baptisms. These were important years before Leo the Great helped solidify the power of the papal office in the early medieval period and set the stage for the rise of Christendom in the West.[6]

As we entered, the building was as still and silent as the dead of night. A large circular marble baptistery immediately greeted us, situated in the center of the room like a stage in a theater-in-the-round. The basin of the baptistery measures almost twenty-eight feet in diameter, roughly the size of a small backyard swimming pool, and was deep enough to submerge an adult.[7] A waist-high railing encircles the font, with two entrances on opposing sides. In front of each entrance are steps leading down into the basin where the catechumens could enter and exit. Above the pool rises a two-story octagonal colonnade consisting of eight dark purple marble columns staged evenly around the basin and topped with a marble entablature. Standing atop those columns are eight smaller white marble columns that supported a central vault with a dove in the center symbolizing the descent of the Spirit. The *Book of Pontiffs* describes the gifts Constantine donated to decorate the baptistery, including the images of John the Baptist and Christ, along with a golden lamb and seven silver stags.[8]

We walked slowly around the font in quiet contemplation, examining every feature. I considered how faithful catechumens preparing for baptism would have paraded into this building early on Easter Sunday morning. They would have assembled in the western ambulatory and slowly made their way down into the water.[9] Then, one by one, they would confess their faith before the gathered community. Their baptism signified that they were no longer born merely of the flesh but of the will of God, and the church, standing around in confirmation, would welcome each new convert into the family of God.

Maybe I was just dizzy with jetlag or hopped up on three shots of strong Italian espresso, but the brilliance of the space was overwhelming. I pondered the fact that early Christians, possibly as early as the third century, had been coming to this place to mark their transition from the kingdom of darkness to the kingdom of light.

Sixtus understood the significance of this place. While refurnishing the building, he had a series of inscriptions consisting of eight distiches chiseled into the marble entablature above the purple colonnade. These lines commemorated the ultimate triumph of Christianity over the empire:

> Here is born from life-giving seed a people, consecrated
>   to another city, whom the Spirit brings forth from the
>   fertile waters.
> To plunge in the holy purifying flood the sinner, whom the wave
>   receives as old but gives forth as new.
> None reborn is different from those it makes one, one font, one
>   Spirit, one faith.
> Mother church as a virgin brought forth those who are born,
>   whom she conceived by the divine breath and brought into
>   being in the flowing water.
> The person who wants to be innocent is here made clean
>   by washing, whether from the guilt of the first parent or
>   one's own.
> Here is the font of life which bathes the whole world, its ultimate
>   source the side of Christ wounded.
> Reborn in this font for the kingdom of heaven, the blessed life
>   does not receive those born only once.
> Be not afraid of the number or kind of your sins, for the one born
>   in this river will be holy.[10]

The first line of the inscription is positioned strategically above the gate where the catechumens would enter the baptistery, with the rest of the inscription encircling the marble entablature. As they entered the pool, the catechumens could easily look up and read the initial phrase, "Here is born from life-giving seed a people, consecrated to another city, whom the Spirit brings forth from the fertile waters."

In that moment, I wondered how a tiny, marginalized Jewish sect managed to become the primary religion of the empire. I walked to the entrance of the baptistery and stood gazing down into the waterless pool. I imagined how many had eagerly come to this very spot. They stepped down into the waters and emerged with a new identity, a new citizenship, a new life born again to walk in conformity to the likeness of Christ, and a new hope to guide them home. This did not mean that they ceased to be Roman but that their Roman identity, with all its social and political entailments, was now refracted through a more fundamental devotion to the King of kings and Lord of lords.

Standing there in the entrance to the empty Lateran Baptistery, I was reminded that the church in the West has reached a similar crossroads but from the opposite direction. The building was, after all, empty. This place, once alive with zealous converts seeking baptism, now lay in silence. No catechumens. No disciples. Just a hollow building with the decaying relics of a lost age. I could hear the faint sounds of the bustling Italian city life outside: cars passing, horns honking, voices shouting, and pedestrians hurrying on to some important destination. The noises filtered in and echoed through the cavernous space. Just then, a few people wandered in, disturbing the silence, but none of them were seeking baptism. Like us, they were just entering a museum to gaze at the ruins of a lost Christendom. No one was coming to join the church. The irony was not lost on me. The world that gave life to this building is gone, and now a renewed secular world once again surrounds it. A haunting reminder that we are back where we started.

We Are the Ancients

As many have observed, there is no longer any debate about the future of the West; it is becoming secular at a steady pace that seems unlikely to turn any time soon.[11] The precise meaning of the term "secular," though, has been a point of much discussion. Philosopher Charles Taylor helpfully frames the definition in three senses. In the first instance, secularity refers to the "common institutions and practices" or public spaces. In this sense, unlike premodern society where religion was the thread that held the fabric of culture together, today churches are entirely separate from political institutions and public activities. One can be fully engaged in society and never encounter reference to God. A second sense refers to the people, not merely the institutions, and the mass deconversion of Western societies away from God. The culture may retain vestiges of its Christian past infused in the political proceedings or cultural events, but they are inconsequential to public life. People simply do not care to believe in God. A third sense, which is connected to the previous two, argues that in a postmodern society, secularity "is a matter of the whole context of understanding in which our moral, spiritual or religious experience and search takes place." According to Taylor, ours is a secular age in search of the moral and spiritual good but not frequently finding it in Christianity or any other traditional religious communities for that matter. This postmodern age recognizes that all moral commitments come with assumptions that inform their social expressions so that, in a sense, everyone is secular, and the public square is filled with a range of moralities competing for the same cultural real estate. Christianity is merely one perspective on life, or what Taylor calls a "social imaginary," among many. Secularity in this third sense, in the words of Taylor, "consists, among other things, of a move from a society where belief in God is unchallenged and indeed, unproblematic, to one in which it is understood to be one option among others, and frequently not the easiest to embrace." Taylor warns that secularity in this third sense means that belief in God is not axiomatic and "it may be hard to sustain one's faith" amid the competing alternatives.[12]

In this context, Christianity faces a new and dramatic challenge. We are no longer living in a modern world where Christianity is intellectually suspect but morally acceptable. We are now in a postmodern world where Christianity is rejected as morally bankrupt (and most of the time still intellectually suspect). In other words, Christianity is not sidelined anymore because it is religious but because its moral claims frequently run contrary to new expressions of social progress and moral diversity. While many moral expressions are applauded in the public square, traditional Christian morality is not often discussed in polite company.

Carl Trueman, building upon Taylor and others, labels this secular moment as the triumph of "expressive individualism," which privileges internal feelings over external norms.[13] Trueman helps diagnose our perilous condition, but most intriguing are his closing lines where he recognizes the resonances between the ancient and postmodern worlds: "we are now living in the second century," he says.[14] We have regressed back to the days before Constantine when pagans held political and social power and wielded it over the church.

Back to the days when the honorable Roman populace filled the amphitheaters to cheer on the suppression of Christianity. Like the quiet irony of the empty Lateran Baptistery surrounded by vibrant cultural life, many have observed that the secular turn described by Taylor and Trueman can feel like a return to the *sitz im Leben* of the ancient Roman world.

Trueman has plenty of company. The British political commentator Ferdinand Mount, for example, declares, "God's long funeral is over, and we are back where we started. . . . We have returned to Year Zero, AD 0, or rather 0 CE, because we are in the Common Era now, the Years of Our Lord have expired."[15] Mount continues, "our present habits, our enthusiasm, our preoccupations and world-view don't just carry in them some interesting traces of the civilization that crumbled when Rome crumbled. In a weird, but exact way, they often *reproduce* the mindsets of Rome under early emperors." In other words, "we *are* them and they are us."[16] Christendom is gone, and a new world has emerged, only with a feeling of déjà vu, like a return to a childhood home after a long journey.

For Mount, like Taylor and Trueman, the road leading back to Rome was predicted years ago by philosophers such as Nietzsche who celebrated a world where secularists excommunicate anyone who does not worship at one of their many altars.[17] Nietzsche's vision did not come true as he expected, however, because the post-Christian utopia never emerged. Instead, we see a return to the past. In one insightful paragraph, Mount lays out the parallels between the ancient and postmodern worlds:

> By the time of the Antonine emperors in the second century AD—that period which Gibbon regarded as the summit of human felicity—Rome was a ferment of religious choice. You could believe in anything or nothing. You could put your trust in astrologers, snake-charmers, prophets and diviners and magicians; you could take your pick between half a dozen creation myths and several varieties of resurrection. Or if you belonged to the educated elite, you could read the poetry of Lucretius and subscribe to a strictly materialist description of the universe. In short, this is a time when anything goes and the weirdest, most frenzied creations of the human mind jostle with the most beautiful visions, the most inspiring spiritual challenges and the most challenging lines of scientific inquiry. It is hard to think of any period quite like it, before or since—until our own time.[18]

The words "until our own time" hang like a cloud over the rest of Mount's work. Each page is filled with resonances and startling connections between the ancient world and today. There is no shortage of common assumptions between modern and ancient views of the human body, sex, domestic life, science, religion, celebrity, art, and nature. Even if some of these connections are less convincing and the danger of anachronism looms, the parallels are unmistakable.[19]

More recently, University of San Diego law professor Steven Smith puts a different twist on the matter in his book, *Pagans and Christians in the City*. Smith posits that our cultural transformation is not so much a return to pagan Rome as a renewed manifestation of an ancient contest between competing religious ideologies. His work is an extended reflection on a series of lectures T. S. Eliot delivered in March 1939 at Corpus Christi College, Cambridge in which Eliot argued that Western culture of the twentieth century was in a struggle between a Christian society and a pagan one.[20] While history has proven that a "Christian society" is far from perfect, Eliot granted, a "Christian society only becomes acceptable after you have fairly examined the alternatives."[21] Since the days of Eliot, the struggle between Christianity and paganism has escalated. Just as in the ancient world, Smith contends, we are learning quickly that paganism and Christianity reflect "basic existential orientations that could not easily coexist in peace."[22] The classical world was a pagan culture in which the religious and civic spheres were inseparable; before the rise of Constantine, the pagan gods enjoyed "centuries of uninterrupted worship."[23] Even the term "pagans" or *pagani*, as they were called by the church, referred to "civilians who had not enlisted through baptism as soldiers of Christ against the powers of Satan."[24] In the recent years, this new form of paganism is becoming "more open and confident" so that now, "modern paganism," as Eliot and Smith call it, is imposing its will upon Western culture in a way that is reminiscent of the days of ancient Rome.[25]

Standing alongside Trueman, Mount, and Smith, a chorus of scholarly voices herald the resonances between the modern and ancient worlds. The Orthodox patristic theologian and historian, John Behr, for example, believes that there is "an uncanny parallel" between the second century and our own day.[26] New Testament scholar Michael Kruger concludes his study of the second century by saying, "We are entering into (and in some ways are already in) a post-Christian world. In order to interface with this world, we do not necessarily need a new apologetic but perhaps an old one—a second century one."[27] American historian John D. Wilsey points to Justin Martyr, an apologist of the second century, as a model for Christian civic engagement.[28] Michael Green's well-known summary of evangelism in the early church was inspired by the postmodern shifts in our culture, prompting his desire "to go back to the beginning and see how the first Christians succeeded in making such an impact."[29] We find the same motivation at work in Gerald Sittser's book on early Christian cultural engagement. He began looking for "models and movements" that could guide the church through the troubled waters of postmodernity and recognized the need to look to the ancient church "before Christendom began to emerge."[30] Finally, author Rod Dreher reminds his readers to take comfort, because in the "first centuries of Christianity, the early church survived and grew under Roman persecution and later after the collapse of the empire in the West."[31] All these writers are sensing the same thing: the present cultural moment reflects a revival of the ancient struggle between paganism and Christianity. It seems there is no question now: God is dead, long live the gods.

CULTURAL ENGAGEMENT: ISOLATION OR CONFRONTATION?

Given these symptoms and diagnoses, we are left to ask, What is the remedy? Where do we go from here? This is where things get a bit complicated. Anyone interested in ancient history knows that the struggle between Christianity and paganism was not easily decided. The problem was that pagan worship of the gods was integral to "an entire social world into which Christianity could not be fitted." The encounter between paganism and Christianity was not some casual friendly afternoon collegiate debate; it was "at bottom a conflict between two religious visions" and took many years and much sacrifice to settle.[32]

There are many voices trying to chart a pathway through these murky waters. Most of the responses fall along two opposing lines: isolation or confrontation. The Reformed theologian John Bolt captures this sentiment when he asks whether Christians today should "acknowledge and more or less accept this changed state of affairs, or do we fight it?"[33] As we stand watching the death of Christendom and the loss of cultural power, should we dig in our heels, grit our teeth, shout a war cry, and charge forward to confront the culture? Or should we cut our losses, fall back into a safe position, and create isolated communities of resistance?

The call to retreat was sparked in significant ways by the image of Benedict of Nursia found in the final lines of Alasdair MacIntyre's influential book, *After Virtue*. MacIntyre, who anticipated Trueman, argues that *emotivism* characterizes the twentieth century, that we live in a world where "all evaluative judgments and more specifically all moral judgments are nothing but expressions of attitude or feeling; insofar as they are moral or evaluative in character that morality is merely driven by preferences."[34] This means that "all moral disagreement is rationally interminable." The logical step, as Trueman observes, is an expressive individualism, where internal feelings and preferences rule our lives. In an attempt to close with some measure of hope, MacIntyre appeals to Benedict of Nursia as a model for cultural engagement:

> What matters at this state is the construction of local forms of community within which civility and the intellectual and moral life can be sustained through the new dark ages which are already upon us. And if the tradition of the virtues was able to survive the horrors of the last dark ages, we are not entirely without grounds for hope. This time however the barbarians are not waiting beyond the fronters; they have already been governing us for quite some time. And it is our lack of consciousness of this that constitutes part of our predicament. We are not waiting for a Godot, but for another—doubtless very different—St. Benedict.[35]

He does not explain how this might work, or how the monastic life will be effective against a cultural emotivism; he just leaves the reader with the lingering hope of the image of a monastic retreat.

Several have taken up the challenge to flesh out MacIntyre's suggestion about Benedict. Take, for example, Jonathan Wilson's book *Living Faithfully in a Fragmented World: From* After Virtue *to a New Monasticism*. Wilson envisions a new movement offering resources for those who want to embrace a contemporary monastic way of life. In his analysis, the society *and* the church are both governed by the same fragmented forces, so the recovery of the church must begin with a new community outside the church, or at least "outside the structures and activities of the church that are deeply intertwined with our fragmented world."[36] Wilson's application of MacIntyre, however, has been dwarfed by the bestseller, *The Benedict Option* by Rod Dreher. Dreher's argument shares the same essential foundation as Wilson and casts a similar vision. He argues that

America, and the West at large, is at the crucial turning point, that conservative Christians can no longer "live business-as-usual lives in America, that we have to develop creative, communal solutions to help us hold on to our faith and our values in a world growing ever more hostile to them." The time has come for believers to be "separate, sometimes metaphorically, sometimes literally," and "to embrace 'exile in place' counter-cultural communities." The church must recognize that "politics will not save us" and that it should no longer "prop up the current order." It is time to construct "new forms of community within which the moral life could be sustained so that both morality and civility might survive the coming ages of barbarians and darkness."[37]

I must admit some sympathy with those encouraging an "exile in place" retreat to the monastery. The call to fall back and form communities of resistance is born of love for one's community and church. The rapidity of cultural change has reshaped churches, educational institutions, businesses, volunteer associations, and other social organizations. These changes do not always bode well for some seeking to make their way by faith. The swiftness of cultural change seems only to be speeding up with no apparent end in sight, nor are prophets around to tell us what will happen.

But MacIntyre has not convinced everyone. Others do not care to follow Benedict into the monastery. They feel that the best path forward is confrontation, and there is no shortage of calls for aggressive postures toward the perceived insanity of our culture. James Davison Hunter popularized the term "culture wars" with his 1991 book, *Culture Wars: The Struggle to Define America*, which described—though did not advocate—this perspective. In this space, there are many works calling for new kinds of theonomy or integralism, where the church becomes the basis for political power in the state. Robert Wilken captures these sentiments when he articulates the views of some who prefer the seizure of political power: "In my wanton and admittingly darker ruminations, I sometimes wonder whether what Christianity needs is not so much a new Benedict as a new Charlemagne."[38] They long for a ruler, such as Stephen Wolfe's "Christian Prince" who will wield the reins of political and social power to usher in a renewed Christendom that will reestablish peace.[39] Streams of Catholic integralism and Christian nationalism have formed alternative approaches to cultural engagement.[40]

Several other studies have noticed this jockeying between isolation and confrontation. Stephen Bullivant's sociological analysis observed this division among Christian leaders' response to the growing rates of American deconversion. Some advocate for a Christian nationalism while others propose an exile-in-place quietism.[41] Bullivant finds the same kind of divisions between an encroaching Christian nationalism and exile-in-place quietism.[42] Likewise in missiology, Paul Williams shows how a volleying between cultural isolation and confrontation has defined missional strategies over the past fifty years. The church struggles in "holding on to unhelpful elements of the modern paradigm or failing to adapt to the huge cultural changes that have occurred since modernity's collapse."[43]

Others seek to craft mediating positions that try to find a balance between isolation and confrontation. Many stress the hope for living peaceably and finding common ground with those who don't share conservative Christian views. Still others hope to transform the culture by renewed activism: *To Change the World* by James Davison Hunter, *Culture Making: Recovering Our Creative Calling* by Andy Crouch, *Created and Creating* by William Edgar, *Joy for the World* by Greg Forster, *I Pledge Allegiance* by David Crump, and *Politics after Christendom* by David VanDrunen.[44] Hunter, for example, aims to be neither overly pessimistic nor overly optimistic and instead advocates a church with a "faithful presence" in the world.[45] He hopes that eventually all sides can find some common ground, call a truce, and live together in peace. Forster argues that God's kingdom is "active not passive," and that non-Christians might well come to the faith when "they encounter the joy of God through Christians' participation in their civilization."[46] VanDrunen believes that "God has instituted and rules political communities, and Christians should be active within them and promote their welfare. But Christians ought not to seek the kingdom within such communities."[47]

In short, we can see from works such as these a spectrum of options for facing the death of Christendom—from isolation to confrontation, with various possibilities of mediation in between. What is left is a sense of division and conflict built on two conflicting assumptions: the tendency to assimilate to the culture or to withdraw to the safety of a confined community.[48] Missiology is indeed to the point: in our post-Christian age, we are all de facto missionaries living among the modern pagans in our neighborhoods, towns, cities, and states, pulled between calls to retreat and calls to confront. Neither option is entirely wrong, and perhaps in specific places and times, the church should gravitate more toward one or the other. But there is another option that neither repeats Benedict nor crowns Charlemagne. If we are living in a world of modern paganism, perhaps we should go back to the earliest centuries and examine the lives of the Christians who thrived in the age of the Caesars.

CULTURAL SANCTIFICATION

When we come to the Christian sources of the earliest days of the church, we do not find the kind of frantic bifurcation found in much of the literature cited above. Instead, we find serious commitments to Christian identity and the distinctiveness of Christian doctrine and practice alongside discussions of good citizenship and public engagement that helped Christians navigate a pagan world. In essence, early Christian cultural engagement was defined not by an isolation or confrontation but by what we might call a "cultural sanctification."[49] Cultural sanctification recognizes that Christians are necessarily embedded within their culture and must seek sanctification (both personal and corporate) in a way that draws upon the forms and features of their environment to transform them by pursuing virtue.[50] This Christian performance of sanctification involves defending the faith, sharing the good news of salvation found in Christ, and visibly embodying all the virtues of the Christian spirituality in ways that persuade others.

In his work on the history of missiology, the famous missiologist Andrew Walls argues that the church has always struggled between two opposing principles: indigenization and pilgrimage. The indigenizing principle, which emphasizes a localism, recognizes that when people convert to Christianity, they do not come as static, isolated individuals but as persons intimately bound to a social world. Conversion does not mean they cease to perform the normative human functions required to live: they drive cars, eat fast food, and enjoy an evening stroll through the woods. "In Christ," Walls writes, "God accepts us together with our group relations; with that cultural conditioning that makes us feel at home in one part of human society and less at home in another." Christians must always endeavor "to live as a Christian and yet as a member of one's own society" and to make the church like a place where we feel at home in this world.[51] In these ways, the indigenizing principle stresses the importance of a locally constituted community of faith walking and working together.

However, in all their indigenizing efforts, Christians are always pilgrims and never fully at home in this world. The pilgrim principle "whispers to him [the Christian] that he has no abiding city and warns him that to be faithful to Christ will put him out of step with his society; for that society never existed, in East or West, ancient time or modern, which could absorb the word of Christ painlessly into its system."[52] Christian assumptions will always help guide the Christian life within the culture, but they will never be fully immersed in its patterns and practices. As Rowan Greer observes, "it looks as though the church is healthiest when the tensions are preserved—so that the Christian lives both in this world and in the light of the next and seeks to preserve both the holiness and the catholicity of the Church."[53]

Vince Bantu unites both of Walls's indigenizing and pilgrim principles under the heading of "cultural sanctification" and suggests that the "gospel simultaneously indigenizes itself to the local culture and reminds the church that she is a pilgrim in this world and must be out of step with the culture where it conflicts with the call of following Jesus."[54] In my estimation, the concept of cultural sanctification, with its indigenizing and pilgrim principles, captures the way early Christians approached the pagan world. They always tried to guard "the newness of the message without isolating themselves from the culture or accommodating themselves to the culture."[55] Far from rejecting or confronting the world, the early church held these two principles together. While we might fear the dramatic cultural shifts of our time, we can draw assurance from the church having been here before. Through the steady process of cultural sanctification, the early church navigated the Scylla and Charybdis of cultural engagement.

AN EXAMPLE OF EARLY CHRISTIAN CULTURAL SANCTIFICATION

Thus, it is reasonable to return to the ancient church to seek a little wisdom from Christians who have walked roads like ours before. The church lived, ministered, and served in an ancient world that was not defined by a cultural Christianity. Instead, through their vision of cultural sanctification, they transformed society through embedded missional efforts preoccupied with the church's identity and persuasiveness. A good example is found in the short second-century apologetic text entitled the Epistle to Diognetus. Calling neither to retreat nor to fight, the text represents the "ambivalent middle way that the majority were to go."[56] Several recent books on cultural engagement even point to this short work as a potential way forward through the morass of postmodern culture, though none of them explores the argument in detail.[57]

Not much is known about the historical situation of this epistle, except that it seems to date to the second century and was written to a pagan named Diognetus who was interested in learning more about Christianity.[58] The argument of the text falls into the genre that scholars call "protreptic discourse," which aims to "persuade an audience in a deliberative manner."[59] In other words, it is an example of cultural engagement that hoped to convince readers to respect Christian theology and reject the false charges brought against it. Its arguments attempted to create a cultural space for Christians to live and worship freely and without fear of retribution.

The author defends the Christian faith with an extended reflection upon the uniqueness of a Christian identity in contrast to that of the Jews and Greeks. He summarizes his understanding of the church and the church's mission in the world in a few key paragraphs:

> For Christians are not distinguished from the rest of humanity by country, language, or custom. For nowhere do they live in cities of their own, nor do they speak some unusual dialect, nor do they practice an eccentric lifestyle. This teaching of theirs has not been discovered by the thought and reflection of ingenious men, nor do they promote any human doctrine, as some do. But while they live in both Greek and barbarian cities, as each one's lot was cast, and follow the local customs in dress and food and other aspects of life, at the same time they demonstrate the remarkable and admittedly unusual character of their own citizenship. They live in their own countries, but only as aliens; they participate in everything as citizens, and endure everything as foreigners. Every foreign country is their fatherland, and every fatherland is foreign. They marry like everyone else, and have children, but they do not expose their offspring. They share their food but not their wives. They are "in the flesh," but they do not live "according to the flesh." They live on earth, but their citizenship is in heaven. They obey the established laws; indeed, in their private lives they transcend the laws. They love everyone, and by everyone they are persecuted. They are unknown, yet they are condemned; they are put to death, yet they are brought to life. They are poor, yet they make many rich; they are in need of everything, yet they abound in everything. They are dishonored, yet they are glorified in their dishonor; they are slandered, yet they are vindicated. They are cursed, yet they bless; they are insulted, yet they offer respect.

When they do good, they are punished as evildoers; when they are punished, they rejoice as though brought to life. By the Jews they are assaulted as foreigners, and by the Greeks they are persecuted, yet those who hate them are unable to give a reason for their hostility.[60]

In a word, what the soul is to the body, Christians are to the world. The soul is dispersed through all the members of the body, and Christians throughout the cities of the world. The soul dwells in the body, but is not of the body; likewise, Christians dwell in the world, but are not of the world. The soul, which is invisible, is confined in the body, which is visible; in the same way, Christians are recognized as being in the world, and yet their religion remains invisible. The flesh hates the soul and wages war against it, even though it has suffered no wrong, because it is hindered from indulging in its pleasure; so also the world hates the Christians, even though it has suffered no wrong, because they set themselves against its pleasure. The soul loves the flesh that hates it, and its members, and Christians love those who hate them. The soul is enclosed in the body, but it holds the body together; and though Christians are detained in the world as if in a prison, they in fact hold the world together. The soul, which is immortal, lives in a mortal dwelling; similarly Christians live as strangers amidst perishable things, while waiting for the imperishable in heaven. The soul when poorly treated with respect to food and drink, becomes all the better; and so Christians when punished daily increase more and more. Such is the important position to which God has appointed them, and it is not right for them to decline it.[61]

In just a few lines, the Epistle to Diognetus casts a vision of cultural engagement that is more relevant and compelling than many current works on the topic. Scriptural terms and concepts pervade nearly every sentence as a vision of the church's life in the world is presented to a pagan audience. The epistle boldly sets forth both the uniqueness of the church and the importance of the church's life in the world.

Consider, first, how the author has a clear, convicted appreciation for the nature of the church. In the closing lines of the excerpt above, the author argues that the church is fulfilling an appointed ministry and occupies an "important position" within the world. The church is uniquely appointed to a divine mission that has providentially embedded them in the world, and the people of God cannot deny their divine appointment to live there faithfully, wherever "each one's lot was cast." They are not "distinguished from the rest of humanity by country, language, or custom," and they are spread out in every known geographical region. The nature and the unity of the church is "invisible," identified not by the outward visible signs of any given culture but through the union and communion with the Spirit. The people of God are held captive and persecuted by the world, but, ironically, they actually "hold the world together." The early Christian community did not see the church as just another voluntary organization or social gathering but as the locus of God's redemptive work in the world.

The author also holds that the church is marked out by two things: doctrine and morality. Christians do not, the author maintains, "promote any human doctrine"; their teachings and beliefs are of divine origin. These were not "discovered by the thought and reflection of ingenious men," such as the Greco-Roman philosophers or rhetoricians. Rather, their doctrine was imparted by Christ to his apostles and handed down to the church. Likewise, their ethics offer the best path to human flourishing. They have distinctive views on sexual ethics, infanticide, wealth and poverty, power and retribution, citizenship, and ultimately, love. Their spiritual lives are characterized by the tension that (alluding to Paul's words in Romans 8:9) they live "'in the flesh,' but they do not live 'according to the flesh.'" Their holiness transcends the civil laws, even though they themselves are rejected. In a word, they "love everyone, and by everyone they are persecuted."

The Epistle to Diognetus is not interested in finding the right method or option for cultural engagement before clearly defining what true Christian belief and practice were and how that practice shaped their understanding of the political and public spheres. Christian cultural engagement was to begin in the church with a well-defined understanding of identity and mission. The church is, again, the focal point of God's redemptive activity and the means by which God is redeeming the world. The church is the soul of the world; while distinct from the body, it animates the body. There is some danger in pressing this analogy too far or reading too much into the epistle's negative portrait of the body. Given the author's situation within a hostile empire intent upon rejecting, persecuting, and eradicating Christianity, this image may be polemical and illustrative rather than a dogmatic explanation of anthropology.

With all this foundational work, however, the epistle is also thinking about the political and social implications of the church's mission. Alongside its implicit doctrine of the church, it provides a basic summary of political and public theology. Early Christians' political theology is evident from the way "they demonstrate the remarkable and admittedly unusual character of their own citizenship." For them, "every foreign country is their fatherland, and every fatherland is foreign." They were simultaneously citizens of the country in which they resided and foreigners whose identity was rooted in Christ as King. Not that they then retreated or denied their citizenship; on the contrary, "they live in their own countries" and "participate in everything as citizens." Simply put, they were active citizens embedded in the life of their communities. They did not confuse their earthly citizenship with their heavenly one, or reject the world and live in isolation, but sought the welfare of the city. The early church had no designated "Christian" country; rather, with Paul, it accepted political authorities as appointed by God and "obey[ed] the established laws." Yet this form of citizenship was qualified by their commitment to Christian doctrine and practice and their understanding that all earthly political rulers were provisional and temporary.

Beyond political theology, the epistle proposes a broader public theology on the premise that Christians "are not distinguished from the rest of humanity by country, language, or custom." In nearly every way, Christians looked like everyone else. They had no special Christian dialect, Christian clothing, or Christian jobs. They did not create their own social sphere to inhabit; rather, Christians "participate in everything like citizens," and they "tolerate all things as foreigners." This tension between participating (*metechousi*) and tolerating (*hypomenousin*) established a paradigm for how the early church thought about social engagement and cultural sanctification. They live in the same houses, says the epistle; they marry, have children, work, eat and drink, and generally enjoy the good things of life alongside their fellow citizens. But their public lives were qualified because, while dwelling within the culture, Christians were "hindered from indulging in its pleasures." They endured paganism and immoral practices as foreigners. Their emphasis on holiness was a way not to remove themselves from the culture but to live within it, yet transcend it by means of a special discipline. Much of the epistle is devoted to persecutions and accounts of how Christians are hated, despised, and rejected for their stubbornness, even though their oppressors "are unable to give a reason for their hostility."

Finally, the author of the Epistle to Diognetus understood that there is a telos to the Christian story, a final goal that colored the whole conversation about cultural engagement: "Christians live as strangers amidst perishable things, while waiting for the imperishable in heaven." They held an abiding love for divine providence and an eschatological hope of the Lord's return. As strangers they were persecuted, but in an ironic twist: "Christians when punished daily increase more and more." Amid their struggles with paganism and living as outcasts of society, they assumed that emperors and empires would rise and fall but that the people of God were to live in hope of the Son's return inaugurating the eternal kingdom of God. The end to the story was not persecution, suffering, and death but Christ's return in glory to judge the living and the dead and to establish a kingdom that will have no end. Fear not, the New Testament enjoins again and again, for Christ now reigns, and Christ will come again.

With its limited scope, this epistle does not touch on the many different ways in which early Christians acted in the political and public spheres. It provides an appetizer for the full-course meal that is served throughout the rest of this book. We will explore many more examples of early Christians preparing for culture engagement through catechesis; defending the faith before gathered crowds, civic leaders, or intellectuals; and serving the outcast and oppressed in social witness to their faith. These forms of cultural engagement cumulatively helped build the structure of the early church's response to a pagan world. The Christian call to cultural sanctification is a call to pursue holiness and conformity to the likeness of Christ *within any and every cultural context*. Neither retreating nor assimilating, firm in their identity and theological and moral convictions, Christians are to live with faithfulness to the truth of God revealed in the Scriptures.

While returning to the ancient world offers us helpful insights, there are some important differences between then and now. We do not live in ancient Rome but enjoy the blessings of a democratic republic and a modern economy. We carry cell phones, drive cars, and benefit from all kinds of advances in health care and technology. Besides such obvious contrasts, some more fundamental and influential differences between the ancient and modern worlds will impact the effectiveness of our cultural sanctification.

First, the modern church is not starting with a clean slate. We have a past, and it is not always pretty. In the days of Christendom, the church had cultural power but did not always exercise that power well. There is no shortage of tragic stories of abuse at the hands of those claiming to follow God. We cannot turn a blind eye to sins committed in the past and need to be honest when sins are exposed. At the same time, this checkered past is not the full story. These atrocities do not change the reality that the church is the locus of God's redemption, nor do they change the essence of the church's approach to cultural engagement and the hope of the coming kingdom of God. I will have much to say about these things in the coming pages. Regardless of our past, with the early church, we must hold fast to our distinctive theological convictions rooted in the teaching of the apostles that call us to the high moral standards of the Christian life.

Second, Western Christians today need to help each other grieve the loss of Christendom. This is no small task. Things have changed fast. Certainly, many Christians feel the secular tide has swept over the landscape almost overnight. Many feel that beloved institutions and organizations have transformed and are unrecognizable. Stephen Bullivant's recent book entitled *Nonverts: The Making of Ex-Christian America*, for example, helps capture the loss of Christendom from a sociological perspective and explains why so many are leaving the church.[62] In the short term, we should acknowledge this loss, lament, and pray. Pastors, ministers, and lay leaders in such situations must learn to manage the loss of Christendom. While grieving this loss, the post-Christian culture should also recognize that it has been influenced by Christianity in a way that pre-Christian culture was not. The Western church should not overlook the positive gains Christianity has made in the past or amid the global church.[63] We should not forget that the church in the West had produced remarkable academic institutions, significant social services, and stable governments. Even if we do not always appreciate the character of these institutions, we do have political and social structures in place that can shape the culture in ways the early church never had. But the revival of paganism is far from the end of the story, and the end of Christendom also presents new opportunities. In any case, the church in the West has a tall task ahead of it. Now is not the time to shrink back from the joy of the high calling to live Christianly in this world.

Third and finally, despite various similarities, there are many differences between ancient and modern political structures and social norms. The early church worked from the margins of the culture and did not enjoy many of our freedoms and opportunities to influence political and social life. We have advantages that can help us make positive contributions to our culture, but it will require creative applications of the wisdom of ancient cultural sanctification. This book is a first attempt to that end and hopes to further the conversation about Christian cultural engagement. When I become discouraged over our cultural context and the frustrations of living in a pagan world, my mind goes back to the moments I have spent with missionaries training to head overseas to some distant remote location. I am always amazed at their joy even when they know that serious challenges lie ahead of them. In the Lord's providence and guidance, we have been placed here in this day and age, and there is no reason for us to decline the call upon all our lives and embrace the challenge of cultural sanctification.

Summary of Chapters

This book interprets early Christian cultural engagement as a posture of cultural sanctification. That is, from the time of the apostles to the rise of Constantine, the church was engaged in a slow and steady process of living faithfully and seeking sanctification both personally and corporately in ways that transform the culture. This united effort entailed cultivating a Christian identity distinct from a Roman one, and an embedded place in the world that promoted distinctive Christian action in both the political and social spheres. Focused on the first principles of the gospel and rigorous catechesis in doctrine and morality, the church lived rooted within the culture, hoping to transform it through their presence.

Chapter 1 illustrates the necessity, first, of crafting a communal identity that draws sharp theological and moral contrasts with the world. The early Christians formed this identity through the regular practices of catechesis and worship prior to and as a basis for cultural engagement. Early Christians had to deconstruct many assumptions guiding their Jewish or Roman identities and slowly begin to construct, through steady discipleship, theological and moral assumptions from the Scriptures to shape a new Christian identity. The early church was no civic club where voluntary association came with immediate social benefits. It was a gathering of those formed and being formed by the beliefs and practices of Christian teaching. This is a point where much of the modern conversation about cultural engagement falls short. Many begin with methods and action strategies without attending to the deep roots of identity formation that provides the theological and moral basis necessary for healthy interactions.

The book then turns from within to without to consider the political and public dimensions of cultural engagement. Chapter 2 explains how the church cultivated a political theology to navigate its cultural situation. Dwelling within a hostile empire, early Christians had to think carefully about political power from a position of weakness. Scripture taught them that God was transcendent and providential over creation and had instituted government for his own purposes. The church accepted their position within the culture and worked as earthly citizens to be active and faithful within it. Early Christians did not assume that some sort of political action would save them but did understand the need for political engagement, even when they had little hope of political victory. The church today has much to learn from this same scriptural framework, even as it has more opportunity for positive political action.

Besides a *political theology* the church also cultivated a rich *public theology* as it reflected on the church's interaction with its neighbors. These exchanges included both the mind and the body, that is, both intellectual and social responses. Chapter 3 discusses the first of these, how the church navigated the prevailing intellectual climate and evaluated the dominant ideas and thinkers of the day. This included engagement with civil authorities as well as public intellectuals. Its witness saw the emergence of the church's own public intellectuals, most of whom were pastors or leaders in the church who used the prevailing thinking of the day to craft their own responses and try to persuade others. Activism and apologetics were balanced within this intellectual engagement.

Chapter 4 turns toward the social side of the church's public witness. Here again the church learned to balance activism and holiness by the practice of cultural discernment. This involved public service, daily work, and social conduct that conformed to their general moral vision. Christians were called to live lives of virtue among their neighbors and to demonstrate the beauty of holiness through their public witness and service. These kinds of conversations should encourage believers today to reflect carefully about our own public theology and witness, in word and deed, in our own times.

Chapter 5 underscores the hope in the coming kingdom of God that pervaded all actions and reflections of the early Christian community. The abiding conviction of the Lord's return resonated through their lives as well as their arguments, for the church worshiped, lived, studied, worked, served, and rested under the enduring hope in Christ's return. Hope is a good thing, one too often lost during times of political and cultural upheaval. If we learn nothing else from early Christian cultural engagement, it is that an abiding hope in the return of Christ should pervade everything we do.

The final chapter ties all these strands together to reflect on what wisdom the contemporary church can gain by studying cultural sanctification in the ancient church. Its example should challenge and encourage the faithful as we begin to chart a better way forward through our new postmodern pagan world. The ancient church did not pull off cultural sanctification perfectly; far from it. As C. S. Lewis reminds us, the ancients, like every other cohort in church history, "made as many mistakes as we." But, he adds, they did not make the same mistakes as we, nor will they "flatter us in the errors we are already committing; and their own errors, being now open and palpable, will not endanger us. Two heads are better than one, not because either is infallible, but because they are unlikely to go wrong in the same direction."[64] May the wisdom of the ancients help, in some small measure, to guide the church today to face our cultural tempests with faith, hope, and love. As the Epistle to Diognetus puts it, Christians today ought to see "the important position to which God has appointed them, and it is not right for them to decline it."

IDENTITY

A Baptismal Confession

Somewhere in Asia Minor in the third century, a Christian congregation began gathering on Holy Saturday, the day before Easter. It was a special time
set aside for baptizing new members. The occasion was solemn, yet a sense
of eagerness suffused the small gathering. Most of the catechumens—those
seeking to become members of the church—had been going through the process of discipleship for around three years, studying Scripture, praying, and
worshiping with the church.[1] All of them had been fasting since Friday. Many
in the church fasted with them, so by now, they were all hungry for both sus-
tenance and baptism.

As the night wore on, prayer and fellowship continued, and the sense of
anticipation grew. When they heard the cock crow at first light and the sunrise
broke through the shadow of night, the community moved to a special place
where the water was cool and flowing.[2] The moving water reminded them of
the way their sins were washed away by the blood of Christ. As they removed
their outer garments to symbolize their new birth in Christ, a deacon moved
down into the water to receive each catechumen for baptism, shivering a little
as the cool water rushed by him.

Finally, the moment arrived. Surrounded by the natural world and living
amid a pagan empire filled with idols and idolatry, the first catechumen joined

the deacon down in the water. The deacon looked intently at him and asked, "Do you believe in God the Father Almighty?" It was the first point of the rule of faith, the basic confession of the church and the theological dividing line between Christianity and paganism. The catechumen replied confidently, "I believe." Then the deacon baptized him in the name of the Father; the water rushed over him, and he stood back up.

The deacon was not done. He asked the catechumen a second question: "Do you believe in Jesus Christ, the Son of God, who was born of the Holy Spirit and the Virgin Mary, who was crucified under Pontius Pilate, and died, and rose on the third day living from the dead, and ascended into heaven, and sat down at the right hand of the Father, the one coming to judge the living and the dead?" Each word of the confession of Christ rang out into the pagan world, adding to the one Father the one Son Jesus Christ, the Lord. These theological claims challenged the basic religious convictions of the empire. The catechumen responded a second time, "I believe." Again, the deacon thrust the neophyte down into the water.

At last, there came a third and final question. The deacon asked the catechumen, "Do you believe in the Holy Spirit and the Holy Church and the resurrection of the flesh?" For a third and final time, the catechumen replied, "I believe." Then he was baptized again. The community stood around in confirmation and agreement and, one by one, welcomed each new member into their church family.

After baptism, the new members dried themselves and dressed. An elder gently touched their foreheads with oil, reminding them that they were now anointed children of God and members of God's family. When the rites were completed, everyone gathered in the church for a service where the Eucharist was served. For the first time, the new members participated in the meal with the whole church. When the moment came, they partook of the bread and wine; for the first time in several days, food and drink touched their lips. It reminded them of the goodness of the world to be found in the gospel and the family of God. From now on, the catechumens were members of the church, sealed by the Spirit, adopted into the family of God, and able to enjoy all the blessings entailed in their new identity.

This description of baptism, found in the early Christian text *On the Apostolic Tradition*, illustrates how the early church thought about baptism in a world where they were working from the margins of the culture. The rite was not a sideshow or insignificant; it was fundamental to their worship and their identity. It enacted the crossing from the pagan religious view to a new understanding of reality. It entailed a new social imaginary or "a radical revision of the first principles" that challenged the very foundations of classical culture.[3] With that new identity, the church slowly began destabilizing the symbiotic relationship between religion and the state in ancient Rome.

CULTURAL SANCTIFICATION AND CHRISTIAN IDENTITY

The early church had no Christendom to support the public lives of the faithful, so these ancient Christians, especially in the first few centuries, understood how important liturgical acts like baptism were. They dug deep roots to withstand, and even thrive, amid the swirling winds of pagan culture. For this reason, catechesis and liturgy are the starting places for our discussion of cultural sanctification. These constituted the double doors of the entrance to the Christian home. When new converts walked through these doors, they were greeted by a faithful community committed to Christian doctrine and virtue.

For us, too, a Christian vision of cultural sanctification must begin with crafting Christian identity through catechesis (or discipleship) and liturgy (or worship). If Christians do not know the basic contours of Christian doctrine and morality, how can we expect them to live Christianly in a pagan world? Unfortunately, much current literature on cultural engagement begins with discussions of methods rather than formation. We are often concerned with *how* to respond to culture without considering the very basis upon which that response must proceed. Methods are essential, but without the right Christian assumptions informing them, we will be tossed about and finally prove ineffectual.

Early Christian identity proceeded from the two key practices of catechesis and liturgy. Catechesis entailed a long period of examination to form new believers in the contours of the church's doctrine and morality. This regular and extended time of discipleship ensured that the right teachings were passed on, and the right ordering of worship ensured that these convictions would be maintained. The church called its people to a distinct set of theological convictions and a different liturgical life with its own rhythms that shaped their lives in contrast to the surrounding world where the activities of the state were always mingled with religion. Like two threads, catechesis and liturgy were woven together to cultivate a Christian identity and prepare new converts to live Christianly in the world.

In his analysis of religious communities, American anthropologist Clifford Geertz explains how these three features of religion—belief, ritual (or symbolic practices), and ethos (or ethics)—are always held together and mutually affirming. "Religious belief and ritual," Geertz writes, "confront and mutually confirm each other; the ethos is made intellectually reasonable by being shown to represent a way of life implied by the actual state of affairs which the worldview describes, and the worldview is made emotionally acceptable by being presented as an image of an actual state of affairs of which such a way of life is an authentic expression." This means, according to Geertz, that "religion is never merely metaphysics. For all peoples the forms, vehicles, and objects of worship are suffused with an aura of deep moral seriousness. . . . Religion is never merely ethics either. The source of its moral vitality is conceived to lie in the fidelity with which it expresses the fundamental nature of reality."[4] Thus, metaphysics, ethics, and ritual must be held together and understood in mutually interactive ways. Noting how these things applied to the early church, Robert Wilken writes, "The Christian religion is inescapably ritualistic (one is received into the church by a solemn washing with water), uncompromisingly moral ('be ye perfect as your Father in heaven is perfect,' said Jesus), and unapologetically intellectual (be ready to give 'a reason for the hope that is in you,' in the words of 1 Peter)."[5] We see how these things flowed together in the story of baptism mentioned above. The catechumens and the community of faith were united in a pattern of conversion and confession that marked them out within their world. In an age when cultural Christianity is waning, there is no doubt that now is the time to revive our basic commitments to discipleship and regular worship together that will testify to the beauty of the community of faith. Living faithfully in a secular world will most certainly require Christians to take their Christian identity more seriously and the specific ecclesiological structures they take.

Conversion in the Early Church

Our discussion of cultural sanctification in the early church must begin at the beginning, at conversion. What made Christianity appealing to outsiders? What were the things that motivated them to join the church? In his work *Understanding Religious Conversion*, Lewis Rambo argues that conversion always "is a complex, multifaceted process involving personal, cultural, social, and religious dimensions." It proceeds across seven "stages," including different environmental factors: context, crisis, quest, encounter, interaction, commitment, and consequences. The first stage, "context," recognizes that "networks of relationships and the cumulative effects of education, training, and institutional structures all influence the potential convert."[6] Conversion is suffused with a complex experience of "socialization," forming the convert spiritually into a new way of life, a new set of beliefs and practices. In sum, while conversion might be personal, it is not individual, because it involves a whole complex set of social relations.

The stages of crisis, quest, and encounter encompass the kinds of experiences and social interactions individuals have with a particular social or religious community that spark some kind of change. For Rambo, "interaction" denotes the way the early church shaped the catechetical process as it began initiating new converts.[7] Catechesis entailed the time to form and test the beliefs of potential new members, like the preseason practices intended to form an athlete's skills and habits. Rambo's work reminds us that conversion, in the ancient world or today, is not merely about coaxing someone to give mental assent to a set of propositions but about a commitment of the whole person to a larger community. Alan Kreider uses the metaphor of fermentation to convey the same idea. Instead of focusing on church growth strategies, the early church grew through the gradual, patient process of developing their "habitus," or "habitual behaviors." They believed that the "enactment of their message," more than anything else, would help draw new members.[8] The church was not interested in a few actors who might drop by for a show but those who were willing to join their community and conform their lives after the teachings of the church.

This model of slow steady identity formation is remarkably different from the rise of conversionism in the nineteenth and twentieth centuries. As the works of William James and Arthur D. Nock show, in this era, conversion was understood as a psychological change, internal and immediate.[9] But the first few centuries of the church saw no outbreaks of revivals, or any mass conversions outside those mentioned in the book of Acts. Having inherited no cultural Christianity, evangelism was more organic and relational. Rather than seeing conversion as a cataclysmic momentary spiritual experience, they saw it as an intensive learning process in which converts were challenged to "experience and enact a new way of life" and a new sense of mission.[10] As Martin Goodman argues, the "biggest agent of transformation for the convert was negative: withdrawal from pagan worship."[11] Outsiders saw the church acting in ways that set them apart. The reasons for this distancing are complex, but Kreider uses the helpful image of "push and pull" to characterize the draw of the church. Sometimes dissatisfaction with other philosophical or religious options pushed people to consider alternatives, while at other times, the attractiveness of Christian morality and the visible beauty of the Christian community pulled them.[12] In either case, these interactions resulted in people joining a different community, a group of fellow travelers defined by certain theological convictions, moral actions, and liturgical practices.

Pagan Conversion

Despite some similarities, the church and other religious and philosophical schools evangelized in different ways. Unlike the Christian (and Jewish) communities, the pagans offered cults that essentially served a civic function. The religious cults were active in all kinds of propaganda, teachings, miracles, and other forms of personal interactions. They did not actively proselytize, because the cults were often tied to the ruling classes and intimately connected with political interests. They offered "a revelation but not a dogma."[13] They were interested in civil religion, not a distinctive view of God or reality that would challenge the political assumptions of other religions. The second-century philosopher Celsus illustrated this point when he compared the outreach of the cults and philosophical schools to that of Christianity. The pagans called the righteous and elite, while Christians called sinners; the Christian message was not for just the upper class but for the populace.[14] Celsus could not imagine a world where a religious community might actually invite a sinner, or a place where the wealthy might gather alongside the broken and the outcast, for the main purpose of religion was to be a tool of the state, not a gathering of those who share serious theological or moral convictions. Religion did not offer enlightenment but satisfaction and provided "a useful weapon in discussion and in the spreading of their tenets."[15] Thus, "becoming religious in the Greco-Roman world did not entail either moral transformation or sectarian resocialization"; it was simply part of the pagan political context, a way to belong and participate within the standing order.[16] According to Nock, Judaism and Christianity offered religions as we understand them; the Romans "offered cults," and they looked to philosophers, not the cults, "for guidance in conduct and for a scheme of this Universe."[17]

If Romans had any notion of conversion, it applied to the philosophical schools, or to the way of life of a particular philosophical system. Two philosophical schools, for instance, the Cynics and the Stoics, offered "conversion to radical individualism" or "austere self-sufficiency," respectively.[18] Philosophy presented both a rational explanation of phenomena and a way of life that produced rigorous self-discipline and cultivated habits and virtues: the Cynics emphasized detachment and freedom, the Stoics stressed taming the passions and conformity to natural law, Epicureanism taught joy in the calm life, and so on. Conversion to these schools was essentially a "turning from luxury and self-indulgence and superstition . . . to a life of discipline and sometimes a life of contemplation, scientific or mystic."[19] While offering a school of life, these communities lacked the liturgical confessional features that marked out the church.

A good example of the radical difference of Christian conversion is found in Pliny's letter to the second-century emperor Trajan. Pliny, the governor in Bithynia, had encountered many converts to Christianity and observed how their evangelistic efforts disrupted the social and economic activities of his region. His letter is evidence that the Romans could not comprehend the nature of Christian conversion. These converts, he wrote Trajan, included "many persons of every age, every rank, and also of both sexes." They stopped patronizing the temples and refused to attend social activities such as the gladiatorial games. He realized that this "contagion" of Christianity would not be cured unless he took legal action against them and "encouraged" them to repent of their commitment to any god that superseded their allegiance to the empire. The conundrum for Pliny, however, was that Christians committed crimes of omission; they simply refused to perform acts contrary to their religious convictions. He did not know what to do with these constant claims to the moral high ground:

> The sum and substance of their fault or error had been that they were accustomed to meet on a fixed day before dawn and sing responsively a hymn to Christ as to a god, and to bind themselves by oath, not to some crime, but not to commit fraud, theft, or adultery, not falsify their trust, nor to refuse to return a trust when called upon to do so. When this was over, it was their custom to depart and to assemble again to partake of food—but ordinary and innocent food.[20]

Pliny had no legal basis for killing these Christians except the grounds of stubbornness. They were not conspiring to commit some crime; they simply gathered to worship, committed themselves to the highest standards of virtue, and refused to sacrifice to the Roman gods. The emperor replied that he had little concern about them. They were not to be sought out, but if they were caught, they should be executed unless they proved they were not Christians by "worshiping our gods."[21] This legal precedent became the standard approach to the church in the second century.[22]

Of course, not all Christians were saints and martyrs. Pliny was probably telling the truth when he reported that many Christians buckled under the pressure of persecution. But we can still assume that many held fast to their convictions. Pliny's very concern tells us that while Christians were being persecuted, many others were finding their theology and morality appealing. The church's patient discipleship program helped lay a solid foundation that could withstand pressure and hostility.

CHRISTIAN CONVERSION

Conversion in the early church was distinct in "unit[ing] the sacramentalism and the philosophy of the time."[23] Like the philosophical schools, the Christian community gave people a way of life and a purpose. But they also gave them a confession, morality, and liturgy. To use Walls's language, the church "indigenized" the culture by Christianizing some of its elements and patterns. The Christian community was similar and yet different. It was marked out not by mere external features but by convictions, lifestyles, and community. Striving toward sanctification while both interacting with their neighbors and living as pilgrims, the Christians slowly transformed their culture.

The ancient apologist Justin Martyr offers a good example of how conversion could happen in the early church. Justin was a philosophically minded pagan inclined toward the deep questions of life. His intellectual journey led him through the doctrines of the Stoics, Peripatetics, Pythagoreans, and Platonists, but without satisfaction.[24] Finally, he tells us, while studying Platonism, he observed some Christians being martyred. He witnessed the visible testimony of their commitment to Christianity, and having "heard the Christians slandered, and saw them fearless of death, and of all other-things which are counted fearful, perceived that it was impossible that they could be living in wickedness and pleasure."[25] The public testimony of Christian fortitude both softened his heart and convinced his mind that Christians could not be crazy if they were willing to give their lives for the sake of their god.

Then, on a chance encounter with an old man by the sea, Justin was introduced to the writings of the prophets and apostles. This elderly Christian engaged him in casual theological conversation that finally came around to the old man telling Justin where to find truth:

> There existed, long before this time, certain men more ancient than all those who are esteemed philosophers, both righteous and beloved by God, who spoke by the Divine Spirit, and foretold events which would take place, and which are now taking place. They are called prophets. These alone both saw and announced the truth to men, neither reverencing nor fearing any man, not influenced by a desire for glory, but speaking those things alone which they saw and which they heard, being filled with the Holy Spirit.[26]

When Justin heard these things, "straightway a flame was kindled in my soul," he tells us, "and a love of the prophets, and of those men who are friends of Christ, possessed me; and while revolving his words in my mind, I found this philosophy alone to be safe and profitable."[27] His conversion entailed a complete revision of his understanding of God and the relationship between God and creation; he found a different metaphysical basis for his identity and understanding of reality. He recognized that the gods of wood and stone offered no ground for a solid religious identity. Just as Christianity was the only sure and true philosophy, Christian theology and morality laid a firm foundation for a conception of reality that can guide a believer home.[28] Thus, the public witness of Christian martyrdom and a chance encounter with an elderly believer led Justin to the testimony of the Scriptures and his conversion to Christianity.

Converts like Justin could be Roman in every visible way and encourage active engagement with their fellow citizens. Such regular organic interactions led to lives that were transformed. Speaking of himself and others who had joined the church, Justin wrote,

> we who formerly delighted in fornication, but now embrace chastity alone; we who formerly used magical arts, dedicate ourselves to the good and unbegotten God; we who valued above all things the acquisition of wealth and possessions, now bring what we have into a common stock, and communicate to every one in need; we who hated and destroyed one another, and on account of their different manners would not live with men of a

different tribe, now, since the coming of Christ, live familiarly with them, and pray for our enemies, and endeavour to persuade those who hate us unjustly to live conformably to the good precepts of Christ, to the end that they may become partakers with us of the same joyful hope of a reward from God the ruler of all.[29]

The church was not merely a philosophical school offering a scheme of life, nor was it a pure civil religion that unified society; it was both and, at the same time, uniquely more. Christians who had been steeped in paganism now dedicated themselves to the "good and unbegotten God" and followed the teachings of Christ. At the same time, they had been turned around ethically. They embodied a theological transformation that rejected the pagan gods and recognized the validity of the one true God, a moral transformation that pursued virtue and conformity to the likeness of Christ, and a social transformation that led different tribes to live together in community and drew others to join them. As Meeks writes, the earliest Christian writings want "to root the moral sensibilities of [their] readers in their consciousness of having turned around."[30] They gathered as a community and worshiped together as they sought sanctification, all the while remaining embedded within their communities.

What are the implications of this model for today? Evangelicals have always celebrated the importance of conversion. According to Bebbington's classic definition, conversionism is one of their defining features, and their history is full of revivals that cultivated spontaneous religious encounters.[31] Yet revivals, at least those of the past three centuries, have presupposed the semblance of a Christian culture, like an old house sitting empty and waiting for a family to move in it and bring life to the residence. Put otherwise, revivalism assumes that the reigning cultural structures are Christian, and that a dead Christendom can be brought back to life. But we live in a different world. The institutions and social structures that supported a cultural Christianity are gone. We may hope and pray for revival and praise God when true revival comes, but in the meantime, perhaps we should consider the slow, steady, everyday evangelistic encounters through a regular visible witness of the community. The church did not strategize to be the church so that they could evangelize—just the opposite. They sought to be the church, and in doing so made the church attractive. They actively welcomed outsiders and patiently disciplined them in the beliefs and practices of the Christian faith. The same can happen today.

Conversion on this model will take time and commitment to an embedded Christian life that offers a regular, visible witness of a living community.

CONVERSION AND CATECHESIS

Given the loss of a cultural Christianity, we should be very interested in embodying the kind of life and arguments that might persuade our fellow citizens. To that end, we need serious catechesis. A proper cultural sanctification begins with shoring up the theological and moral commitments that strengthen our communities. Before we start complaining about outside worldliness, we need to do some healthy self-examination and consider the doctrines and morality by which we actually live to better know how to offer true light in the darkness. Cultural engagement begins in the hallowed hall of the church with good instruction in the contours of Christian faith and practice.

Catechesis simply means discipleship, the process of training a person in the basic doctrines and morality of Christian teaching.[32] The early church always provided some measure of this.[33] It knew that for Christians to cultivate virtue to live in the pagan world, "they needed time, the friendship of mentors, and the opportunity to grow in patient ways of living that were normal for Christians."[34]

The importance of doctrinal and moral formation was already emphasized in the apostolic writings that early Christians read. They knew the scriptural commands to disciple others (Matt 28:19–20; 2 Tim 2:2) and so established gatherings to train potential converts. An array of catechetical manuals written in the first few centuries after Christ give us a window into the curriculum for these sessions. It included a rich diet of theological and moral instruction. The goal was to disciple the whole person, not just some hypocritical know-it-alls who boasted of their theological acumen or people with good moral impulses who lacked a coherent theological commitment.

The important second-century bishop of Lyons, Irenaeus, made whole-life discipleship the basis of his ancient catechetical text, *On the Apostolic Preaching*. In his opening paragraphs, which provide the anthropological basis for discipleship, Irenaeus argues that "since man is a living being composed of a soul and a body, it is fitting that" following the right path "should happen in each case; and because stumblings can arise from both of these, holiness of body is the abstention from all shameful things and from all lawless deeds, while holiness of the soul is to keep the faith in God whole, neither adding nor subtracting from it."[35] The Christian catechist must attend to both soul and body, both doctrine and morality; these are dancing partners that move in step, stride for stride, together.

Irenaeus also argues that the disciple should seek purity in both. Neglecting holiness in either brought sin and loss. Irenaeus asks his readers, "what use is it to know the truth in words, only to defile the body and perform evil deeds? Or what profit indeed can come from holiness of body, if truth is not in the soul? For these rejoice together and join forces to lead man to the presence of God." Hypocrisy and heresy destroy true religion, but when doctrine and morality are held together in due measure and proportion, Irenaeus tells us, it is a beautiful thing to behold.[36]

As happens today, there were Christians in Irenaeus's community who fell off along either side of this divide—Christians either who wanted to stress doctrine over practice or who celebrated Christian practice while neglecting doctrine. There were plenty of reasons to do either, especially given the reality of persecution and rejection, and Irenaeus's community was no stranger to both. The fourth-century church historian Eusebius preserved a letter, written around 177, that records a period of vicious persecutions of Christians in and around Lyons. Plothinus, the bishop at the time, and many of the members, both women and men, were tortured and killed. Some buckled under persecution and renounced their belief, but the community celebrated others who remained faithful. Their suffering, as Irenaeus's catechetical manual attests, did not discourage the community from discipling others in the faith. When Irenaeus encouraged purity in doctrine and ethics, he had this persecuted community in mind. Christians have nothing and lose everything if they do not preserve the basic contours of Christian doctrine and practice.

Under Christendom, Christian mores filtered through the fabric of the culture. With that support lost, Christians today must hold fast to religious convictions that are both sincerely held and well informed. We cannot just assume that our churches have a firm grounding in Christian doctrine. For too many years, Evangelicalism has elevated conversionism and church-growth movements with simple processes of membership (if any at all) and have boasted about their inflated church rolls. They have embraced performance over formation and opened up the Christian community to vices that preclude a culture that values and instills whole-life discipleship. Irenaeus and the ancient church remind us that we must be formed, body and soul, to the truths of the Scriptures before we should begin thinking about the world around us.

Catechesis and Doctrine

But what was the substance of Christian doctrine and morality? What exactly did the early church seek to pass on, and how? We can find the church's central confession already in the New Testament writings themselves. Christ asked the disciples in Matthew 16:13, "Who do people say that I am?" While other options such as John the Baptist, Elijah, or Jeremiah were around, Peter confessed Jesus to be "the Christ, the Son of the living God" (Matt 16:16). This simple confession marked out the disciples from others. Likewise in Acts 17, when Paul conversed with the Epicurean and Stoic philosophers, he did not discuss religious experiences or social distinction but the theology of the resurrection (Acts 17:18). Other short confessions are found in passages such as 1 Corinthians 8:6: "for us there is one God, the Father, from whom are all things and for whom we exist, and one Lord, Jesus Christ, through whom are all things and through whom we exist," or 1 Corinthians 15:3–4: "For I delivered to you as of first importance what I also received: that Christ died for our sins in accordance with the Scriptures, that he was buried, that he was raised on the third day in accordance with the Scriptures."[37] Such were the theological dividing lines between Christian and pagan from the start.

The early church formulated this emphasis on doctrine into what is called the "rule of faith."[38] The rule was an essential summary of the church's main theological commitments and presaged the creeds that would develop later: the Apostles' Creed, Nicene Creed, Athanasian Creed, among others. These were the doctrines communicated in catechesis and confessed at baptism. When we examine the various early versions of the "rule of faith," two important attributes stand out. the rule offered a confessional standard that knit the community together, and it provided a summary of the faith that defined doctrine, summarized the narrative of salvation history, and addressed heresies. These three attributes, sown together, helped the Christian disciple see the world anew and reenter it with confidence.

The rule or "canon" of faith served as a confessional standard. It supplied "a condensed summary, fluid in its wording but fixed in content, setting out the key-points of the Christian revelation."[39] These key points set the basic theological contours of the faith and most often comprised statements related to the doctrine of God, Christ, the Spirit, and the church. No single articulation of the rule of faith was universally recognized and used in all liturgical contexts throughout the ancient world; instead, we find different articulations in the writings of the fathers, from Irenaeus to Augustine. The rule of faith being "fluid in its wording but fixed in its content" means that its basic structure and general content were constant, creating steady theological coherence, while also allowing for philological diversity. There was a "family resemblance" among them all like the traits or characteristics shared by a biological family.

The rule of faith provided a general metaphysical description of reality, a kind of social imaginary. This included the true nature of God, the world, and the relationship of people to both.[40] All theological and moral judgments depended upon the objective truth presented in the rule. The metaphysical assumptions of the rule informed their epistemology (what they know to be ultimately true) and ethics (how they are to live). This might be hard for us to grasp because the modern world often elevated epistemology over metaphysics as the basis for knowledge, while the postmodern world prioritizes ethics. The early church's right ordering of authorities, by contrast, made God the source of knowledge and the basis for knowledge and ethics. From that starting point, the church built an ordered structure of their vision of reality and determined the right moral patterns.

Irenaeus's catechetical manual draws this important connection between the rule of faith and reality. Faith, Irenaeus argues, "is established upon things truly real," and the Christian should "believe what really is, as it is, and believing what really is, as it is, we may keep our conviction of it firm." The rule of faith is God as God is understood and articulated by the preaching of the apostles. Reality is not determined finally by sensory experience or rational inquiry; it is given by God to the prophets and apostles who proclaim the word of God. Irenaeus's rule of faith itself, articulated in his catechetical manual, goes like this:

> This then is the order of the rule of our faith, and the foundation of the building, and the stability of our conversation: God, the Father, not made, not material, invisible; one God, the creator of all things: this is the first point of our faith. The second point is: The Word of God, Son of God, Christ Jesus our Lord, who was manifested to the prophets according to the form of their prophesying and according to the method of the dispensation of the Father: through whom all things were made; who also at

the end of the times, to complete and gather up all things, was made man among men, visible and tangible, in order to abolish death and show forth life and produce a community of union between God and man. And the third point is: The Holy Spirit, through whom the prophets prophesied, and the fathers learned the things of God, and the righteous were led forth into the way of righteousness; and who in the end of the times was poured out in a new way upon mankind in all the earth, renewing man unto God.[41]

In introducing it, Irenaeus stipulates the rule to be the "order" (*ordo-dispositionis*) of our faith. In other words, it is the basic arrangement of theological truth given to the church. It emerges out of the Scriptures and formulates an organized summary of Christian doctrine. This order of faith is the "foundation" (*fundamentum*) of doctrine upon which the building of the church is constructed. For this reason, Irenaeus implores Christians to "keep the rule of faith unswervingly and perform the commandments of God."[42] Upon this summary of faith, the people of God can order their lives, so that whether surrounded by ancient stoics or modern secularists, this rule orders reality. Finally, the rule is the "stability" (*firmamentum*) beneath every conversation. The rule stabilizes every sermon, every worship service, every small-group Bible study, every evangelistic encounter, and every apologetic defense. The rule secures the faithful, so that come hell or highwater, they are delivered safely to the other shore.

Irenaeus witnessed Rome at its height in the second century, but he was not fooled into thinking that this imposing appearance was the very definition of reality. In that imperialistic culture full of gods, his alternative basis for knowledge was radical; so it is today. Many in the ancient world scoffed at the revealed truth of the Scriptures and mocked the Christian confession. So also we find ourselves in a world that has untethered "the human from metaphysical framework."[43] We frequently see that "secularization's intrinsic tendency to close the world off from transcendence drives a wedge between the transcendent source of Christian beliefs and the secular values generated by them," writes scholar Jens Zimmerman.[44] There was, and is, no transcendent reality upon which moral claims were based; instead reality and morality were tied to the present world order and the glory and growth of the existing establishment or a would-be rival. Christian cultural sanctification was guided by a different framework arrayed around different metaphysical assumptions that could set the church's moral compass.

Alongside the content of the rule came other attributes that gave it order and structure. The rule of faith was propositional (most often triadic), salvation-historical, and polemical, with clear implications for cultural engagement.

First, the rule was almost always triadic and organized around the headings of Matthew 28:19: Father, Son, and Spirit. This gave it a propositional, or doctrinal, structure that made basic assertions about the nature of God and discussed both missions and processions. For many, Matthew 28:19 is concerned with Jesus's followers going out to the nations to share the gospel, but for the early church, it first spoke to the nature of the God who commands us to go. The titles of "Father, Son, and Spirit" were not just placeholders but had ontological antecedents. The connection between the rule of faith and baptism in Matthew 28:19 meant that this confession was the fundamental boundary marker for the community. The converts had to confess a doctrine of God that is Trinitarian, along with defining the key attributes of God and the distinctiveness of the divine persons. There is no space here to trace out all the divine attributes included in the rule of faith, but Irenaeus's language above provides a good sampling. God is uncreated, invisible, simple, and the Creator of all things. There is no one else to whom creatures should look to understand their salvation. Then the Word of God, through whom all things are created, is proclaimed among the prophets and apostles and appeared in the flesh to provide salvation. From beginning to end, the Word of God was with the Father, working to abolish death and produce a community of those devoted to God. Finally, the Spirit of God, through whom the prophets spoke, was poured out in a new way upon believers all over the earth and leads God's people back to God.

Other articulations of the rule of faith, such as those found in the writings of Tertullian and Origen, reflect the same propositional or doctrinal character. Tertullian's rule of faith has a triadic structure focused on the Father, Son, and Spirit.[45] The Father creates all things by means of the Son and sends the Son and the Spirit. Origen begins his basic theological work, *On First Principles*, by expanding on the rule of faith. He explains that Christians by his third century have come to disagree on a whole host of theological matters even if they share some basic doctrinal commitments: "many of those who profess to believe in Christ differ not only in small and trivial matters, but even on great and important matters." That being the case, Origen lays down "a definite line and clear rule regarding each one of these matters" before he continues on to specific theological differences.[46] The rule of faith, for Origen, is the boundary marker that both distinguishes the faith of Christians and frames the borders of the field wherein the Christians can safely compete in rigorous theological debate.

2 Second, besides its triadic structure, a salvation-historical narrative binds the rule together. As Paul Blowers puts it, the rule "served the primitive Christian hope of articulating and authenticating a world-encompassing story or metanarrative of creation, incarnation, redemption, and consummation."[47] The rule typically began with a reference to creation and then moved through a christological narrative including Christ's preexistence, incarnation, life, death, resurrection, ascension, and second coming. Finally, a statement about the Spirit and the church often accompanied the christological narrative, along with a description of the hope of resurrection and the life of the world to come. These marked the key turning points of the history of salvation, moving from creation to Christ to consummation and defined the true narrative of God's work in the world; all other narratives marched under this banner. In this story, the Christian disciples found and could find themselves.

Third, the rule of faith often bore a polemical spirit shaped by the hostile cultural context in which it was fashioned. Whatever was the theological issue du jour facing the church, the rule included an implicit response to it. For example, Irenaeus was dealing with a group of gnostic heresies. They sprang up in various sects with different nuances but collectively tended to devalue the body and creation.[48] Thus Irenaeus's rule emphasized the body and incarnation, stressing that Christ was "made man among men, visible and tangible" to abolish death and bring life to the people of God. In another presentation of the rule of faith in his larger work, *Against Heresies*, Irenaeus again emphasizes the material and incarnation aspects of the rule.[49] Thus, the rule of faith did not create doctrine but articulated it in specific places to address specific theological errors.

Likewise with other examples of the rule. Tertullian wrote against several heresies, including Monarchianism, also known as modalism. Monarchianism denied any distinction among the divine persons and rejected any sense of Christ's divinity. So, Tertullian's rule of faith stressed the deity of Christ and relationship of the Son to the Father, saying the "one only God has also a Son, His Word, who proceeded from Himself," and this Son is "both Man and God, the Son of Man and the Son of God."[50] Origen, on the other hand, had the philosophers in mind: "although many Greeks and barbarians promise the truth, we gave up seeking it from all who claimed it for false opinions after we had come to believe that Christ was the Son of God and were persuaded that we must learn it from him."[51] Situated in the cosmopolitan center of Alexandria and engaged with the various philosophical schools, Origen naturally emphasized the fact that in Christ "are hidden all the treasures of wisdom and knowledge" (Col 2:3). His rule of faith, he stipulates, is the "elementary and foundation principles" of the faith and the basic guide for all theological reflection.

The rule of faith, therefore, served as a consistent confessional standard across the ancient Christian community. These theologians believed they had received the apostolic testimony and attempted to pass it on to the church. Thus, across the diversity of communities and beliefs ran a unity in doctrine that comprised the basic confession made at baptism. Wherever Christians found themselves in the ancient world, the rule of faith marked them out and distinguished them from the other religious and political options in the world around them. Not a particular religious experience, then, or a particular rhetorical style but a distinct confession was the test of faith.

Our journey to understand early Christian cultural sanctification thus begins here: there is no *Christian* cultural sanctification, either in the ancient world or today, without *Christian* confession. Unless we have a clear understanding of the basic contours of the faith, we have no hope of healthy cultural engagement. Whatever form this takes at the local level, our churches definitely need to give serious attention to catechesis and discipleship. The loss of Christendom means that Christians need to be able to understand and articulate the basic contours of the faith. With the early church being under constant cultural pressure, the rule of faith, in Irenaeus's image, provided the foundation for truth and the stability within every conversation. These doctrines marked out early Christians and held them fast, and they can do so for us as well.

CATECHESIS AND MORALITY

The early church emphasized morality as much as doctrinal fidelity. Recall that Irenaeus said that catechesis was not complete until a person was formed in both soul and body, both doctrine and practice. Living in a pagan world meant that they could not afford hypocrisy, so they had to be deeply concerned about the performance of their faith in the public eye. For "what use is it to know the truth in words," Irenaeus wrote, "only to defile the body and perform evil deeds?"[52] Alan Kreider calls this *habitus* or "reflective bodily behavior." He posits that early Christianity grew not because it always won arguments but because its "habitual behavior (rooted in patience) was distinctive and intriguing."[53] In every encounter, the church aimed to offer a steady public display of their teaching that, on balance, was winsome and persuasive.

In the first few centuries of the church, this vision of Christian morality was cast in something called the "two-ways tradition."[54] The premise of the two ways is fairly straightforward; there are two paths laid before us, like the two roads diverging in a yellow wood. Scripture uses such images several times—Jeremiah 21:8, for example, "Behold, I set before you the way of life and the way of death," and Psalm 1:1–2, "Blessed is the man who walks not in the counsel of the wicked, nor stands in the way of sinners, nor sits in the seat of scoffers; but his delight is in the law of the LORD, and on his law he meditates day and night."[55] Matthew 7:13–14 implies this distinction when it contrasts the narrow and wide gates: "Enter by the narrow gate. For the gate is wide and the way is easy that leads to destruction, and those who enter by it are many. For the gate is narrow and the way is hard that leads to life, and those who find it are few." The church knew these passages and used them to call the Christian to live differently in the world.

The "way of life" is not defined by external qualities such as clothing, food, or entertainments (though these may have some moral implications) but by moral attributes. Pursuing the way of life is a call not to run from the culture but to live active Christian lives *within* it, with all the political and social implications that held. Step by step, little by little, in a thousand ways, people choose to walk down one of these roads. If the church participates in the same immoral activities as the society around it, there is nothing to point to a better life, no distinctive code that marks out the beauty of the Christian way of life. So how did the early church understand the two ways?

THE TWO WAYS: THE WAY OF LIFE

The way of life comprised the virtues necessary to live the Christian life, the affections of the heart toward the good things of God. This was clearly spelled out in the early Christian text called the Didache, one of the earliest church manuals composed to help lead ministers through the basic elements of catechesis and worship. It opens starkly: "There are two ways, one of life and one of death; but a great difference between the two ways." The two ways are as opposed as night and day or up and down. The central impulse in the way of life is the double love command: the love of God and love of neighbor. As the Didache declares, Christians should "love God who made you" and "second, your neighbor as yourself; and all things whatsoever you would not occur to you, do not also do to another."[56] The double love command forms the basis of all other moral actions, impelling "duty toward God through reverence, and sanctity and duty towards people through humanity and justice."[57] The Christian should perform the double love command in and through every activity, both inside and outside the church, with an eye toward God and others. The Didache explicates the double love command with a long list of moral exhortations toward holiness that reads like a blend of the second table of the Decalogue, apostolic exhortations toward holiness in the New Testament, and the Sermon on the Mount in Matthew 5–7. Together this biblical mosaic lines out the path of the way of life, calling the Christian to live faithfully in this moral matrix.

The love for God is set in a tension between outward activities and an inner holiness, a balance between purity and activism. Living out the first command, the love of God, mandates blessing, prayer, and service toward neighbor. Given that we are all God's creatures, there should be no hint of pride in the life of the church. Instead, says the Didache, we should "bless those who curse you, and pray for your enemies, and fast for those who persecute you." Bless others, be holy; pray for others, avoid immorality, seek the good of others, strive to live holy lives as we live under the watchful care of God. Yet active and outward activities are not everything; the faithful are also called to love God through a life of purity and abstinence "from fleshly and worldly lusts." The text here appeals to the Sermon on the Mount:

> If someone gives you a blow upon your right cheek, turn to him the other also, and you shall be perfect. If someone impresses you for one mile, go with him two. If someone takes away your cloak, give him also your coat. If someone takes from you what is yours, ask it not back, for indeed you are not able. Give to every one that asks you, and ask it not back; for the Father wills that to all should be given of our own blessings.[58]

These actions distinguish the church's way of life. Humility, service, compassion, and mercy are all virtues that characterize a family but need to be extended to others, especially among those *in the church*. Even if Christians wear the same clothes and work at many of the same jobs as everyone else, their lives should be different. A vibrant holiness should distinguish them. This was the early church's vision of the good life, and as we shall see, it was ultimately more attractive and compelling than what the Roman world had to offer.

The second commandment, to love your neighbor, was defined in similar terms but with more emphasis on horizonal relationships with others in their community. It forbad stealing, committing abortion, coveting your neighbor's possessions, bearing false witness, speaking evil, holding grudges, or being double-minded or double-tongued. Neither might the faithful be covetous, rapacious, hypocritical, evil disposed, or haughty. Instead, Christians "shall not hate any man; but some you shall reprove, and concerning some you shall pray, and some you shall love more than your own life." These moral exhortations go on for several more paragraphs in the Didache and detail many specific and practical ways that Christians were called to virtue. The text challenged the faithful to "flee from every evil thing, and from every likeness of it." Christians must avoid anger, jealousy, quarrelsomeness, lust, fornication, filthy talking, idolatry, lying, theft, and blasphemy. Instead, they should be meek, long-suffering, gentle, good, and humble, receiving everything that comes to pass in their lives as good, "knowing that apart from God nothing comes to pass."[59]

Besides the Didache, several other ancient Christian texts stress the importance of the moral life and the two ways. Irenaeus posits that there was only one way "leading upwards for all who see, lightened with heavenly light" and to "the kingdom of heaven, uniting man to God."[60] He contrasts this with the many roads that lead to death. The image invokes Jesus's dictum about the narrow road that leads to true life and the broad road that leads to destruction. Similarly, the Epistle of Barnabas, also from the second century, repeats that "there are two ways of doctrine and authority, the one of light, and the other of darkness. But there is a great difference between these two ways."[61] In these texts, as in the Didache, the "way of light" entails the double love command with many biblical passages in support.[62]

The constant call to holiness coming from early Christian writings owed in no small part to the pagan culture around them. The pursuit of holiness was both personal and corporate, in the sense that there seems to be no division between the calling upon individual Christians and the exhortations toward a collective holiness. The church was a new family and became the "fundamental unit of urban Christianity" and learning to navigate between separating from all things that are depraved and a profound and sincere love for neighbor. Christians treated each other like brothers and sisters: "It was altogether appropriate that, just as in a natural family, moral training, advice, and admonition would take place in those household 'meetings.'"[63] In text after text, one can hear the voices of the early church urging their people to live lives of sanctifying beauty that season the culture with the salt of Christian morality. At every turn, there is a simultaneous call to be distinct and holy *and* an assumption that their lives are embedded with their neighbors'. While there are dangers on all sides, the church learned the art of walking this tight rope, balancing between holiness and activism.

THE TWO WAYS: THE WAY OF DEATH

The alternative to the way of life in God's economy is the way of death. Like the way of life, it is defined not in external terms but by orientations of the soul that are evil or sinful. The way of death is in every way antithetical to the way of life and ultimately leads to the separation from God that is true death. The way of death recalls many vice lists in the New Testament and similar commands throughout Scripture.[64] Galatians 5:19–21, for example, describes the works of the flesh as "sexual immorality, impurity, sensuality, idolatry, sorcery, enmity, strife, jealousy, fits of anger, rivalries, dissensions, divisions, envy, drunkenness, orgies, and things like these." Paul stresses that those who do these things will not inherit the kingdom of God. Similarly, the Didache blends many of these kinds of biblical passages; the way of death is lined with

> murders, adulteries, lusts, fornications, thefts, idolatries, magic arts, witch-crafts, rapines, false witnessings, hypocrisies, double-heartedness, deceit, haughtiness, depravity, self-will, greediness, filthy talking, jealousy, over-confidence, loftiness, boastfulness; persecutors of the good, hating truth, loving a lie, not knowing a reward for righteousness, not cleaving to good nor to righteous judgment, watching not for that which is good, but for that which is evil; from whom meekness and endurance are far, loving vanities, pursuing requital, not pitying a poor man, not labouring for the afflicted, not knowing Him that made them, murderers of children, destroyers of the handiwork of God, turning away from him that is in want, afflicting him that is distressed, advocates of the rich, lawless judges of the poor, utter sinners.[65]

The text then simply exhorts the reader, "Be delivered, children, from all these."[66] This list is intended to be descriptive, not exhaustive. The early church understood that what distinguished them was not a particular style of clothing or occupation but a particular way of life incommensurate with anything contrary to God's law.

Again, the Epistle of Barnabas, also from the second century, contrasts the way of darkness and the way of life. The first is "crooked and full of cursing" and leads to "eternal death and punishment." What defines the way of death are not political allegiances or economic activities but "things that destroy the soul," including "idolatry, over-confidence, the arrogance of power, hypocrisy, double-heartedness, adultery, murder, rapine, haughtiness, transgression, deceit, malice, self-sufficiency, poisoning, magic, avarice, want of the fear of God."[67] To follow the way of darkness is to reject compassion, mercy, kindness and every other fruit of the Spirit. Those on this path celebrate persecution, heresy, unrighteousness, immorality, oppression of the needy and lowly; they are wicked, arrogant, greedy, indulge in gossip, murders, oppression, and so on. In his catechetical manual, Irenaeus describes the way of death as the "many and dark and contrary" roads that "lead down to death, separating man from God."[68] In sum, those who are seeking salvation needed to remain firm in their moral as well as doctrinal commitments, always minding the way of life in their daily walk.

The two-ways tradition is a no-nonsense reading of the spiritual life. Early Christians were very concerned about whole-life discipleship and whole-life sanctification. They did not separate their spiritual lives from their weekly activities. To be Christian was to live Christianly, not just on Sunday morning in worship. The Christian life is a journey, a way of life, an upward-leading path that is often arduous but worth every step. This emphasis in the early church became something of a moral apologetic that offered the visible beauty of the gospel lived out in community. These Christians believed that their lives would be a living sacrifice to the glory of God. In this way, the early church created a "'counterculture' that shifted people's loyalties and drained their energies away from the larger society."[69] Not in ways that removed themselves from society, but in discernment choosing how to participate in ways that did not offend the Christian conscience.

It is possible to read this emphasis on the holy life through the lens of legalism, and the early church was accused of moralism often enough.[70] But set against the backdrop of the pagan world, the apologetic and evangelistic functions of the community become more understandable. The church today should couple the emphasis on the holy life with a good process of church discipline and pastoral care. Whatever strategy for cultural engagement we employ, there is no substitute for the holy life. We need to recover this vision of a moral apologetic, remembering the caution against moralism, as a way of living that distinguishes the church and creates a community that is a living testimony to the goodness of Christian faith and practice.

The Way of Life: Contingency, Sanctification, and Improvisation

The two competing paths of life and death rest on contrary sets of metaphysical assumptions and open into contrary visions of life. There is no method or strategy for the way of life, only a path and the moral framework around it. But how did the early church discern the right moral choices within their various geographical and cultural contexts? By a process of moral reflection marked by contingency, sanctification, and improvisation.

Let's focus on the first two, contingency and perfection. These established the conditions and goal of the moral life behind and beyond specific behaviors. In his book *Ethical Patterns in Early Christian Thought*, Eric Osborn does not simply survey the moral codes of the early church but stresses its patterns of ethical demonstration, four in particular: righteousness, discipleship, faith and freedom, and love. Together, these help to organize the spiritual life. Ethics in the early church was not just about observing moral propositions but picturing the kind of life that Christians ought to embody. These patterns always point beyond themselves to the perfections of God. In other words, the Christian life is to go beyond behavioralism; the command to "be holy as I am holy" imagines a pattern of living that reflects the beauty of the divine, refracted by the work of the Spirit into the specific circumstances of the life of the Christian.

The ethical patterns in Christian life, in Osborn's analysis, are always committed to "both a sense of perfection and a respect for the contingent." The early church showed both "sensitivity to the demands of contingency and perfection, and distortion when the tensions between them failed." *Contingency* involved variations in geographical, political, and cultural situations, but through this contingency, the church sought *perfection*, or what we are calling *sanctification*. The contingency of the moment reflected evolving cultural factors and challenges, amid which the church sought to live righteously. The pursuit of righteousness emphasized a way of life focused on "moderation, harmony and regulation." Thus, "righteousness is practical, Christians are co-workers with God in his world, daily work is important, and there is no part of life without moral relevance." Today, too, the church must assess the moral and theological assumptions guiding our pagan culture to seek holiness in this world. As Osborn writes, "Where an ethic is serious about contingency and perfection it always runs the risk of losing one for the other. There is no general rule for all cases except the important principle that no rule can be more than half-right. The demands of contingency or perfection cannot be generalized and kept together." Further, as Osborn notes, "perfectibility is not a present possibility."[71] We face an ongoing struggle that amounts to a process of sanctification and culminates in glorification in the eternal state. Beatitude and the resurrected life await the faithful who will, at long last, inherit the kingdom and behold the glory of God.

In thinking about how the ethical life is conducted, ethicist Samuel Wells adds as well the importance of improvisation amid the tensions between contingency and sanctification. There is no script for the Christian life that comprehends every possible engagement with the world. Those who improvise draw upon their skills and past learning to perform their role in the drama. Wells says they "are schooled in a tradition so thoroughly that they learn to act from habit in ways appropriate to the circumstances."[72] Frances Young uses musical improvisation in a similar way to describe Christian scriptural interpretation. "In order to improvise effectively," Young writes, "the performer not only has to have technical competence, but also needs to understand music theory, the rules of harmony and counterpoint, the accepted conventions of development, the stylistic character of the work within which the cadenza is to figure." Thus, to improvise well, the Christian exegete needs a variety of competencies: philological, linguistic, contextual analysis, and imagination.[73]

Analogously, the Christian ethical life relies upon catechesis in the tradition to provide the theological and moral competencies that enable improvisation. Wells describes how Scripture and tradition, and perhaps reason and experience, "provide the boundaries of their performance" in the drama. The early church drew upon internalized habits of virtue to perform the holy life in whatever situation it found itself. The church cultivated scriptural habits and virtues "to improvise within its tradition" and form a community "in the right habits trusting itself to embody its tradition in new and often challenging circumstances."[74] In sum, nestled between contingency and perfection, the church should learn the art of improvising, or living Christianly, through the cultivation of faith and virtue organically embodying a cultural sanctification.

For all the ethical commands recounted above, the early church never prescribed specific cultural scenarios to explain virtuous living. It expected believers to cultivate virtue and then learn the art of expressing that virtue in any situation. Christians' lives were so thoroughly infused within the culture that they had to employ discernment in every facet of their lives: personal relationships, employment, recreational activities. This kind of improvisation, aiming for perfection among the contingencies of the moment, helped the church strive for faithfulness in the pagan world, holding to the straight and narrow path, so that, in Tertullian's poetic imagery, "amid these reefs and inlets, amid these shallows and straits of idolatry, Faith, her sails filled by the Spirit of God, navigates; safe if cautious, secure if intently watchful."[75]

LITURGY AND GATHERED WORSHIP

Liturgy was just as important as catechesis in the early church for doctrinal and moral formation. Liturgy strictly speaking meant the proper regulation of worship; as traditionally defined, it entails "a corporate religious service rendered to God by the people" that involves "a drama involving both God and the people, the 'exchange of prayers and graces, taking place in sacred time and sacred space."[76] This includes Sunday worship, the daily office, and other regular gatherings of the church's calendar. These rites unite the church's life and beliefs in ways that strengthen its identity and practice. Liturgy thus is the ongoing performative expression of the church's doctrine and morality. But this traditional definition still assumes too much distinction between the sacred and secular. In his book on cultural liturgies, James K. A. Smith reminds us that we are all *homo liturgicus*, or liturgical animals, because we are "embodied, practicing creatures whose love/desire is aimed at something ultimate." Liturgy, in this sense, takes on a broader definition to include both the performance of worship within a Christian service and the patterns of living according to love. These "liturgies—whether 'sacred' or 'secular'—shape and constitute our identities by forming our most fundamental desires and our most basic attunement to the world."[77]

Following Smith, we can see that the early church cultivated a distinct pattern of worship *and* living that distinguished it amid the regular patterns of life around it. Early Christians practiced cultural rhythms that defied Roman society in an alternative life of worship. To recall Walls's indigenizing principle, converts do not join the church as bare individuals but with a whole host of social relations, and Christians need to learn the art of living within these relations as Christians. The doctrine and morality they confess cannot remain theoretical and abstract; it needs to shape an embedded life so that the world can see the church as a place for human flourishing. Christian identity is not some lofty idea removed from lived Christian experience; rather it frames that experience in this present life. Catechesis and liturgy are like two hands working in tandem to guide believers through the pagan world while they perform their virtue in worship.

The church arranged regular communal worship that was performed in continuity and contrast with the cultural patterns of Rome. Charles Taylor's concept of the "social imaginary" is helpful here. In his analysis of the modern secular age, Taylor analyzes the way "ordinary people 'imagine' their social surroundings," an imaginary that is "carried in images, stories, legends, etc." Though only a few might know this theory, the whole society participates in an imagined world. It is "the common understanding which makes possible common practices, reflecting a widely shared sense of legitimacy."[78] It also entails "the way people think about the world, how they imagine it to be, how they act intuitively in relation to it."[79] The liturgical patterns of the early church challenged the "social imaginary" of the Roman world on many fronts. Amid the Roman world, Christians performed their holy lives by way of liturgical opposition. They *enacted* a rule of faith that confessed a distinctive, transcendent God who ruled providentially over creation and who was actively leading the church through a history of salvation that would not culminate in the glory of Rome but of God.

Since Christians were newcomers on the religious scene, many Romans struggled to understand what was happening in their gathered settings. The Roman governor Pliny, for example, described early Christianity as a "superstition" (*superstitio*) and "political club" (*hetaeria*). Galen, the Roman philosopher, thought it was a philosophical school.[80] Both descriptions were conscious attempts to fit the Christian community into known categories. But the church defied these categories because they sewed together things that were often separate in the Roman mind: the liturgical, the religious, and the philosophical. They were working from different metaphysical assumptions, different standards of morality, expressed in alternative patterns of worship.

This liturgical opposition is already evident in the New Testament, where Christians are described observing regular patterns of prayer or devotion, as well as the basic practices of baptism and Eucharist.[81] From the start, the regular patterns of Christian worship animated and defined the community, promoting a distinctive view of time that followed what Gerald Sittser calls a "liturgical script."[82] By the middle of the second century, this pattern was well established, as evident, for example, in Justin Martyr's *First Apology*. Vicious rumors were circulating in Rome, where Justin was ministering, that the Christians were participating in cannibalism, incest, and other sadistic practices. Justin refuted these charges by describing what was really going on in Christian worship; the pattern he laid out follows some of the same basic practices found in Scripture (Acts 2, 4, etc.) and in Christian worship today:

> And on the day called Sunday, all who live in cities or in the country gather together to one place, and the memoirs of the apostles or the writings of the prophets are read, as long as time permits; then, when the reader has ceased, the president verbally instructs, and exhorts to the imitation of these good things. Then we all rise together and pray, and, as we before said, when our prayer is ended, bread and wine and water are brought, and the president in like manner offers prayers and thanksgivings, according to his ability, and the people assent, saying Amen; and there is a distribution to each, and a participation of that over which thanks have been given, and to those who are absent a portion is sent by the deacons. And they who are well to do, and willing, give what each thinks fit; and what is collected is deposited with the president, who succors the orphans and widows and those who, through sickness or any other cause, are in want, and those who are in bonds and the strangers sojourning among us, and in a word takes care of all who are in need.[83]

This was not a church manual for how to perform worship but an apologetic description to calm the fears of those who thought something nefarious was going on in the church's gathering. The very fact that Justin had to explain these gatherings attests to their distinctiveness. Notice that all the elements of worship are present: gathering on Sunday, Scripture reading, preaching and exhortation, prayer, Lord's Supper, and tithing. Justin Martyr's description of the worship service followed a standard pattern and "its basic shape differed little from place to place."[84] These threads wove a distinct Christian pattern for worship, a structure that "is as fundamental to the church as its doctrine."[85] Choosing to worship on Sunday, for example, set the Christians apart from the Jewish community and commemorated the resurrection in the Lord's Supper. They worship on Sunday, Justin said, because "Sunday is the day on which we all hold our common assembly, because it is the first day on which God, having wrought a change in the darkness and matter, made the world; and Jesus Christ our Savior on the same day rose from the dead."[86] Among all these practices, baptism and Eucharist were clearly the rituals that "reinformed for the early Christians a special sense of identity."[87] Each of these elements served to mark out the Christians' vision of time, authority, and discipleship or sanctification. In short, for early Christians, and for us today, worship is the primary way the moral imagination is formed.[88]

In his work *On Prayer*, Tertullian provides a summary of liturgical practices in North Africa that shows liturgical formation in process. Which was the proper day to perform baptism, for instance? He gave theological reasons for baptizing at Easter, connected to the Lord's passion. "Passover," Tertullian writes, "affords a more than usually solemn day for baptism; when, withal, the Lord's passion, in which we are baptized, was completed." Tertullian likely had in mind passages such as Romans 6:4: "We were buried therefore with him by baptism into death, in order that, just as Christ was raised from the dead by the glory of the Father, we too might walk in newness of life." Yet Pentecost, too, was a good time for baptism, given its significance for the Lord's ascension and the Spirit's descent. Indeed, he saw no problem with baptizing on any day in the liturgical calendar, for "every day is the Lord's; every hour, every time, is apt for baptism: if there is a difference in the solemnity, distinction there is none in the grace."[89] Ultimately specific days were not the point; the point was that the church was thinking theologically about the liturgical calendar and how it spoke to the distinctive ministry of the church in opposition to the civil religion. Theirs was no Hallmark calendar that cycled through the popular holidays but a religious ordering that moved through the seasons celebrating the salvific acts of Christ and the Spirit. Christians tried to capture time and organize it around the rhythms of the Christian gospel.

LITURGY AND DAILY LIFE

The church did not prescribe liturgy only for gathered settings but tried to inculcate a daily spiritual life shaped by regular patterns of devotion. Their days and weeks were to be sprinkled with observance of prayer and fasting. Many early Christian works link prayer to the spiritual life and appeal to the Lord's Prayer as the paradigm to promote daily progress in sanctification.[90] The Didache, for example, encourages the church not to pray like the Jews or the Romans but to pray the Lord's Prayer "as the Lord commanded in the Gospel." Indeed, this should be done "three times a day," morning, noon, and evening. The Didache encouraged special fast days as well. If the Jews and Romans fasted on Mondays and Thursdays, the church should fast on Wednesdays and Fridays.[91] This kind of regular prayer and fasting was living in expectation of the Lord's return and following Paul's command to "pray without ceasing" (1 Thess 5:17). The early Christians understood that "they prayed as they lived: as citizens of two worlds." Prayer was "the daily confession of faith in a spirit of eschatological readiness of the Second Coming or for martyrdom, and of intercession for the needs of the church and the world."[92] These personal acts organized the days and weeks in regular patterns of personal worship that reinforced the larger liturgical patterns of the church.

The liturgical acts recorded in early Christian writings all helped to set the Christian life apart from the "social imaginary" of the Roman world. They performed their liturgy in defiance of the dominant rhythms around them, sprinkling them with a distinct Christian scent. This liturgical formation reminds us that the early church was not interested just in evangelizing and preaching but in forming a community. Christianity is "a culture-forming religion, and the planting and growth of Christian communities led to the remaking of the cultures of the ancient world."[93] Close-knit communities defined by the regular practices of worship and discipleship helped establish a pattern of living that ran contrary to the dominant cultures. Christianity is not just about what we believe and how we act but how we perform these things in public. The early church sought to become a living and visible manifestation of the beauty of the Christian gospel, and eventually this became a powerful apologetic.

Like the ancients, we flow in the stream of the postmodern world, but we need not give up our paddles and let the river take us where it wills. We can cultivate different rhythms of liturgy that shape our communities. Any discussion of cultural engagement today must give some serious thought to rival patterns of worship and examination of our own liturgical script. How does our worship form our people and create a sense of community? Does our worship distinguish us from the culture or simply reflect it? For far too long, evangelicals have imbibed alien forms of worship with the goal of exciting, entertaining, or evangelizing. But the liturgical focus of the early church reminds us of the importance of worship for community formation. Liturgy and worship shape the people of God, guiding them along the virtuous path of righteousness. Theirs was not an empty liturgy born of traditionalism but liturgy in contemplation of doctrine and practice and expressed in opposition to the patterns of the dominant culture. Our gathered worship and daily acts of devotion ought to mark out the faithful similarly as we live within a pagan world.

CONCLUSION

Hippolytus's account of baptism cited at the opening of this chapter shows that it was a serious occasion marking the transition out of the kingdom of darkness into the kingdom of light. Baptism was the moment when pagans who lived in a world infused with idolatry formally confessed their faith in God and committed to a life of holiness. The catechumens and the community of faith were united in a rhythm of conversion and confession by way of a different ritual that marked them out and challenged them to living faithfully within an alien world. This is where Christian vision of cultural engagement begins, with a Christian identity forged in a synergy between catechesis and liturgy. Early Christian thinkers such as Irenaeus or Origen never announced that they had, at long last, found the best method for taking over the empire. Instead, they wrote treatises on catechesis and the spiritual life that were serious about discipleship and spiritual formation. Like two threads, catechesis and liturgy were intertwined to fashion a distinct Christian identity and to prepare new converts to live Christianly in the world.

In catechesis, the church discipled new converts by the rule of faith and the way of life that promoted virtue. The rule entailed both doctrine and narrative. It set out the basic framework of reality, including both the substance of theological commitment and a metanarrative that moved from creation to recreation. The early Christian way of life aimed for virtue by improvising through all the contingencies of changing contexts to seek sanctification. The liturgical life supported this quest with a theological and moral performance in regular acts of worship. Thus was the church distinguished while organically intermingling with the surrounding world.

If there is any wisdom to be found in the basic vision of early Christian cultural engagement, it begins with how the church viewed its own identity and the call to cultivate a serious commitment to doctrinal conviction, moral formation, and the liturgical life. We need discipleship and catechesis now more than ever, the kind of slow steady discipleship that builds a bulwark of faithful followers who do not live in fear or anger but in holiness. We also need to think about liturgical practices that construct a different pattern of living in the culture. The early church had no political and social structures to come alongside the church and support its ministry, so the church had to cultivate patterns and rhythms of their own distinct from those of the pagan community. Through catechesis and liturgy, the church learned how to worship and serve, work and play, live and die. There is no doubt that the Christian community is facing a challenging future. But the church has been here before, and we need to focus our energies on cultivating our Christianity identity with all the theological and moral convictions it entails and a liturgical life that prepares us to live with conviction in our evolving world.

CITIZENSHIP

POLYCARP'S DEFENSE

"Away with the Atheists! Find Polycarp!" the crowd shouted.[1] They had already tortured and murdered several Christians, but now the mob craved the life of the beloved elderly bishop of Smyrna, hoping that his death might quell the insidious Christian movement. They dispatched a group of soldiers to arrest him. When the news reached Polycarp, he was not alarmed but waited for the soldiers to arrive and welcomed them into the house. He called for a feast to be set before them, requesting only a few hours for himself to pray in the next room. While he prayed, the soldiers listened in amazement. When they finished their meal, they took him back to the city. On the way, they tried to convince him to worship Caesar: "Why, what harm is there in saying, 'Caesar is Lord,' and offering incense (and other words to this effect) and thereby saving yourself?"[2] Why would Polycarp not placate the gods to survive? To them, Roman religion was one with Roman civic identity. How could Christians worship a transcendent God who reigns over all and at the same time honor the emperor?

Upon their return to the city, the soldiers led Polycarp into the stadium. The crowd roared in anticipation. They ushered him to the proconsul, who began a careful interrogation. "Have respect for your age," he said. "Swear by the Genius of Caesar; repent and say, 'Away with the atheists!'" At that moment, Polycarp, gazing around at the bloodthirsty crowd, turned his eyes toward heaven and said—ironically referring to the crowd—"Away with the atheists!"[3]

The proconsul was not amused. He entreated Polycarp again: "Swear the oath, and I will release you; revile Christ." Polycarp replied, "For eighty-six years I have been his servant, and he has done me no wrong. How can I blaspheme my King who saved me?"[4] Polycarp had served God faithfully, but now here he stood before an earthly ruler, living in a temporary empire, and surrounded by a seething mob who threatened him with torture and death. But Polycarp welcomed the opportunity to honor God with his life. For him, divine authority superseded any temporal political allegiance. He could not imagine denying the one true God and Creator who had saved him, gave him the hope of eternal life, and would one day establish an eternal kingdom.

For a third time, the proconsul turned to Polycarp and insisted he swear by the genius of the emperor and renounce Christ. The bishop responded plainly; as a Christian, he could not worship the emperor. Polycarp offered to explain the doctrines of Christianity so that the proconsul could understand, but to no avail. Instead, the proconsul gestured to the crowd and encouraged Polycarp to persuade *them*. But Polycarp invoked the teaching of the apostles: "You I might have considered worthy of a reply, for we have been taught to pay proper respect to rulers and authorities appointed by God, as long as it does us no harm; but as for these, I do not think they are worthy that I should have to defend myself before them." That is, there was no compelling reason for him to justify his beliefs before the angry mob calling for his death, but the proconsul was different. He was a ruler "appointed by God," and the church, following Romans 13:1, had to respect those in political authority. This fundamental political dualism had defined Christian citizenship from the very beginning, and in a hostile pagan environment, the church had to learn how to apply Paul's words quickly. For Polycarp, this meant that Christians were to respect earthly political rulers, even in the face of persecution.[5]

Polycarp's argument did not satisfy the proconsul or the crowd, so the good bishop was sentenced to death. With that—in the words of his pagan opponents—this "teacher of Asia, the father of the Christians, the destroyer of our gods, who teaches many not to sacrifice or worship," was removed from this earth, and the people were relieved that they would soon be freed of this foolish sect that undermined their way of life.[6] But Polycarp, as he was burned at the stake, offered a final prayer that reaffirmed God's reign over all things:

> O Lord God Almighty, the Father of your beloved and blessed Son Jesus Christ, through whom we have received the knowledge of you, the God of angels and powers and of all creation, and of the whole race of the righteous who live in your presence, I bless you because you have considered me worthy of this day and hour, that I might receive a place among the number of the martyrs in the cup of your Christ, to the resurrection to eternal life, both of soul and of body, in the incorruptibility of the Holy Spirit. May I be received among them in your presence today, as a rich and acceptable sacrifice, as you have prepared and revealed beforehand, and have now accomplished, you who are the undeceiving and true God. For this reason, indeed for all things, I praise you, I bless you, I glorify you, through the eternal and heavenly High Priest, Jesus Christ, your beloved Son, through whom to you with him and the Holy Spirit by glory both now and for the ages to come. Amen.[7]

As he drew his final breath, Polycarp worshiped the God who had created the very people calling for his death.

This narrative comes down to us in the text entitled the Martyrdom of Polycarp, which served as a model for early Christian apologetics and martyrdom. Of course, some may question the historicity of the account or quibble over some of its hagiographical details, but that would distract from its larger theological and political argument. The narrative is more than a wonderful tale about a good bishop who was faithful to the end; it taught political theology. The bishop of Smyrna, the Roman crowds, and the proconsul had competing visions of citizenship and the dynamics between God and world, and from their interaction, we can begin to grasp some of the basic contours of the church's political theology. The church developed a vision of cultural sanctification that situated political authorities in their rightful place under the providence and authority of God.

As seen in the previous chapter, early Christian identity was shaped through the interwoven threads of catechesis and liturgy to guide them through the world, including the political world. The relationship between the church and politics poses a perplexing question, for us as for that ancient crowd. How do Christians understand their identity in relationship to civil society, and upon what basis? Conversion to Christianity entailed a new understanding of citizenship and a new posture toward society, a new set of assumptions and orienting first principles. Like tourists traveling to a new land, early Christians found themselves needing to reacclimate to a new environment; that included reorienting their understanding of political power.

Political theology in the early church rested on three core assumptions: a firm conviction in divine transcendence and providence, a belief that God granted political authority to certain earthly rulers, and an active citizenship that proceeded from a political dualism. First, the church's approach to the political sphere was framed by its understanding of the nature of God and God's present reign over this world. The West has long assumed that political thought is something quite separate from theology or religious activity. But for the early church, theological claims about the nature of God had political implications. Second, given divine transcendence and providence, the church believed that all imperial authority was bestowed by God for specific purposes, primarily to maintain peace and security, to promote justice, and allow religious liberty. When ancient Christians thought about the emperor or civil authority, they respected them and their position, even as they appealed to a higher authority. They understood that God is sovereign even when, as Hebrews states, "we do not yet see everything in subjection to him" (Heb 2:8). Third, under this canopy, Christians were active citizens, which compelled them to honor civil authorities, pray for them fervently, pay all taxes, defend religious liberty, and promote virtue. Early Christians dwelt in the tension of this dual allegiance and learned how to live faithfully amid a pagan culture. So might we, even as there are some important differences between a modern liberal democracy and ancient imperial rule. The early church lacked the opportunity to contribute to politics by activism and voting. We should not take these things for granted but keep them in mind as we draw upon the ancient church's vision of political theology.

For these various attributes communicate a solid Christian vision of citizenship and a healthy perspective on the state. Even when they were outcasts, Christians respected politics and political authorities, because God still reigned over all. As Christendom crumbles, this vision of citizenship should assure us that even in our darkest political moments, God is the Creator and sustainer of all. This is his world, and we are sheep of his pasture. This point must encompass us and settle into our lives. That does not mean that we turn a blind eye toward sin or passively accept the status quo. We must become active citizens who both honor the state and seek to shape it according to the goodness of divine law. In the world of Christendom, Christians often focused their efforts on transformation, hoping to change the culture through political means. But our only hope in life and death lies not in such political victories but in the basic theological confession that we belong to God.[8]

DIVINE TRANSCENDENCE, PROVIDENCE, AND POLITICAL THEOLOGY

The early church's view of the state did not begin with the state but with God. Any conception of good citizenship must ask the more fundamental question, Who or what is God? When we proclaim to love God, we should ask, like Augustine, "what do I love?"[9] Is there a transcendent creator, or is this world all there is? What is the highest authority that commands our allegiance and worship? If God, according to the Scriptures, is the Creator of all things and reigns over all, then there is nothing that exists outside of his providential care. This metaphysical reality should unite the people of God and inform their vision of political and social life. The doctrine of one God and Creator "formed the background and indisputable premise of the Church's faith" in the face of a pagan world, forming a "bulwark against pagan polytheism" and other religious communities.[10] Furthermore, if God reigns over all, there is nothing to fear; the faithful can stroll down the street with all confidence, knowing that the Creator of all things is watching over them and providentially administrating creation toward an appointed end.

PAGAN AND CHRISTIAN POLITICAL THEOLOGY

Roman views of religion were closely tied to the power of the state. Any notion of divine transcendence and providence was domesticated into earthly political structures. We find the term *providentia* on Roman coins, for example, which assumed that the gods ensured the cycles of the seasons and peaceful transitions of political power.[11] Christianity, on the other hand, held to a "transcendent religiosity" that distinguished God from the present world.[12] For Christians, the sacred is not fused with the created world, nor does a pantheon of gods that struggle against each other for preeminence have to be placated.

Like ancient Rome, the postmodern world "cuts us off from any agreed upon transcendent metaphysical order" and offers no unambiguous moral framework for political activity.[13] Drawing off the model of the early church's cultural engagement must begin with our recovering the concept of real and honest interaction between divine and human acts within "one public history."[14] History was the "crux of the issue" between Christianity and the classical world.[15] This world, not just part of this world, "is the theatre of God's saving purposes and mankind's social undertakings."[16] God reigns providentially over creation, administering everything within and outside the church. This means that early Christians stood in awe of God, not Jupiter or the emperor or any other civic official. God reigned, so there was no reason to run and hide, no fear of political oppression, and no need to capitulate or compromise. As the "doctrine of one God, the Father and creator, formed the background and indisputable premise of the Church's faith,"[17] so many church fathers joined Polycarp in proclaiming their confidence in the Lord's transcendent providence, also under the pressure of opposition and persecution.[18] This differed fundamentally from a mindset oriented exclusively to this present world. For the Christian, divine transcendence offers an eternal and objective basis for their political and social order.

Every apologist in early Christianity, surrounded as they were by pagan gods and temples lining the streets, consistently appealed to the first principles of divine transcendence, of God as Creator over all, and of the appointed telos of creation.[19] Scriptural passages such as Romans 13:1–7, Titus 3:1, and 1 Peter 2:13–17 guided their understanding of living the Christian life under the authority of earthly rulers appointed by a sovereign God. This was, after all, the first point of the rule of faith and the basic difference between the pagan and Christian views of reality. Christian monotheism entailed not only a singular God but also a distinction in divine attributes. As Smith argues in *Pagans and Christians in the City*, "the ultimately crucial difference is not so much that the Jewish and Christian God is solitary while the pagan gods are plural. What matters, rather, is the relation of those deities to the world and even, we might say, their metaphysical status."[20] God rules and reigns, there is no one like him, and he shares his glory with no one.

A good example of early Christian political theology is found in a letter commonly known as 1 Clement, sent by Clement, the bishop of the church at Rome, to the church at Corinth. A faction of younger men in the Corinthian church had revolted against the older leadership and splintered the community, even as the church experienced persecution from the outside.[21] The letter, likely composed late in the first century during the reign of the hostile Domitian, encouraged the congregation in Corinth to remain unified despite these internal and external struggles.[22] The first twenty chapters trace the faithfulness of God's people in the face of persecution throughout salvation history. Just as these had trusted in divine sovereignty and providence, so now, Clement argues, the church must do likewise: "Let us see him [God] in our mind, and let us look with the eyes of the soul on his patient will." God is not hostile toward creation; no, the "heavens move at his direction and obey him in peace," while the "earth, bearing fruit in the proper seasons in fulfillment of his will, brings forth food in full abundance for both men and beasts and all living things which are upon it, without dissension or altering anything he has decreed." Everything, Clement concludes, "the great Creator and Master of the universe ordered to exist in peace and harmony, thus doing good to all things, but especially abundantly to us who have taken refuge in his compassionate mercies through our Lord Jesus Christ" (1 Clem 20). Everything is arranged and governed as God's will determines, even down to the smallest things. Thus, there is no reason to fear.

In his closing lines, Clement drew the practical implications of divine transcendence with a thoroughly political prayer meant to encourage and motivate his readers. He invokes the Lord, who rules wisely and mercifully over creation, to "save those among us who are in distress; have mercy on the humble; raise up the fallen; show yourself to those in need; heal the godless; turn back those of your people who wander; feed the hungry; release our prisoners; raise up the weak; comfort the discouraged. 'Let all the nations know that you are the only God'" (1 Clem. 59; Acts 4:27). Clement repeats that the sovereign Lord has been "given power of sovereignty" through God's "majestic and inexpressible might" (1 Clem. 61). This was a doctrine of comfort; we live in God's world as the sheep of his pasture (1 Clem. 59; Ezek 34:31).

Many other ancient Christians underscored the political importance of divine transcendence and providence. Amid Christian heresies celebrating a pantheon of gods, Irenaeus held fast to the "absolute transcendence" of God.

His rule of faith, discussed above, begins with "God, the Father, uncreated, uncontainable, invisible, one God, the Creator of all."[23] For Irenaeus, "it is a matter of necessity that God, the Fullness of all these, should contain all things in His immensity, and should be contained by no one."[24] Hence, his formula: God encloses all things but is enclosed by nothing.[25] But if "God exists in a completely different order of being than humanity and material creation,"[26] then nothing exists outside of God's providential care. If this seemed baffling from the pagan point of view, Irenaeus pointed his followers to passages like Isaiah 55:8: "For my thoughts are not your thoughts, neither are your ways my ways, declares the LORD."

Like Irenaeus, the Epistle to Diognetus observes that the one true God was revealed to God's people not as another god to add to the pantheon but as "God, Himself, who is almighty, the Creator of all things and invisible."[27] The language of "almighty" communicated "God's all-pervading control and sovereignty over reality."[28] This is the God who "made heaven and earth, and all that is therein, and gives to us all the things of which we stand in need."[29] The Shepherd of Hermas, a widely read early Christian apocalyptic text, describes "God who dwells in the heavens, and made out of nothing the things that exist and multiplied and increased them on account of his holy church." Then it adds, "the name of the Son of God is great, and cannot be contained, and supports the whole world. If, then, the whole creation is supported by the Son of God, what think ye of those who are called by him?"[30] Origen said in response to the pagan Celsus, "So completely does Divine providence embrace all things, that not even the hairs on your head fail to be numbered by him."[31] Again and again, the early fathers cycled back to this fundamental assumption: there is one, true God who reigns over all things, and this one, true God is leading creation toward an appropriate end. Those faithful to him are citizens of the kingdom of God, and their ultimate hope lay not in the glory of Rome but in the glory of that kingdom.

This tenet should resonate from every pulpit and permeate every Bible study gathering today. Like the early church, we need to be continually re-assured that God is the author and preserver of creation. We should say it so often that it sinks into our souls and inspires us to live with confidence. Loving parents remind their children that though the trials of life may toss them about, they will do everything in their power to protect and provide for them. So also does the transcendence and sovereignty of God remind his people that God reigns over all things and that the earth stands silent before him. Certainly societal problems, sin, and death mar God's world, but the most important theological prolegomenon for cultural engagement today is the transcendence and providence of God.

This also must inform any proper view of citizenship. The early church's discussions of the transcendence, sovereignty, authority, and singularity of God were fundamentally political and pervaded their political interactions and arguments going forward. Without divine transcendence, there is no Christian political theology. Historian Paul Veyne recognizes that "the originality of Christianity lies not in its so-called monotheism, but in the gigantic nature of its god, the creator of both heaven and earth: it is a gigantism that is alien to the pagan gods and is inherited from the god of the Bible."[32] Once believers were baptized into the church, they held a new set of first principles that became a dividing line separating them out theologically and ideologically. They had, to put it simply, very different conceptions of reality, power, and authority from their pagan neighbors. Even though this may have led to breakdowns in communication, since there were few common metaphysical assumptions from which dialogue could proceed, proper Christian cultural engagement still proceeded from a love of God's transcendence, sovereignty, and providence in and over creation.[33]

POLITICAL AUTHORITY BESTOWED BY GOD

With such a high view of divine providence, the early church had a positive view of the state even amid persecution. God's sovereignty and providence had delegated some authority to earthly rulers for a purpose. The early church operated by a persistent conviction that God had granted authority to the state and that Christians ought to submit to the just rule of earthly kings. As Polycarp said to the proconsul, "You I might have considered worthy of a reply, for we have been taught to pay proper respect to rulers and authorities appointed by God, as long as it does us no harm."[34]

Early Christian theologians cited Scripture to the point. When Joseph or Daniel found themselves in a foreign land ruled by a pagan king, they did not sit around complaining; they lived virtuously and worked within the structures of the civil authority to become leaders worthy of respect. In the New Testament, Peter and Paul prescribed the same approach. Paul told the church to recognize that God had installed political authorities (Rom 13:1–7), and he fearlessly engaged political authorities such as Felix and Festus with the gospel whenever he stood before them.[35] Peter, too, instructed the people, "Fear God. Honor the emperor" (1 Pet 2:17). Jesus himself called the faithful to render to Caesar what is Caesar's and to the Lord what is the Lord's (Matt 22:21). Declares Old Testament wisdom, God "makes nations great, and he destroys them; he enlarges nations, and leads them away" (Job 12:23).

Given their situation, it is most striking that early Christians were not anti-imperial. Yet the early church did not remain idle when the actions of the state or its representatives lacked virtue. Nor did they regularly pass glowing praises of the state's actions or laws. They performed civil disobedience and critiqued the laws with the good rhetorical flourishes they had learned from their classical education. When the state promoted unrighteousness, they proclaimed, with the apostles, that Rome was Babylon (1 Pet 5:13). But even then they did not forget the apostles' other injunctions and regard the state as wholly evil.

Living within a pagan empire, the church understood the primary functions of the state to be promoting peace and security, enacting just laws to curb sin, and allowing the free exercise of religion for the promotion of virtue. If there was no authority except that which comes from God, and if God in his sovereignty had empowered the state to provide for the security and safety of its citizens, then the state had been granted the sword to bring peace and security. Many in the early church believed that the "sword was the state's real vocation . . . dialectically link[ing] Roman submission to emperor and Christian submission to God."[36] Alluding to Romans 13:4–6 and related passages, Irenaeus observes that "earthly rule" has been "appointed by God for the benefit of nations, and not by the devil, who is never at rest at all, nay, who does not love to see even nations conducting themselves after a quiet manner."[37] Like Irenaeus, the apologist Athenagoras, writing to the Stoic emperor Marcus Aurelius, states that we Christians "are of all men most piously and righteously disposed toward the Deity and towards your government."[38] Tertullian put it simply: "we respect in the emperors the will of God, who has made them rulers of the nations."[39] Even the prayer of 1 Clement teaches that God gives "to sons of men glory and honor and authority over those upon the earth."[40] The Epistle of Barnabas teaches, "You shall be subject to the Lord, and to [other] masters as the image of God, with modesty and fear." At the same time, "You shall seek out every day the faces of the saints, either by word examining them, and going to exhort them," and, "You shall remember the day of judgment, night and day."[41] Even when they struggled with it, early Christians heard a constant refrain to respect the state's authority.

Besides providing safety and security for its citizens, the state was ordained to impose laws to suppress lawlessness, limit sin, and thereby promote virtue in its citizens and justice in society.[42] Early Christian theologians such as Origen saw continuity between civil laws and the divine law. He reasoned that since the Scriptures did not list out every vice covered by the civil law, therefore "all the crimes that God wants to be punished, he has willed that they be punished not through the priests and leaders of the churches, but through the worldly judge. And aware of this, Paul rightly names him a minister of God and an avenger of the one who does what is evil."[43] For Origen, these associations between the just rule of God and earthly rulers were remarkable. Pondering the claim of Romans 13:4 that the emperor is "God's servant," he writes, "Paul troubles [me] by these words, that he calls the secular authority and the worldly judgment a minister of God; and he does this not merely one time, but he even repeats it a second and a third time."[44] Further exploring the connection, Origen reasoned that the apostles only concerned themselves with divine laws because the civil laws were already sufficient to regulate general crimes. The apostles had to stipulate avoiding meat sacrificed to idols (Acts 15:29) but not various other commands concerning murder, adultery, and so on, because these things were already covered by civil law. In this way, Origen argued, a "worldly judge fulfills the greatest part of God's law."[45] There is no spiritual partitioning in this kind of reasoning; the church was to obey civil laws as a way of revering and respecting "God's servant," God's chosen leader.

Early Christian theologians well knew that political power could be abused, even though it was meant to curb sin. Not all civil leaders are virtuous, and, in the Lord's providence, people experience different types of political governance. Some rules, Irenaeus observes, "are given for the correction and the benefit of their subjects, and for the preservation of justice; but others, for the purposes of fear and punishment and rebuke; others, as [the subjects] deserve it, are for deception, disgrace, and pride; while the just judgment of God . . . passes equally upon all."[46] Origen likewise saw both the benefit and the exploitations of political power. Just as the senses of sight, hearing, and touch are natural inclinations given to the body, so is the authority bestowed upon human rulers a gift of God. Power, though, just like the natural senses, might be used for either good or evil purposes. God bestows power, but "the judgment of God will be just in respect to those who govern with the authority they have received in accordance with their own impieties and not in accordance with God's laws."[47] Like a tool that can be used for both constructive and malicious purposes, the state is not inherently evil but can be used to promote virtue or vice. In sum, to the early church, the state was essential to the work of God and the unfolding of God's redemption. The church was not rebellious or cynical toward the state and agreed with its pagan neighbors that those who rebel against the king and dissolve public order should be justly punished.

Third, the church argued for the free exercise of religion so that it might promote public virtue. The two went hand in hand. When the church engaged political authorities, it stressed the need for virtuous rulers to administer justice and honor the conscience by recognizing religious liberty. The people of God held the state accountable to the virtue assumed in the natural law, and to the normative arrangement of justice given by divine command in Scripture. It hoped that as the state provided for the safety and security of its citizens, it would not curtail religious activity. It worried about the various ways that the state might compromise the purity and liberty of the church. Following the reign of Constantine and the rise of a cultural Christianity, this became less a serious concern. In the pre-Constantinian period, however, the freedom to worship according to conscience was the bigger issue.[48] As the Martyrdom of Polycarp testifies, that freedom was not observed consistently among the populace or by government officials. To be a Roman citizen was to worship the gods, and rebellion against that seemed tantamount to treason and insurrection.

Christians living in the first few centuries were the first to articulate the importance of religious freedom and the injustice of coercing the conscience. They rejected any state that hopes "to build only in this world a kingdom of definitive happiness or in absolutist fashion seeks to force religion into a legal system that alone has full jurisdiction."[49] Tertullian warns hostile authorities, "see that you do not give a further ground for the charge of irreligion, by taking away religious liberty, and forbidding free choice of deity, so that I may no longer worship according to my inclination, but am compelled to worship against it." He complained that while the Egyptians worshiped "gods of birds and beasts," and while Syria, Arabia, Africa, and other Roman provinces had their own gods, both denied Christians opportunity to worship according to their conscience. Ironically, "liberty is given to worship any god but the true God, as though He were not rather the God all should worship, to whom all belong."[50] Hippolytus makes a similar point in his commentary on Daniel. The faithful "ought not dissemble or fear the powerful, especially those who use power for evil. If they are compelled to do something opposed to their belief, their better choice is death rather than submission." Then, treating the injunction of Paul in Romans 13:1, he commented, "the words of the apostle—to obey the authorities that are over us—enjoin us not to obey human commands against our belief and God's law, but to avoid doing evil while respecting authority in order to escape punishment as lawbreakers."[51] In the second century, Justin Martyr was not shy about condemning Roman authorities for their treatment of Christians. On one occasion, he criticized the way Roman authorities handled the case of a female convert to Christianity who divorced her pagan husband because of his excessive immorality.[52] Urbicus, the prefect of Rome, had condemned the woman's pastor, Ptolemaeus, to death simply for being a Christian. Justin's public censures did not go unnoticed. At some point, he, too, was arrested, dragged before the authorities, and ultimately martyred.[53]

These three—promoting peace and security, enacting just laws that curb sin, and allowing the free exercise of religion—were not the only functions of the state envisioned by the early church, but they did frame their political theology. The church continually cycled back to these points and challenged political figures when they did not uphold them. When the state neglected them, moved beyond them, or imposed upon religious conscience, they encouraged the faithful not to submit to the state. The early church recognized that these functions, well performed, allowed for the church to live virtuously and get on with the good work of ministry.

As we think about political engagement today, these are important guidelines for us too. The West may be becoming increasingly pagan, and the state may enact laws contrary to God and God's word, but this does not mean that we reject the state. Nor should we cower and hide from it. Significantly, in our democratic republic, we have a greater degree of influence over the political systems than did Christians in ancient Rome. Christian citizens, whether then or now, recognize that civil leaders and emperors, no matter how brutal and wicked, have been appointed by God for divine purposes. Politics thus is not the problem, nor is it the solution. The church should respond to leaders who do not allow the church to practice its faith. Likewise, we can support political action that helps promote virtue. Yet it is not finally civil laws that make people virtuous but the Spirit of God working through catechesis and liturgy. As we maneuver in the public square, we must never assume a posture of despair that forgets divine transcendence or seek a utopia that forgets human sin but remember that God is sovereign and mandates the church to work for the public good.

POLITICAL DUALISM AND ACTIVE CITIZENSHIP

Political engagement in the early church went beyond reciting first principles to take up how Christians were to act within the political arena. The church hardly yielded to the state in all things, shutting its mouth and avoiding civil disobedience. It "never confronted the state with a 'no' of inflexible refusal dictated by an otherworldly mysticism or with a 'yes' of unqualified acceptance based on political indifference."[54] Ancient Christians, out on the margins, perhaps more than in any other era of church history learned the art of living simultaneously in the "yes" and "no." They could affirm the authority and role of the state, while at the same time recognizing that God was in charge. The state could not ultimately offer the life of virtue, so the church had to cultivate it on its own and encourage it where it could in public life. The church remained actively engaged in public affairs—now in dialogue, now in service, now in conscientious resistance.

ACTIVE POLITICAL DUALISM

The early Christian approach can thus be described as an active political dualism. "Active," because their apologists claimed Christians to be the most faithful and dedicated citizens precisely because God had appointed the emperor and reigned providentially over all things. Thus, they did not break the law or commit acts of immorality, and if anyone in their community did so, they expected them to be punished to the full extent of the law. At the same time, they rejected any political monism. They did not meld religion and the state as theonomy or integralism. They accepted the arrangement of rendering to Caesar what belonged to Caesar and to the Lord what belonged to the Lord.

The church rooted its political theology in key biblical passages, applying them to their own context. Romans 13 provided a theological basis for its political dualism, while Matthew 22:21 ("render to Caesar") and Matthew 6:24 ("No one can serve two masters") helped define the limits of submission to the state. The church fathers saw a marked difference between earthly and heavenly citizenship. Tertullian, for example, told pagan observers that the Christian is a "foreigner in this world" but a "citizen of Jerusalem, the city above"; he continued, our "citizenship, the apostle says, is in heaven [Phil 3:20]. You have your own registers, your own calendar; you have nothing to do with the joys of the world; nay, you are called to the very opposite, for 'the world shall rejoice, but you shall mourn' [John 16:20]."[55] In other places, the fathers pointed to the figures of Joseph and Daniel as models for a political engagement that supports the state while remaining spiritually faithful. Daniel was submissive to Darius in every way except those that were a "danger to his religion." Yet both biblical figures were able to administrate with "dignity and power" in Egypt and Babylon.[56]

This political dualism posed a serious problem for their pagan neighbors. They saw Christians as desecrating Roman culture, especially Roman religion. For Rome, the head of state was the "supreme priest" and "stubbornly insisted on treating religion as an exclusively political factor."[57] Religion was an important way to unify the empire, bringing all people under a single set of ultimate commitments. It created a way of belonging in the state. It was defined by deference to the civic authorities and other benefactors, fear of the gods, and tolerance of many different religious expressions that could dwell together in a cultural mixture.[58]

Though many of the pre-Constantinian fathers talked about political dualism, the clearest explanation came many years later in Augustine's portrait of two cities created by two loves: the heavenly city from the love of God, and the earthly city from the love of self.[59] Smith lays out the neat paradox: "pagan religious polytheism was consistent with a sort of political monism; Christian monotheism, conversely, led to a kind of political polytheism—or at least political dualism."[60] This dualism was the precursor to the modern pluralism or divided sovereignty that covers the political landscape today. These competing visions of allegiance, as Smith notes, comprise distinct conceptions of the divine, which might be best understood in terms of competing metaphysical assumptions.

The church, by contrast, sharply distinguished between church and state. The institution of the state was willed by God, but the church "remained on the defensive in order to protect her freedom from any stifling embrace of the state, even at the risk of death."[61] Celsus, the second-century critic of Christianity, charged, "You say that it is not possible for one to serve two masters, but is this not the language of revolution, the language of a people who wish to build a wall between themselves and all others and to separate themselves from the rest of the world?"[62] The abiding problem for early Christianity, besides frivolous rumors and various mundane squabbles, was this clash of competing political ideologies. The Romans viewed Christians as subversive, as "a sect that hates the human race," in the words of the Roman historian Tacitus.[63] The "very existence of Christianity, with its perverse and sacrilegious doctrines— sacrilegious relative to pagan piety, that is—was a kind of desecration, or 'de-sacralization.'" Christians "actively and affirmatively subverted the foundations of Roman authority"[64]—even of the whole society, according to Celsus.[65]

Early Christians would have us today master this art of political dualism, to learn to walk the careful line between earthly and heavenly citizenship. We can never lose one for the other. We should avoid the dangers of both the warrior mentality that can lead to anger and the passivity that can generate separatism and seclusion. This is no mushy middle but a stalwart high ground on which one will not lose footing or tumble off in either direction. Walking this tight-rope requires the pursuit of virtuous living that demonstrates Christians to be the best citizens. No doubt our encounters with the state will sometimes demand clear and direct critiques of its actions. But we cannot reject God's good creation or the call to active public participation, celebrating good citizenship and seasoning the earth with virtue. At the same time, we cannot become so enamored with creation as to forget the home that awaits us in the coming kingdom of God. At bottom, we demonstrate good citizenship precisely *when* we live in hope of the coming kingdom.

ACTIVE CITIZENSHIP

What contribution did early Christians make in their earthly citizenship? Besides respecting the proper functions of the state, they honored civil authorities, prayed for peace and stability, paid their taxes, defended religious liberty, and generally promoted virtue. These were the columns, standing upon the foundation of Divine transcendence and respect for political authority, that upheld Christian activity within the political sphere. Each of them might help us consider how the church ought to approach the state today.

Honor Civil Authorities

First, the early church honored those in positions of political authority. Honor does not imply capitulation, compromise, or agreement, but it does entail respect, and the early church gave that to the emperor even during the reigns of the most brutal of them, such as Nero, Domitian, and Diocletian. As Polycarp said in his public defense, this honoring held up to the borders of offending conscience or worshiping false gods. Polycarp recognized that the Roman official standing before him, holding his life in his hands, was in power only because God allowed it. With dramatic flair, Tertullian argued that the emperor, "since he has been chosen by God," actually "is more our emperor than yours, for our God has appointed him." Christians bowed their heads to a holy God and prayed for the welfare of political authorities "with hands outstretched" because the "emperor gets his scepter where he got the breath of life."[66]

Sometimes early Christians hoped for an emperor who honored God and ruled righteously, but they were more concerned with living righteously under the reign of even evil rulers than in exploiting political power or undermining political authorities. They did so out of allegiance to God as the ultimate sovereign. Thus, while Celsus's materialist assumptions held that all things begin and end with the emperor as the sole authority, Origen rejected that pretension; Christians deny "that all things that are on earth have been given to the king, or that whatever we receive in this life we receive from him. For whatever we receive rightly and honorably we receive from God, and by his Providence, as ripe fruits and bread from the earth and wine to gladden men's hearts (Ps 104:15)."[67] Likewise, Theophilus argued that just as "the emperor would not allow his subordinate officials to be called emperors, for that title belongs to him alone and no other may use it legally, so neither is it lawful for anyone but God to be worshipped." The king was to be "revered with due honor, for he is not a god but a man appointed by God, not to be worshiped but to judge justly."[68]

Christians were very realistic about the virtue or abilities of civic leaders. They did not ignore their failures and vices. In his commentary on Romans 13, Origen reminded his readers that Paul was speaking of "just author-ity," the kind of leadership that manifested the classical virtues and ruled in wisdom commensurate with scriptural teaching. The "one who resists them procures condemnation for himself for the quality of his own deeds."[69] With Origen, "just power" would be measured by the standards of natural law and scriptural revelation.

What would such respect for political authorities look like today? What does it say when Christians scornfully mock political figures? We can still cri-tique and disagree with political officials, but if Polycarp could respect the office of the man threatening him with death, Christians today can be known for their political respect, even in disagreement. Here Christian views of di-vine transcendence meet the real world. Recovering a vision of early Christian cultural sanctification means that we look at politics through the lens of God's providential care. However unsettled current events might make us feel, the fathers' reading of Scripture reminds us again and again that this is God's world and that we are his people. When political authorities make poor decisions and fail to lead well, we may arise in protest, but we may not in fear or indignation fail to fear God and honor political authorities.

Pray for Civil Authorities

Second, early Christians prayed fervently for the state and for wise and just rule by earthly authorities, not only the emperor but all in positions of power. In a world where partisan lines are sharp and everyone is quick to post on social media and slow to listen, there is nothing that better reminds the faithful of the reality that this is God's world than the simple act of bowing for prayer. The posture of prayer points to a transcendent view of reality and recognizes that God is at work. In their prayers, the fathers included matters that define the proper goals of the state: peace, stability, and sound judgment. They prayed that those endowed with political authority might rule and reign and enact laws that served the common good. They hoped that in all his actions, the emperor would carry out the good work of administration with all virtue.

All this is to simply follow the commands of Scripture as in 1 Timothy 2:1–4 and Matthew 5:44. A good example of a prayer oriented toward the political world is found in 1 Clement, which first pleads that God would give "harmony and peace to us and to all who dwell on earth" and "to our rulers and governors on earth." Second, that God would give political leaders "the power of sovereignty" so that Christians, "acknowledging the glory and honor which you have given them, may be subject to them, resisting your will in nothing." Third, that the Lord grant these pagan rulers "health, peace, harmony, and stability, that they may blamelessly administer the government which you have given them." Finally, that the Lord might "direct their plans according to what is good and pleasing in your sight, so that by devoutly administering in peace and gentleness the authority which you have given them they may experience your mercy."[70] In line with these exhortations, Polycarp, in his letter to the Philippians, exhorts his fellow Christians, "Pray for all the saints. Pray also for kings and powers and rulers, and for those who persecute and hate you, and for the enemies of the cross, in order that your fruit may be evident among all people, that you may be perfect in him."[71] And Theophilus of Antioch told his critics that instead of honoring the gods, "I prefer to honor the emperor, not by worshiping him but by praying for him."[72]

Since early Christians believed in God's providential reign, they also believed their prayers were upholding the state and the world. This is why Hippolytus wrote, "This is always the devil's way in persecuting, in afflicting, in oppressing Christians: to stop them from lifting their blameless hands in prayer (1 Tim 2:8) to God, knowing that the prayer of saints obtains peace for the world, punishment for wrongdoers." Hippolytus pointed to the story of Moses fighting Amalek in Exodus 17:11; when Moses's hands were raised, Israel prevailed, but when they were lowered, the people were pushed back. "Today too," Hippolytus continued, "this happens to us and among us; when we stop praying, our enemy prevails; when we are faithful in prayer, the strength and power of the evil one weakens."[73] The prayers of the faithful are spiritual devices against the assaults of the evil one and the means by which God works within creation.

Like Tertullian, Hippolytus used Daniel as an example for the faithful. Although Daniel was absorbed in royal affairs, he remained faithful to his daily prayers, giving to Caesar what was Caesar's and to God what was God's (Matt 22:21).[74] Justin Martyr assured the authorities that Christians prayed for them: "we adore only God, but in other things we gladly serve you, acknowledging you as emperors and sovereigns, praying that along with your royal power you may be endowed too with sound judgment."[75] That kind of judgment would be conducive both to the faith and worship of the church and to maintaining peace in the empire. Theophilus called the church to "honor the emperor, be subject to him, and pray loyally for him" in accordance with Proverbs 24:21–22: "fear the Lord and the king, have nothing to do with those who rebel against them, for suddenly arises the destruction they send."[76] The call for prayer positions the church as a community gathered, head bowed, as citizens of heaven imploring God in fervent hope to guide earthly rulers toward peace and justice.

That peace might rule the nations was a major point of prayer. We already saw this in 1 Clement, but Tertullian, too, noted that Christians pray "for the complete stability of the empire, and for Roman interests in general." The prosperity of Rome and the ministry of the church were in some ways tied together; the church had no wish for chaos. Christians, therefore, prayed not just for the emperor but for peace and stability in the whole empire, which would enable the church's ministry. The fathers often had a sense of optimism, deriving from their belief in divine transcendence, that the church would be able to serve and grow. As Tertullian continued, "Without ceasing, for all our emperors we offer prayer. We pray for life prolonged; for security to the empire; for protection to the imperial house; for brave armies, a faithful senate, a virtuous people, the world at rest, whatever, as man or Caesar, an emperor would wish." Some of their contemporaries doubted Christians' sincerity and argued that they simply pretended to pray for the emperor while actually hoping for the destruction of Rome and the fall of the empire. For those who doubted the Christians' loyalty to the state, Tertullian urged these critics to read Scripture: "Do you, then, who think that we care nothing for the welfare of Caesar, look into God's revelations, examine our sacred books, which we do not keep in hiding, and which many accidents put into the hands of those who are not of us. Learn from them that a large benevolence is enjoined upon us, even so far as to supplicate God for our enemies, and to beseech blessings on our persecutors [Matt 5:44]." He adds that the Scriptures say clearly, "Pray for kings, and rulers, and powers, that all may be peace with you [1 Tim 2:2]."[77] As disorder in the empire hindered the church's opportunity to minister, in this sense "faith was joined to Roman patriotism and Christians accepted the State, assisted its progress, treasured it in their moral life, in their prayers, in their social ideals, because the state kept at bay the fearful day of universal upheaval."[78] Origen, too, argued against the pagan Celsus, saying that Christian prayers "are made in secret in the mind itself, and are sent up as from priests on behalf of the people in our country." Through these prayers, "Christians do more good to their countries than the rest of mankind, since they educate the citizens and teach them to be devoted to God, the guardian of their city."[79] While the church would survive instability, imperial stability allowed the opportunity for growth and expansion.

Reading the fathers is a lesson in the political application of Jesus's general injunction to pray even for our enemies. It is possible to pray fervently for political authorities with whom we disagree that they might lead in wisdom and righteousness. How many times do Christians today pause to pray for their leaders? Some liturgical traditions have a long history of praying for those in political authority during worship. That act does not make them complicit in whatever the authorities do wrong, nor does it condone such acts, but it does situate the heart and mind in the right order. What would it look like if the church started praying fervently and regularly for political authorities? Can we even pray for political figures from any political party in our churches where divisions are so sharp? At the very least, this act would remind Christians of their conviction that God is sovereign over all and show others that we are a people who are always praying for our leaders, even for those with whom we disagree.

Pay Taxes

The church also demonstrated loyalty to the state by paying taxes. As the saying goes, taxes are as certain as death; where there is a civil society, there will be taxes that support the work of the government. The fathers knew the commands of Scripture in passages such as Matthew 22:17–21 and Romans 13:6–7 that exhort Christians to pay taxes. Paying taxes is part of being a good citizen, but the issue goes beyond the payment itself. Taxes symbolize support for the political institutions, and political powers always respect those who are exemplary citizens.

Throughout the second and third centuries, Christian writers encouraged the faithful to do this. Writing to Emperor Antoninus Pius in the second century, Justin Martyr reassured him that Christians were exemplary citizens on just this point: "everywhere we try to pay to those appointed by you, more readily than all people, the taxes and assessments, as we have been taught by Him [Christ]." Justin added a summary of the narrative in Matthew 22:15–21

(Mark 12:13–17; Luke 20:20–25) where the Lord is asked whether it is necessary to pay taxes. He responds with the basic distinction: "give to Caesar the things that are Caesar's, and to God the things that are God's."[80] The notion of paying taxes lay at the basis for the church's call to good citizenship.

Christians do not undermine society through active rejection of the state. We can debate and support different forms of taxation and the church's role in society. But Christians pay their taxes and continue to support the work of good governance. The concept of political dualism wrapped up into a summary statement and the refusal to pay taxes was a form of civil disobedience or fraud. The church always encouraged the faithful to give to Caesar and the empire money, prayer, and allegiance.

Tertullian had to address the complaint that revenue from the temple taxes was falling. Contrary to what some might suggest, he said this was not solely the fault of the Christians. Christians were not called "to give alms both to your human and your heavenly mendicants." Yet the compassion of Christians as they spent money in the street amounted to more than the taxes otherwise paid in the temples, because the Christians were called to give to those who ask for it. In all other taxes, however, Christians were to be commended, because they did not cheat the state out of money: "But your other taxes will acknowledge a debt of gratitude to Christians; for in the faithfulness which keeps us from fraud upon a brother, we make conscience of paying all their dues."[81] If the state wanted to levy taxes, the church would be prepared to pay.

Likewise, Origen. Reflecting on Romans 13:5–6, he wrote, "with these words Paul rules that the Church of God exercise its mission of justice and mercy without opposing princes and earthly authorities but in peace and tranquility." He warned the faithful, "if we suppose that believers in Christ are not subject to secular authorities, that they do not have to pay taxes, that they are not required to pay out revenues, and that they owe no one fear or honor, would not the weapons of leaders and rulers deservedly turn against them? Would [such Christians] not make them justified persecutors, but themselves guilty?"[82] Because, Origen continues, in this case Christians would be attacked for their rebellious spirit, not their faith.

Taxes are always a point of contention and fraught with challenges, especially in a modern context where there is so much disagreement over tax structures. But paying taxes is part of a larger issue of good citizenship. Christians are called to support the state and not reject the country in which they live. They should, as far as it depends upon them, live at peace with those around them (Rom 12:18). There are, of course, other ways Christians support the state, including military and diplomatic service, political office, and other social services. Even though the political activity of Christians in the ancient world was limited, and they often questioned the possibility of serving in the military for a pagan ruler, they never questioned the importance of paying taxes. Again, what would it look like if Christians were known as good citizens who willingly paid their taxes and supported the good work of civil service that their tax dollars supported?

Defend Religious Liberty

With all this, the church was consistently vigilant about the ways that the state might impinge upon their religious sensibilities and convictions. This would not have been an issue if the church were part of a philosophical school or accepted religious cult, so the theologians and apologists of the early church rose to regularly defend their right to practice their way of life in the public square. Since it had little, it needed to chart a path forward; religious freedom was a strategic necessity. It was also a basic human right, early Christian theologians argued, so the state should stop persecuting Christians for their religious convictions. Besides Tertullian's defense, covered earlier,[83] similar defenses of religious liberty are found in other early Christian thinkers up to Lactantius. Alongside these arguments, many descriptions, some rather fantastic, of early Christian interrogations and martyrdoms point to acts of civil disobedience when worship was coerced. The church would never "swear by 'the fortune of the king,' or by aught else that is considered equivalent to God."[84] Tacitus complained about how stubborn Christians were in resisting the pressure of the state.[85] This was, of course, an ideal, and some certainly abandoned the faith upon interrogation or quickly bowed to the image of Caesar or an idol. But there are enough stories of Christian resistance to appreciate the conviction by which the early church postulated limits to the state's authority.

This is an important lesson for our own time. With the early church, we can hold up religious liberty as a fundamental and essential human right for all people of faith, even non-Christian religious communities, especially when pagans control the political structures. Above all else, the right to worship according to our conscience is needed so that the church has a place to flourish. This includes the right to practice our faith within the public square and promote virtue within political structures. Christians do not live bifurcated lives but live as citizens, earthly and heavenly, in both the social and private spheres.

Promote Virtue

Yet laws and political structures do not make people virtuous; that is the work of the Spirit. Political structures can help facilitate that work and provide a more or less healthy environment where people can live virtuously, and Christians are called to promote virtue through our presence and political influence. This entails above all that we embody virtue. Many early Christian apologists address the need for virtuous living. The Christian community itself was to be a living testimony to true human flourishing. At the same time, it is right and good for Christians to encourage political figures and polices that promote virtue among all citizens. Our democratic republic allows for more opportunities on this score than citizens of the Roman Empire ever had. But if the political structures are different, the fundamental call to virtue is the same. Government should function to promote virtue, and Christians should encourage just political rule and structures.

The five features of citizenship discussed in this chapter—honoring and praying for civil authorities, paying taxes, defending religious liberty, and promoting virtue—all have immediate application in our time. If the times are different, the basic tenets of Christian citizenship remain. And so we return to spiritual ground. Do we, as a matter of habit and conviction, believe that God is transcendent and providential over creation? Does this conviction frame our lives and our political actions? If we believe that God reigns over all, then we must pray for those in political power and pray specifically for peace, stability, and wise judgment. We pray for just laws that conform to the natural law and uphold divine law. Christians also aim to be the best citizens by paying taxes and participating in the civil sphere in ways that promote the good of society. These points challenge Christians today to reflect upon our vision of citizenship and how we perform within a matrix of laws enacted by those who do not always live by Christian virtues.

CONCLUSION

The early Christian vision of cultural sanctification started inside the hallowed walls of the church where catechesis and liturgy forged a distinctive Christian identity. So armed, they cultivated a different vision of citizenship guided by an active political dualism instead of the Roman Empire's political monism. This dualism operated by three essential features: a firm conviction in divine transcendence and providence, honor for civil authorities, and respect for the state. Citizenship, as conceived in the early church, did not proceed from simply political or anthropological assumptions but from a theological understanding of God's sovereign reign and redemptive work within creation. This conviction was reiterated every time the church recited the rule of faith at baptism, beginning with an affirmation of a transcendent God who governs all things.

Their active political dualism encouraged Christians to be good citizens by honoring civil authorities, praying for political officials and structures, paying taxes, defending religious liberty, and promoting virtue through their lives and influence. Early Christians affirmed that the basic role of the state was to maintain the order and structures of society, so their Christian identity did not undermine their place as citizens. They strove to respect the state within the limits of Christian conscience. By these means, Christians slowly learned how to live faithfully amid a pagan culture. They had to view their earthly citizenship through the lens of a new fundamental understanding of heavenly citizenship. The early church rejected political Gnosticism, which imagines the state to be evil and enjoins retreat from the responsibilities of citizenship; nor did it embrace the Roman world and all its customs and mores. Certainly, early Christians did not always live up to these ideals. Some capitulated to the culture, assimilated paganism into their views, or worshiped Caesar to spare their lives. But they also understood, in ways that can instruct us today, that oppression and persecution do not necessitate either rejecting the culture or capitulating to its ideologies. Citizenship in the early church meant learning to navigate the earthly kingdom while living in devotion to a transcendent God who providentially reigns over all things.

As Polycarp stood before the proconsul, he defended a vision of Christian citizenship gathered from the writings of the apostles. The threats of the crowds and the warnings of the authorities did not sway him from his firm convictions. There was no fear in him, no posture of disrespect or capitulation. The same attitude should mark our engagement with the world beyond politics itself. We now turn to consider how and why the early church engaged with its broader intellectual and social worlds. There, too, we have much to learn from those who have walked these roads before.

3
INTELLECTUAL LIFE

A Casual Debate

Minucius Felix and his friends Octavius and Caecilius found themselves together in Rome and decided to take a trip out to Ostia.[1] The fall was coming on, and temperatures were just turning pleasant. The three walked together toward the sea along the Tiber, when the pagan Caecilius observed an image of Serapis and paused to worship it with a simple gesture of a kiss. This created an awkward moment between the friends. Felix and Octavius were Christians, and the act of worship bothered them; that in turn irritated Caecilius, so he encouraged them to join him on a rock wall for a casual theological debate. Octavius sat on one side and Caecilius on the other, while Felix positioned himself between them to moderate the dialogue.

For some time, Caecilius rehearsed his objections against Christianity. They were the standard talking points. He argued that the world was not ruled by a transcendent, providential God who created all things. The Roman gods, he continued, were the reason for Rome's ascent to power. He mocked Christians' hope in an afterlife and argued that they only invented this belief to help them deal with their personal struggles. He also argued that Christians gathered in secret so that they could carry on all kinds of sadistic rituals and acts of immorality. Caecilius concluded by arguing that Christianity was a newcomer to the ancient religious scene and not worthy of a place in Roman life. Christians presumed to speak on religious matters that lay beyond them—really beyond all understanding or reason. They should, instead, simply follow the wisdom of Socrates: "What is above us is nothing to us."[2] After he concluded, Caecilius smiled, confident in the evidence he presented.

Before he began his defense, Felix reminded Caecilius that the purpose of the debate was to attain truth, not praise, so that there was no reason to gloat before hearing the other side of the story. Then Octavius walked through each of Caecilius's charges in turn. He argued that reason was given to all people as a gift of the Creator, as even the philosophers recognized. He explained that the gods had nothing to do with the flourishing of Rome and that even the ancient historians knew that stories about them were fables with no basis in reality. The strength of its military, not the gods, brought glory to Rome. Christians also lived exemplary lives of virtue, Octavius contended; if anyone would examine the lives of Christians, all ridiculous charges of immorality would melt away. Finally, it was the philosophers, not the Christians, who failed to live virtuously! They were "corrupters, and adulterers, and tyrants, and ever eloquent against their own vices." While the philosophers searched vainly for it, the lives of Christians testified that they had found virtue. At the very least, Octavius argued, Christians should be granted freedom to worship according to their conscience, and foolish arguments against them should be set aside: "Let us enjoy our benefits, and let us in rectitude moderate our judgments; let superstition be restrained; let impiety be expiated; let true religion be preserved."[3]

When Octavius finished, the three sat in silence. Tension hung in the air as they mulled over arguments. Finally, Caecilius conceded that there was something compelling about the Christian life and that the arguments for Christianity were persuasive. Perhaps there was a transcendent and providential God; certainly there was no doubt of Christian piety.[4] There was much more to discuss, but the sun was setting, and they needed to start heading back. But they all left with a sense of gratitude for the debate and for Octavius's winsome and compelling responses.

■ ■ ■

This story comes down to us in a text called the *Octavius*, written by a second-century Christian apologist named Minucius Felix. Surrounded by pagan gods whom one of the friends paused to worship, the three moved organically into an apologetic debate. This dialogue represented a casual meeting of the minds that occurred frequently throughout the ancient world.[5] The main sources for their debate were "the school authors" they had encountered in their elementary education.[6] Octavius met Caecilius on his terms and with his sources, and he used his authorities to persuade him. Scholars debate many things about this exchange and the polemics of Felix's presentation, including the historical accuracy of the account, the attitudes of each of the characters, and the legitimacy of the arguments. While these are important historical questions, they are peripheral to our basic point here: this early Christian dialogue represents the way that the early church valued intellectual engagement with culture around them.

In these instances, the early church was following the precedent laid down by the Lord and the apostles. In many different casual interchanges, Christ, Paul, and others defended their ministry before Jewish leaders, philosophers, political officials, and the populace. There was no avoiding serious intellectual engagement in a pagan world. This meeting of the minds, however, was not like a friendly quiz bowl gathering at the local pub. The Romans had little respect for Christian intellectual life. Even in the New Testament, Jewish leaders alleged that Peter and John were "uneducated, common men" (Acts 4:13). They also questioned the Lord's intelligence when they asked, "How is it that this man has learning, when he has never studied?" (John 7:15). From the earliest days of the church, Christians conducted their intellectual engagement from a position of weakness, which helped to reinforce their convictions and sharpen their arguments. It did not matter whether they were culturally marginalized; they believed that they had received divine revelation. The Lord declared that he hid his teaching from the wise and gave it to little children (Matt 11:25), and the apostle Paul comforted the church by reminding them that God chose what is foolish in the world to shame the wise (1 Cor 1:27). Early Christians took solace in such passages. The ancient intellectual Origen of Alexandria, whom I will discuss in detail later, produced an eight-volume work against the pagan intellectual Celsus; he began it by reminding his readers that when the Lord "was accused by the chief priests and elders, he gave no answer" (Matt 27:12–14).[7] The Son of God, the one through whom all things had been created, did not owe anyone an account. Christians should take comfort in this; yet, Origen reasoned, since many may be led astray by foolish arguments, Christians should take time to defend the faith. Origen was not alone. Many second- and third-century theologians, such as Justin Martyr or Tertullian of Carthage, committed their lives to intellectual engagement for the sake of Christ and the church.

We have already seen that early Christian cultural engagement began with the formation of a Christian identity based in theological and moral commitments and framed within a liturgical life. From that emerged the early church's political theology and its navigation of a new understanding of citizenship. Now we will trace the contours of the church's *public* theology, the way Christians engaged the broader world around them. This chapter focuses on the intellectual part of that engagement, leaving the social dimension for the next. That is, Christians had to learn to deal with the intellectual winds blowing all around them, especially with philosophical and theological critiques of Christianity and rumors of immorality. The church had to defend its faith and also evangelize through arguments. The early Christians were not the best and the brightest of their generation—given their pursuit of virtue, I suspect they would reject that claim anyway—but they were sure they had divine revelation on their side, and when their doctrine and morality were challenged, they rose to the occasion.

Many books stress the pragmatic and practical sides of the matter but neglect the intellectual. When the church was living on the margins of the culture, they did not place all their hopes in political influence or social action; they valued intellectual engagement. They knew that when believers walked out of their worship services, they would enter into a culture set against them. They had to be prepared for casual conversations that raised questions about matters of ultimate concern. So they cultivated an environment that honored Christian thinking and encouraged an apologetic and evangelistic posture embedded in the culture.

I will begin with pagan perspectives on Christianity and criticisms of the church. Though their disdain for Christian life and practice was wide-ranging, their basic concern was that Christianity undermined the sacred Roman traditions that unified the empire. Thus, Roman intellectuals defended their philosophical schools and religious traditions with passion. Amid such mockery and hostility, and with pagans holding institutional and cultural power, the early church had to make appealing moral and theological arguments.

In this environment, there emerged Christian intellectuals who embodied an apologetic life. They arose organically, meshing their clerical duties with the philosophical life to respond to critical charges. This kind of early Christian pastor-theologian usually mounted a conservative, and sometimes a creative, response. They were under no illusion that the pagan world would find their arguments convincing, but they rose to the occasion anyway in an effort to create a space where the church could worship and serve. At times, they created new organizations or institutions that could do the good work of defending the faith and discipling the faithful. Among the many figures we could discuss, Origen, a controversial figure to be sure, was widely recognized then and now for his intellectual acumen. His vision for theological education, his methods for engaging philosophy, and his devotion to virtue all compel our attention in recovering the vision of the pastor-theologian prepared to meet the intellectual challenges of our day.

The Christian apologists and theologians in the early church cultivated various strategies that both criticized pagan philosophical ideas and used philosophical writings to establish common ground with their opponents. They defended the uniqueness of Christianity, argued that Christian doctrine and morality were more intellectually satisfying than the alternatives, appealed to the antiquity of Christianity, and showed how Christianity served the public good. Their goal was always persuasion, and their toolkit included the full set of rhetorical devices. If the Christian arguments did not always convince the philosophers, they did demonstrate that Christians were not interested in hiding or shirking away from intellectual challenges. Their response was commensurate with their lives. This is a lesson not only for the ancient church but also for pastors today.

As in the story of Octavius, we live in a world with gods on every corner; yet evangelicals are not known for intellectual rigor. As Mark Noll has argued, the scandal of the evangelical mind in the twentieth century is "that there is not much of an evangelical mind."[8] While Noll has pulled back from such a harsh critique in recent years in view of many important scholarly contributions in evangelical circles, he remains largely unrepentant about his original thesis.[9] Evangelicals have been far too interested in pragmatic effectiveness and spiritual experience to value the intellectual life. But for life in a pagan world, this priority needs to change. Now more than ever, we need Christians who can defend the faith in the public square. I am not suggesting that every Christian needs a degree in theology, but all Christians should be ready for challenging intellectual encounters. As the church moves beyond a cultural Christianity, conversations like the one between Caecilius and Octavius will become commonplace. Christians must learn, in the words of the apostle, always to be ready to give an answer for the hope that lives within (1 Pet 3:15).

Ancient Intellectual Critiques

The early church was hardly the cosmopolitan center of Roman public life. Christians were not the most popular figures, and their communities were often relegated to the cultural sidelines. Theologians like Tertullian remarked that Christians were universally hated and their doctrine and practices largely unknown.[10] In that light, Christians felt compelled to engage the most important intellectual charges and were not shy about responding to leading philosophers, emperors, rhetoricians, and other civic leaders. Scattered across the ancient world, the church undertook organic intellectual interactions with the hope that some of their pagan neighbors might find its arguments convincing and come to respect Christianity. If not, they at least created space for articulating their views and establishing a basis for their theology.

The leading charges against Christianity fell into three broad classifications: Christians undermined society, were anti-intellectual and immoral, and offered no public good. All of these appear in Celsus's scathing critique of Christianity, *On True Doctrine*. Celsus was the Richard Dawkins of the second century, and his work was clearly influential since Origen felt compelled to offer a detailed response to his criticisms long after his death. Celsus's arguments are a great example of the church's struggle to maintain credibility in a hostile pagan culture.

The first complaint against Christianity constantly charged that it was undermining the stability of state and the rule of law. The classic example occurred in the interchange between Pliny, the governor of Bithynia, and the emperor Trajan. Pliny was a bit perplexed and unsettled by the growing number of Christians in his region, for in his eyes they constituted nothing more than a superstition, a foreign cult begging to be eradicated. In frustration, he wrote Trajan that, though he could not charge them with a crime, their private associations promoted factionalism that grew into political and social unrest.[11] Their gatherings were private, yes, but nonetheless had the public consequence of undermining the Roman gods. If Roman culture was united around the Roman identity, then Christian refusal to capitulate to its ultimate authority was politically subversive.

Second, pagans argued that Christians were morally depraved and so a threat to the public good. Rumors about Christianity were rife in the ancient world, rumors of incest, cannibalism, and other grossly immoral acts. Obviously, these accusations were based upon misconceptions about baptism and the Eucharist as well as perverse understandings of the church as the family of God. Unfounded as these charges were, they percolated down into popular perceptions of Christianity. The Christian retort was, ironically, that pagan immorality was perverting the culture. Justin Martyr, for example, wrote several works defending the notion that Christians were the best citizens. On a few occasions, he debated a Cynic philosopher named Crescens, who thought Christians were "atheists and impious." Justin claimed that their debates revealed that Crescens, in fact, knew nothing about the doctrines of the church. For Justin, Crescens was no real philosopher but an opportunist who mocked Christianity "to win favor with the deluded mob."[12]

Third, besides being cast as threats to order and the public good, by the end of the second century, Christians were also scorned as anti-intellectual. Many pagans questioned the theological and moral commitments of Christians and wondered why anyone would find these views convincing. This critique gained traction as Christians became more prominent and their teaching more widely known. Caecilius's arguments, mentioned above, had already rehearsed this point. Christians had nothing to offer the intellectual community of philosophers and rhetoricians, he argued, because they were unskilled, uneducated, and spoke about things they did not know.

The second-century pagan philosopher Celsus captured many of these points in his scathing work *On True Doctrine*, one of the earliest intellectual rebukes of Christianity. Celsus wrote to teach Christians "the nature of the doctrines which they affirm, and the source from which they come,"[13] hoping that they thereby would recognize the stupidity of their doctrine and morality, repent of their commitment to the gospel, and affirm their allegiance to Rome and the gods. With rhetorical flourishes and bombastic arguments, Celsus moved from rebuke to rebuke, mocking Christians' folly all along.

To his credit, Celsus recognized Christianity for what it was: a serious threat to the traditions of the Roman Empire. He focused his fire on social and theological issues. In the first place, he attacked the very basis of the Christian theological method, the authority of divine revelation. "The Greeks," Celsus wrote, "are better able to judge the value of what the barbarians have discovered, and to establish the doctrines and put them into practice by virtue."[14] There were no special divine texts that ought to be privileged above the philosophers, because knowledge came through philosophical inquiry, not revelation. The "barbarians," whether Christian or Jewish or whomever, must set aside their sacred texts and realize that the Greek mind, especially Plato, provided the basis for truth.

Christians, by contrast, said they followed the "demonstration of the Spirit and of power."[15] As Origen later argued, Christians believed that "the gospel has a proof which is peculiar to itself, and which is more divine than a Greek proof based on dialectical argument."[16] The gospel was the lens that brought clarity to the visible world and all it entailed. This epistemological difference marked the dividing line between Origen and Celsus; the two were operating under different intellectual paradigms. Just as socially the church lived on the margins of the culture, so the reigning philosophical ideas presented challenges for Christians' theological method. Christians needed to learn to navigate among these competing authorities and, like Octavius in the story above, use the pagans' own sources against them.

Second, alongside his intellectual critique, Celsus could not hide his disdain for the low status and blatant ignorance of Christians. As an influential Roman proud of his philosophical acumen, Celsus believed that the purpose of religion was to promote virtue and that the most virtuous were to be found within the various philosophical schools. By contrast, being unable to persuade the intelligent, Christians peddled their views among people who lacked basic cognitive ability and moral aptitude. Celsus jeered that Christians had to turn away anyone who was "educated" or "wise" or "sensible." Instead, "anyone ignorant, anyone stupid, anyone uneducated, anyone who is a child, let him come boldly." In saying such people are worthy of their God, Celsus continued, Christians "show that they want and are able to convince only the foolish, dishonorable, and stupid, and only slaves, women, and little children."[17] His critique of the Christian community was merciless: their dwellings are full of "wool-workers, cobblers, laundry-workers, and the most illiterate and bucolic yokels, who would not dare to say anything at all in front of their elders and more intelligent masters."[18] Celsus was relentless, circling back to these themes again and again throughout his work.[19]

The comparative outreach of the philosophical schools and of Christianity was starkly different and of no uncertain conclusion, Celsus continued.

The mystery religions and similar groups reached out to the righteous and well placed, beginning with this proclamation: "Whosoever has pure hands and a wise tongue" or "Whosoever is pure from all defilement, and whose soul knows nothing of evil, and who has lived well and righteously." Christians were just the opposite: "Whosoever is a sinner, they say, whosoever is unwise, whosoever is a child, and, in a word, whosoever is a wretch, the kingdom of God will receive him."[20] Celsus cannot imagine a world founded on such principles.

His next step was to ridicule the various tactics that Christians employed to persuade such simpletons. Since Christian texts are silly and foolish, Celsus had little time for prophecies that linked the Old Testament revelation with the person and work of Christ, and laughed at how Christian teachers had to interpret them allegorically.[21] Celsus described the "miscellaneous ideas" that Christians invented to persuade pagans to follow their teaching, such as the eschatological judgment of God. This was the tactic of terror, he objected, threatening people with fearful retribution. The words fit the venue, he observed, for Christians liked to "display their trickery in the market-places and go about begging" but "would never enter a gathering of intelligent men, nor would they dare to reveal their noble beliefs in their presence; but whenever they see adolescent boys and a crowd of slaves and a company of fools they push themselves in and show off."[22] The Greco-Roman philosophers and intellectuals did not deign to so lower themselves; as Peter Brown states, "philosophers tended to be peripheral figures on the political scene in late antiquity; some, indeed, were fierce recluses, proud of their ability to avoid all contact with public life."[23] The church's pursuit of ordinary people everywhere, by contrast, turned up many who found the doctrines of the church convincing. Perhaps Celsus scorned the church's doctrines all the more because of their appeal.

When Celsus did find a rare reasonably intelligent person among the Christian fold, the teacher or pastor who led the campaign of deception, he scored them as amateurs: "the man who teaches the doctrines of Christianity is like a man who promises to restore bodies to health, but turns his patients away from attending to expert physicians because his lack of training would be shown up by them."[24] In his dangerous naivete, this novice made outlandish promises to restore his patients but lacked the knowledge and education to do so. Also, when Christian teachers tried to communicate, they babbled on like a drunk person who has just stepped out of a tavern.[25] Celsus's cure for this disease was to have the Christian get out of the way and let the philosophers come in and heal the simple with education.

While ancient academic discourse is filled with criticism of Christianity, the critiques of Celsus remain some of the most developed and scathing. His unrelenting ad hominem attacks demonstrate the Roman fear over losing the intellectual and political struggle for the empire. Rome wanted to preserve unity and saw Christianity as an affront to that agenda. In a certain sense, however, reading Celsus's *On True Doctrine* is comforting. It reminds us that pagans have found Christianity ridiculous for a long time. Modern secularists are not the first to laugh at Christian revelation and reject Christian doctrine and morality as foolishness. So let us take heart, because "the foolishness of God is wiser than men, and the weakness of God is stronger than men" (1 Cor 1:25). We also need to recognize that some of Celsus's points had merit. Christians did not always live up to their moral ideals, could make foolish decisions, and did not always provide a coherent and developed response to their opponents. But this does not take away from the important intellectual work they did generate, for in the face of Celsus and others like him, Christians rose to the occasion and promoted the growth of the intellectual life.

THE RISE OF THE CHRISTIAN INTELLECTUAL

Any number of Christian intellectuals emerged in the first few centuries of the church to defend the faith over against reigning philosophical ideas. Theophilus of Antioch, Justin Martyr, and Origen are outstanding examples. They exemplify a key moment in the church's intellectual history. At least part of the growth of the early church can be attributed to these Christian teachers who worked against the grain of the philosophical discourse to defend the apostolic testimony. They had to prove themselves against the special contempt that Celsus, among others, held for them as deceivers of the gullible.

Thus, the early church's cultural engagement required theological education and discipleship to marshal a chorus of voices ready to provide the populace with a compelling Christian vision. Put more broadly, since the church then lived on the margins of the culture, Christian intellectuals organically emerged from the worshiping community to cast a vision of Christian doctrine that could compete with the Romans'. A church that existed as a marginalized community needed Christians with rigorous theological and intellectual arguments to challenge the very basic assumptions of the surrounding culture. "From the very beginning, the church has nurtured a lively intellectual life," historian Robert Wilken tells us.[26] In some ways, it does not matter whether the arguments are intellectually satisfying to everyone, especially not to those in power who will probably reject the ideas anyway. The arguments need to offer a basic vision of the spiritual life that is ultimately more satisfying.

Christians as Organic Intellectuals

Early Christians, being outside the important institutions and centers of cultural creation, had to find alternative fertile ground where they could grow. That is, to use Fernando Rebaque's terms, they had to be "organic" intellectuals opposed to the dominant "traditional" type.[27] The traditional intellectual in the ancient world, says Rebaque, "is an 'employee' of the socially dominant group, someone who functions to maintain its social hegemony and political power through the creation of social and 'spontaneous' consensus, to legitimate its rule and to discipline the groups that disagree with this power."[28] These thinkers sought to maintain their cultural influence and assumed that their ideals were "natural, immutable and everlasting."[29] Theirs was a work of preservation insulated from outside influences.

By contrast, Rebaque says, Christians were "organic intellectuals . . . created and established by a social group in order to achieve homogeneity and consciousness within economic, social, cultural and political fields."[30] Organic intellectuals are often connected with emerging social movements, and any group that wants to increase its social standing "must assimilate and conquer the ideology of traditional intellectuals."[31] The strategy of *assimilating* and *conquering* the ideologies of the competition comprised the aim of early Christian apologists in response to the prevailing intellectual world.

Rebaque uses Justin Martyr as an example of an organic intellectual from the middle of the second century. Justin hosted a Christian school in his home in Rome, gathering around himself a group of students to prepare them to address the culture of their day.[32] He composed texts that aided the construction of the Christian identity (*Treatise against Heresies*) and defended Christianity against pagan and Jewish outsiders (*1–2 Apology* and *Dialogue with Trypho*). Celsus may have written his critique in response to Justin's works and, if so, may have been aware of Justin's conversion narrative.[33] Justin's conversion, however, was much more than a report of an experience with God; it was a pointed critique of the major philosophical schools of his time and an exaltation of Christian doctrine above their arguments.[34]

People like Justin were not given scholarships to major academic institutions, nor were they sought out for their intellectual capabilities. The community of Christian intellectuals developed out of the need to defend the faith and prepare the faithful for a wide range of apologetic or evangelistic encounters. No doubt, the academic environment in the modern world is complicated and fraught with challenges, but the same fundamental point remains: the church needs intellectuals willing to address the prevailing issues of the day. Today universities, think tanks, and research centers are the hubs of the intellectual life. Traditional intellectuals are the major influencers in these institutions and are often antagonistic to Christianity. In the coming years, Christians will need to think carefully about education and the choice between building new institutions and redeeming old ones. At what point do we cut our losses and start new educational initiatives where the Christian intellectual life can thrive? Where can we best prepare men and women for service in the church and world? Should we choose to remain in the ruins of Christian institutions and continue to work to redeem them? No kind of general rule fits either of these scenarios, and I think a good mixture of both will probably be involved. But we can trust that, just as organic intellectuals in the ancient world tilled the fertile soil where they found it, many more will do so today. Either way, the challenge that lies before us now is learning to cultivate the Christian intellectual life from a position of the margins of the culture. As with Felix, Octavius, and Caecilius walking along the road, casual meetings of the minds will happen every day among Christians who live their lives faithfully in a pagan world.

Conservative and Creative Intellectuals

From the second into the third century, not all organic intellectuals were clergy, though they were nearly always closely associated with the church. In Greco-Roman circles, most priests were simply civic officials, and any writers or philosophers who also happened to be priests held their position for civic, not intellectual, reasons.[35] But as the church flourished and the posture of the empire toward Christianity grew more militant, the function of the organic Christian intellectual merged with the growing institutionalization of the church and the role of the bishop. This marriage between the intellectual life and the spiritual activities of the clergy was distinctive within the Greco-Roman world.[36]

According to William Countryman, the bishop in the third century "enjoyed a special intellectual pre-eminence." Yet the intellectuals among the Christian community were not all alike. Countryman particularly found a contrast between "conservative" and "creative" types. The former include figures such as Justin Martyr, Irenaeus, and Tertullian that were often Christian clergy or leaders concerned with the "maintenance of boundaries," while the later were figures such as Marcion and the gnostic teachers and other "innovators."[37] Those outside the church did not always understand the difference between gnostics and Christians, just as today nonreligious people might not be able to distinguish between Presbyterians and Mormons.[38]

The conservative and creative intellectuals formed a spectrum defined by their attitudes toward the church's faith and practice and prevailing philosophical ideas. The conservative intellectuals held fast to Christian doctrine and practice and communicated it in intelligible ways; they "guarded the community's social boundaries by strengthening ideological definitions." The creative teachers, on the other hand, were more open to assimilation of pagan philosophy. They had little concern for boundary markers and were more focused on "the endless elaboration of the inner world."[39] The danger here is syncretism or the blending of pagan and Christian thought in ways that misconstrue orthodoxy. In the end, the church would come to appreciate the conservative teachers more than the creative ones, because the former were passing on the doctrinal, moral, and liturgical features of the faith that defined the nature of the community.

In any case, the early church mounted an organic response to culture via intellectuals who took it upon themselves to respond to the prevailing philosophical challenges of their day, whether in a conservative or a creative mode. If they were sometimes ridiculed, they did not shy away from serious intellectual and theological engagement. They worked to assimilate and conquer prevailing philosophical ideals. These thinkers were closely associated with the church and especially the emerging role of the Christian clergy, though they were not always clergy and not always orthodox given that their creativity would place them beyond the confessions of the church's tradition. The clerical thinkers aimed to maintain the boundaries of doctrinal fidelity. The more innovative tended to be more speculative and willing to assimilate philosophical ideas, often challenging some features of the church's doctrine and practice. Not all creative thinkers were gnostics, though gnostics stood at the extreme edge of the spectrum when they syncretized Christianity with various philosophical systems. The presence of these thinkers shows that many in the early church were not retreating from the intellectual environment of their world, nor simply capitulating to its philosophical methods and perspectives, but actively engaged paganism for the sake of evangelism, apologetics, and, at times, theological construction.

Today the church needs Christians who will work organically in and among the institutions and churches to cultivate the intellectual life. But those seeking to do so in this pagan world have their work cut out for them. To glean the resources found in the ancient church will require research, education, writing, and teaching—an important work that all must share for effectively communicating the faith in this generation. There is no time to be bothered by scathing critiques of Christianity; they will come and go. Christians must get on with the business of educating and training up the next generation that God provides us. There is little hope that their views will be respected and appreciated when the very basis lies in the special revelation of Scripture that pagan intellectuals reject. Though they can find common ground in natural law, working purely from general sources via empirical observation or intellectual analysis, such thinkers have no time for old tales found in ancient dust-covered books. Those who choose to remain in traditional academic settings might find things to be hard and will require a measure of fortitude and resilience. Yet even there, some can still be persuasive. Though the difficult work of redeeming lost institutions is not for everyone, it is possible with the right theological and ethical grounding to move among them. Wisdom will guide us in knowing the difference. God can always work in ways we least expect or imagine, and good arguments and moral lives have a way of convincing even the most hard-hearted.

The Example of Origen

Among early Christian intellectuals, no one before the fourth century compares with Origen of Alexandria. He was far and away the most widely read and influential of that era. He was—and remains—a complicated and controversial figure.[40] His theological speculation often got him into trouble, but his legacy of serious biblical and theological reasoning continued to shape the Christian tradition for many years.

Origen was born around 185 and spent the first part of his life in Alexandria, Egypt. Sometime around 232, when he was forty-seven years old, he moved to Caesarea Maritima after a dispute with his bishop in Alexandria, Demetrius. He was invited to come to Caesarea by Alexander, the bishop of Jerusalem, and Theoctistus, the bishop of Caesarea, who had created that dispute in the first place by letting Origen, then a layman, preach during a service. Both bishops respected Origen's intellectual gifts and scriptural insights. When Origen moved to Palestine, he was ordained and began preaching on a regular basis. He also set up a catechetical school that accepted students interested in spiritual and intellectual formation. For Origen, "a commitment to scholarship ought to be an intrinsic feature in the profile of aspiring scriptural interpreters."[41] The world was, after all, filled with Celsuses, and the church needed to respond.

According to Origen, Christians who interpret Scripture ought not shy away from serious intellectual questions but be conversant with a whole range of academic disciplines both to better understand the Scriptures and communicate them in an intelligible way. This included a range of philological scholarship such as "defining words, resolving homonyms and ambiguous expressions, distinguishing between literal and figurative uses, and solving problems with punctuation."[42] Origen assured his readers that such education did not pose a problem but was a vital opportunity because "education is the way to virtue."[43]

There are several key lessons to learn from Origen's approach to the intellectual life. First, Origen emphasized theological education as a means of cultural engagement in a pagan world. This is a more institutionalized form of catechesis discussed in chapter 2. Origen gathered a community and established a broad curriculum with different levels of instruction ascending to the heights of intellectual rigor. Second, Origen engaged all the philosophical ideas of his day and taught his students the art of exploiting philosophical insights for the sake of the gospel—what he called "plundering the Egyptians." This is another example of Walls's "indigenizing principle" or what I describe in the next chapter as "cultural discernment." Third, throughout all instruction, virtue remained the purpose of the intellectual life. Education and virtue were fused together in a holistic vision of the good life. A life of virtue is worth more than all the wisdom of the philosophers. Not everyone found Origen's vision of education persuasive. He was scorned by other pagans, and those who want to pursue the Christian intellectual life today should not expect our lot to be much different. But through honest and serious intellectual engagement, there will be many who must take Christianity seriously and the healthy vision of the spiritual life it proposes.

Even in the ancient world, Origen was known for his intellectual acumen. Trained in the Scriptures and the disciplines of Greek education, he earned his living as a grammaticus after his father died. Already in "his eighteenth year," says the fourth-century church historian Eusebius, Origen "became head of a school of catechetical instruction, and there he progressed [spiritually] during the persecutions at the time of Aquila, the governor of Alexandria."[44] He went on to form several schools in Alexandria and Caesarea with his multidisciplinary curriculum. His first school in Alexandria, Eusebius records, had been founded by Pantenus but needed to be revived by Origen. In these years, we can see the formal vision of theological education begin to emerge.

The curriculum offered several levels of instruction, which provided a fertile ground for recruitment. According to Eusebius, whenever Origen "perceived that any persons had superior intelligence he instructed them also in the philosophic disciplines—in geometry, arithmetic, and other preparatory studies—and then advanced to the systems of the philosophers and explained their writings."[45] One student from the school in Caesarea, Gregory the Wonderworker, was seemingly destined to a life studying law; then an encounter with Origen confronted him with divine persuasiveness:

> I cannot recount here how many such words he uttered in favor of the life of philosophy, not just one day but most of those first days when we went to hear him. We were pierced as by a dart by his discourse even from the first, for he combined a kind of winsome grace with persuasiveness and compelling force. . . . For he said that . . . no true piety at all, properly speaking, was possible to anyone who did not lead a philosophic life. As he poured out more arguments like these one after another, and by his arts brought us in the end to a complete standstill like men under a spell, he was supported in his words, I know not how, by some divine power.[46]

Origen's arguments, Gregory continued, were like "a spark landed in the middle of our soul." What he found in Origen was "the love for the most attractive Word of all, holy and most desirable in its ineffable beauty" and through this biblical scholar, Gregory (and many others) discovered a love for the Word of God that "was kindled and fanned into flame."[47] That fire changed Gregory's life, his plans, and his desires, and not his alone. The second and third centuries was an age of conversions, especially among the literate class.[48] Gregory was converted by Origen's defense of the Christian faith, but more than that, he was converted because the *Christian* "philosophical life" was more enticing than the success track of the law and more beautiful than the pagan alternatives in philosophy. It involved a whole way of life, not the mere intellectualism of the pagan schools.

Grateful for Origen's tutelage, Gregory delivered an address of thanksgiving, also known as a panegyric, in honor or Origen and gave a striking memoir of Origen's methods and impact. He recounted how Origen had encouraged the broadest reading: "We were permitted to learn every doctrine, both barbarian and Greek, both the most mystical and the most pragmatic, both divine and human; we pursued the ins and outs of all these more than sufficiently and examined them closely, taking our fill of everything and enjoying the good things of the soul."[49] In Origen's school, there was no attempt to water things down. It is easy to see how this perspective on theological education blossomed in other periods, whether under scholasticism or amid the challenges of modernity. Origen reminds us that the best theological education is done in and through a tradition that willingly engages all forms of knowledge. For apologetic and evangelistic, not to mention dogmatic, purposes, the church should be learning and engaging the prevailing philosophical attitudes and postures of its age.

While they engaged a wide range of disciplines, the Scriptures were the main textbook. In a letter written to Gregory, Origen reminds him, "chiefly give heed to the reading of the Divine Scriptures.... For we need great attention when we read the Divine writings, that we may not speak or form notions about them rashly."[50] Comparing the philosophical writings with the Scriptures, Origen accepts that some might learn certain points of truth from the philosophers, but the writings of the Old and New Testaments offer the highest truths.

Show me teachers who give preparatory teaching in philosophy and train people in philosophical study, and I would not dissuade young men from

listening to these; but after they had first been trained in a general education and in philosophical thought I would try to lead them on to the exalted
height, unknown to the multitude, of the profoundest doctrines of the
Christians, who discourse about the greatest and most advanced truths,
proving and showing that this philosophy was taught by the prophets of
God and the apostles of Jesus.[51]

The Scriptures are the source and fountain of true knowledge. There are many
voices claiming the right path, but only the Lord has the words of eternal life
(John 6:68).

Through knowledge of God and the "doctrines of Christ,"[52] Origen employed the pedagogical practice of dialectic reasoning.[53] Proverbs 10:17, "education that is unchallenged goes wrong," is one of Origen's guiding passages
for this kind of education.[54] But he also appeals to Plato's words, "proofs are
friendly," and argues that there are "even more among us who have learnt that
a leader of the gospel must be 'able to refute the adversaries' [Titus 1:9]."[55]
Gregory gives a fairly detailed account of this practice. He compares Origen's
dialectical institution to a gardener pruning the plants and preparing them
to grow and mature. He writes, "he cut out and thoroughly removed by the
processes of refutation and prohibition; sometimes assailing us in the genuine
Socratic fashion." This style of teaching prepared his students "successfully
for the reception of the words of truth," and the twin goals of the dialectic
experience are "knowledge of God" and "piety."[56] These things are derived
from the Scriptures, which helped form a canon or criterion for truth, or what
Origen calls the rule of faith.[57] Origen knew that "without a criterion or canon,
knowledge is simply not possible, for all inquiry will be drawn helplessly into
an infinite regression."[58] Together these things—persuasion, dialectics, knowledge, and piety—shaped Origen's style of eduction.

Origen was also distinctive for the way he encouraged the faithful to "plunder
the Egyptians." As the Israelites escaped Egypt, they acquired gold, silver, and
clothing (Exod 12:35–36). From these items, Origen observes, they fashioned all
the contents of the tabernacle: the ark, cherubim, mercy seat, golden pot, and so
on. "These things [the sacred objects] were made from the best of the Egyptian
gold," Origen writes. Similarly, the writings of the philosophers possess truths
that could be harvested and applied to a good theological method. Subjects
such as rhetoric and grammar become the handmaidens to Christian theology.[59]

Origen imagined that Christian doctrine stood above all philosophical schools and simply bent over to gather the scattered truths found among them—and not just one. Just as the church was not identified with the empire, so it was not bound to the reading or study of just one or two of the philosophers.

The story of Origen's plundering of the Egyptians is part of a larger narrative that Frances Young describes as "a cultural take-over bid." At the heart of this revolution lay the Bible and theological education. I do not imply that the early church embarked on a "culture warrior" agenda in the modern sense of the term, but the image of plundering the Egyptians had an indigenizing effect that shaped their missional approach to philosophy. In the Roman world, "ancient revered literature and civic pride" worked together "to create a living culture in which people inhabited a socially constructed world with a population of visible and invisible beings, a sacred order that has to be respected, and appropriate rituals performed to maintain natural and social harmony." The Romans constructed their worldview on the "'imitation' of the classics which provided models of sublime style and diction, but also with proper critical attention, appropriate moral exemplars, employing virtue and *eusebeia* (piety)." The early church, and in this case Origen, offered an "alternative literary culture" fashioned upon the Bible.[60] In the ancient world, this meant that they focused some of their efforts on redeeming Hellenism and especially the Hellenistic literature.

Beginning with the apostles (Acts 17), pre-Nicene theology made use of pagan literature and the arguments of the philosophers "to serve their exposure of traditional religion and philosophy, and to condemn the whole integrated literary and symbolic culture that surrounded them."[61] Origen's work was a "pivot of the story," because Origen moved "to professionalize the exegesis of Scripture and adopt methods from the schools so as to turn Scripture into the basis for a complete educational system with primary, secondary and tertiary levels." In Origen, "the Christian Bible had truly become a classical canon, replacing for Christian pupils the texts which traditionally had pride of place in the schools of the Hellenistic world."[62] These Christian thinkers leaned on the Bible and slowly engaged the world as they inhabited the culture formed from reading Scripture. They also confronted critics like Celsus. Yes, the church called sinners to the gospel, Origen wrote in response to Celsus's jibes, but in addition, "we attempt to convert philosophers to Christianity."[63]

Gregory tells us that Origen encouraged his students "to take up and become conversant with all the rest, neither biased in favor of one nation or philosophic doctrine, nor yet prejudiced against it, whether Hellenic or barbarians, but listening to all."[64] He believed this was a wise method "lest one isolated doctrine from one group or another be the only one heard and promoted" and a person fail to see the weakness of that school and become taken in by it. This was the problem with the philosophers, said Gregory. Each student "likes the opinions he first encountered, and since he is, as it were, fettered by them, he can no longer accept others."[65] Their pride thus leaves these haughty philosophers swept away in a single philosophical stream.

Changing metaphors, Gregory compared the philosophers' sectarianism to people stuck in a swamp or lost in a forest or labyrinth. The first get stuck in the thick mud of their system and cannot move forward or go back. The second cannot navigate their way out through the dense trees or find the path out of a confusing labyrinth. In fact, Gregory concludes, "there is nothing—no labyrinth so involved and complicated, nor thicket so dense and tangled, nor marsh or bog so perilous—that holds those who enter it so fast as a doctrine, if it be one held by philosophers like these in their isolation."[66]

Origen, by contrast, did not leave his students stuck in one or another stream but like a skilled docent led his students across every philosophical terrain: he "gathered and presented to us everything which was useful and true from each of the philosophers, but excluded what was false."[67] Thus, his students could discern the things that were helpful for both apologetic and dogmatic purposes. Gregory should also "extract from the philosophy of the Greeks what may serve as a course of study or a preparation for Christianity."[68] Halfway through his critique of Celsus, Origen invokes the words of the prophets and exhorts his readers saying, "we also need words to root out ideas contrary to the truth from every soul which has been distressed by Celsus' treatise or by opinions like his."[69] The only stream of philosophy that Origen refused to engage was that of the atheists. Since they denied the very first premises of Christian doctrine, indeed, beliefs that all human beings hold in common—namely, the existence of God and the working of providence—there was no merit in trying to engage them.[70] He felt there needed to be some kind of common ground for them to be intellectually and spiritually profitable.

Origen's strategy of plundering the Egyptians provides an important suggestion for living in a pagan world. The Christian community cannot hide socially or intellectually but must learn the art of engaging its philosophical context; this is part of the famous "indigenizing of the gospel." Origen demonstrated the missionary and apologetic impulse of using available cultural forms for the purpose of persuasion in evangelism, apologetics, and dogmatic construction. He was able to persuade some to follow Christ. If others rejected him, he used their own sources against them to defend Christian revelation. Finally, sometimes philosophical construction helped him bring clarity to Christian revelation for dogmatic purposes. This third use often served the first two as well. All his discourses honored the Scriptures as the primary sources of truth and the authority to which all philosophical reasoning must bend. At the same time, they yielded a memorable lesson in the value of Christian intellectuals knowing their philosophical contexts.

Besides lauding the curriculum, Gregory also expanded on Origen's primary concern of promoting virtue or spiritual growth through the study of divine things. The central feature of Gregory's panegyric of Origen, and what he commends him most for, is his emphasis on moral formation in education.[71] His purpose was not to study philosophy for the sake of philosophy or to improve one's social standing or career prospects; rather, everything was oriented toward the study of the Scriptures for growth in holiness and godliness. "The topmost matters of all," Gregory says, are "the divine virtues concerning how to act, which bring the soul's impulses to a calm and steady condition." These virtues free us from grief and evil, discipline us, make us happy, and conform us to the likeness of God. Gregory mentions Origen's emphasis on wisdom, moderation, justice, and fortitude, and, as the instructor, he led by example. "This man did not explain to us about virtues in that fashion, in words, but rather exhorted us to deeds," Gregory writes. Origen was no hypocrite. Origen taught his students that "learning is vain and unprofitable, if the word be unsupported by works."[72] Throughout these discussions, Christ is the "model and prototype" of all the virtues. He "has set us an example of justice, of temperance, of courage, of wisdom, of piety, and of the other virtues."[73]

This holistic vision of theological education assumes that the life of virtue is worth more than all the learning in the world. Origen does not seek education for the sake of knowledge, as if learning is mere data dump. He recognizes that "the little faith of a Christian is better than the abundant wisdom of the world."[74] In one homily on Psalm 36 (Psalm 37), Origen contrasts someone who is learned—a point directed at pagan intellectuals—with a simple pious Christian who must not hold back on virtue.

> There are some who, in the course of life, have been educated in the education of the cosmos and have known extensively the learning of this age, so that the wording is preeminently for their benefit, because it is not stupid; but if one is a lover of logos, sometimes it is possible to find such people filled with all bad things, being rich in this expressive logos, being rich in learning, being poor in justice, and poor in good deeds. In fact, I often know orators, teachers of literature, and those who give promise of philosophy and dialectic who are not only idol-worshipers, but also persons who sleep with boys, frequent prostitutes, and commit adultery. But it is possible to see someone acting as a member of the Church, faithful, but in some manner stupid: he cannot open his mouth, but he fears God. Held in custody by fear, he does not sin, but holds back from sins, while the wise man of this world does not hold back.[75]

Others, like Origen, frequently condemn the pagan's lack of virtue. The philosophers' lives did not match their words. These sentiments were echoed by many theologians before Origen. The second-century apologist Minucius Felix wrote, "We who bear wisdom not in our dress, but in our mind, we do not speak great things, but we live them; we boast that we have attained what they have sought for with the utmost eagerness, and have not been able to find."[76] The identical phrases appear in Cyprian also.[77] The continuity of this message suggests it may have been some sort of a slogan among early Christian communities.[78] They believed that the church and the populace would agree that their hypocrisy undermined their philosophy.

Finally, Origen saw intellectual formation as a gradual and graded development.[79] One might compare this to the transitions from primary to secondary education or beyond. But Origen's attention was more focused on the cultivation of virtue and not mere programmatic development. Habits and repetition were essential tools for spiritual growth. Gregory writes that the goal is to be conformed to the likeness of Christ and to live a godly life. "I think that everything has no other goal than to come to God, having been conformed to him in purity of mind, and to remain in him."[80] Origen emphasizes the spiritual journey through a cycle that was "circular and repetitive," where "basic skills and fundamental sources were acquired and then regularly revisited" so there was a progression of growth advancing toward spiritual maturity.[81] This all points to the intellectual formation of students, who would, like Gregory, receive the instruction and then venture out to become leaders and pastors guiding the churches.

THE PAGAN REACTION

There was a mixed reaction to the teaching of Origen and others. Some, such as Gregory, were persuaded; other pagan philosophers and intellectuals found him unconvincing. Porphyry is a good example. He composed the biography of the famous Neoplatonic philosopher Plotinus and was himself a highly influential philosopher. He was born around 233 in Tyre in Phoenicia, and his family was apparently wealthy enough to afford him a good education. Porphyry was clearly well acquainted with Christianity and, in the words of Robert Wilken, "the most learned critic of all." His writings against Christianity made such an impression that Augustine was still responding to him in the fifth century. Porphyry's criticism of Christianity followed several different lines of argumentation. At times, he praised Jesus for his ethical teaching, while also pointing out inconsistencies in the Old Testament and the foolishness of believing the gospel accounts.[82] But more fundamentally, quite unlike Origen, he held Christianity and philosophy to be incompatible.

When Porphyry was a young man, he traveled down the coast to hear Origen lecture. Unlike Eusebius and Gregory, he was not taken with what he heard. He recognized that Origen was a student of Ammonius, the reputed founder of Neoplatonism, and "attained the greatest proficiency in philosophy of any in our day, [and] derived much benefit from this teaching in the knowledge of the sciences." However, Ammonius had been raised by Christian parents, only to abandon the faith in preference for a life studying philosophy, while Origen went the opposite direction. Origen was thus, in Porphyry's mind, an intellectual traitor, "educated as a Greek in Greek literature," but going "over to the barbarian recklessness." He carried with him philosophical learning only to mingle "Grecian teachings with foreign fables."[83] Porphyry could never forgive Origen for this kind of betrayal, or accept his theological claims. Philosophy could not be mixed with Christianity; Origen "contaminated this *paideia* when he later converted to Christianity."[84] If Christians like him earned a measure of respect for their morality, their borrowing from the philosophical schools to bolster the faith reeked of treason.

Such was the ongoing struggle between Christian and pagan intellectuals within the pre-Constantinian world. The second and third centuries saw a clash of the minds that intensified as the years passed and the church expanded. There was something about the intellectual arguments for Christianity that convinced figures like Justin, Caecilius, and Gregory. The method of argumentation, however, was neither pure confrontation nor isolation but assimilation oriented toward conversion through intellectual encounter. While Origen looked to engage and assimilate the insights of various philosophical systems, he was at once critical of pagan literature and viewed the Scriptures as the supreme authority, while at the same time not engaging in "complete condemnation."[85]

Origen's approach to the intellectual life does not mean Christian education must be formalized with titles and degrees. Depending upon the circumstances, it might happen within the church through mentoring relationships, discipleship ministries, theological education initiatives, or other parachurch organizations. We are already seeing a significant rise in church-based theological education, which is a positive development. I think Origen, along with the whole ancient apologetic tradition, offers an inspiring model for these initiatives. The current models of theological education have been—and will continue to be—effective, but times are changing. The apologists remind us that good theological education does not always (or only) happen within the traditional cultural institutions. The Christian intellectual life is something that can transcend these things. Origen reminds us that the highest forms of theological education are not always sanctioned by the elite cultural institutions, but neither should theological education shy away from the rigor of serious reflection upon divine things. Some fear that new educational initiatives might lead to lower standards or a watered-down curriculum, and rightly so. But there is no doubt that all educational institutions are evolving in various ways, driven especially by the online revolution. And as education moves more online, perhaps locally based educational initiatives will have a significant advantage over other models.[86] While Origen did not deal with modern technology, his emphasis on virtue and theological education fits well with newer locally constituted educational initiatives. Either way, the experience of the early church reminds us that public engagement in a pagan world requires some to embrace the call to a discerning intellectual life that engages the world around us for evangelistic and apologetic purposes and for the construction of Christian doctrine.

ARGUMENTS OF THE CHRISTIAN APOLOGISTS

Given the need for Christian intellectuals to respond to today's prevailing philosophical streams, let's consider some of the main themes and strategies of ancient intellectual engagement.[87] First, early Christian theologians worked hard to show the distinctiveness of Christianity and the weaknesses of the prevailing philosophical systems. This almost always entailed a defense of the Scriptures, the very basis of their theological systems, while also casting the Christian life as more intellectually satisfying than that of any other contender. Second, they argued for the antiquity and originality of Christian doctrine. Contrary to learned traditionalists' complaints, the church was not really a newcomer since the Christian God had created all things and directed salvation history toward the coming of Christ. Third, they insisted that the church was a public good for society. Their presence in the culture was a living witness to the goodness of the gospel. These are not the only arguments—apologetics in the ancient church was varied and complex—but these features reflect some of the most important strategies for furthering a cultural sanctification.

The Uniqueness of Christianity

First, Christian intellectuals in the ancient world worked to establish the uniqueness of Christianity, or what we might also see as the distinction between orthodoxy and heresy.[88] Aristides, for example, divided humanity into groups: Greek, barbarian, Jewish, Egyptian, and Christian. Then he characterized each group and demonstrated the distinctiveness of Christianity. This contention is rather controversial today because the hunt for influences, or *continuity* between Christianity and the Roman culture, is the dominant approach in much of the modern study of ancient Christianity. This tendency can be traced back to nineteenth-century critical scholarship's quest "to highlight ways in which early Christianity undeniably shared features with its wider historical context, and not adequately note differences."[89] In a recent work, New Testament scholar Larry Hurtado argues instead for a renewed appreciation of the distinctiveness of early Christianity. Hurtado recognizes that the scholarly prejudice against this position was born from a "reaction against, and/or desire to avoid, simplistic or exaggerated claims of Christian uniqueness in the service of evangelistic or apologetical aims." In other words, modern scholars did not concern themselves with the obvious fact that the early Christians actually believed their message and wanted to persuade others to join them. But as Origen and others made clear, the use of and appeal to the intellectual contributions of the wider culture was itself *serving apologetic aims*. To ignore the early Christian theologians' aim of distinguishing themselves from their Greco-Roman context is to distract from the actual assumptions of the ancient authors themselves.[90]

In the discussion of the uniqueness of Christianity, the Scriptures played an important role. They were the authoritative divine revelation given through the prophets and apostles and set apart from the other philosophical streams.[91] They defended the unity and coherence of the Scriptures against the diversity and contradictions of the philosophers. This comes alive in Justin's conversion, and he writes this narrative for apologetic and not merely evangelistic purposes. He wanted to show that Christianity was not part of any school but offered its own distinct way of life based upon a distinct cosmology and set of theological assumptions. He discovered this when, after dabbling in each of the major philosophical schools, he encountered an old man who explained the doctrines of Christianity:

> when he [the old man] had spoken these and many other things, which there is no time for mentioning at present, he went away, bidding me attend to them; and I have not seen him since. But straightway a flame was kindled in my soul; and a love of the prophets, and of those men who are friends of Christ, possessed me; and while revolving his words in my mind, I found this philosophy alone to be safe and profitable. Thus, and for this reason, I am a philosopher. Moreover, I would wish that all, making a resolution similar to my own, do not keep themselves away from the words of the Saviour. For they possess a terrible power in themselves, and are sufficient to inspire those who turn aside from the path of rectitude with awe; while the sweetest rest is afforded those who make a diligent practice of them. If, then, you have any concern for yourself, and if you are eagerly looking for salvation, and if you believe in God, you may—since you are not indifferent

to the matter—become acquainted with the Christ of God, and, after being initiated, live a happy life.[92]

Justin forthrightly declared that the Scriptures were formative in his conversion to Christianity. It was these writings, not those of Plato and Porphyry—perhaps for us, Foucault or Derrida—that sparked a flame in his soul. In this way, the Scriptures were central to the distinctiveness of the mission of the church; they were the special revelation given by God to the people of God. These writings, and these alone, led to the happy life. So also, Origen warned those who may have been deceived by the things of the Egyptians: "my son, diligently apply yourself to the reading of the sacred Scriptures. Apply yourself, I say. For we who read the things of God need much application, lest we should say or think anything too rashly about them."[93] Many other apologists, including Theophilus and Athenagoras, likewise pinned their conversion to an encounter with Scripture and emphasized the uniqueness of Christianity.

Distinguishing the uniqueness of Christianity also entailed distinguishing between orthodoxy and heresy. Many of the early Christian thinkers recognized that wrongheaded thinking about God began in the church through those that veered off from the faith that was handed down. Tertullian appeals to Paul (Gal 5:20; Titus 3:10–11), who compels the reader to avoid false doctrine. Tertullian observes that the Greek term *haeresis* entails "the sense of that choice which a man makes when he either teaches [false doctrines] or takes up with them."[94] Origen, too, argues that "all heretics begin by believing, and afterwards depart from the road of faith and the truth of the church's teaching."[95] Along the way, these Christian thinkers used the "same language of the Platonists to stress 'the youth' of these heresies" and "that they were born out of (and away from) the 'orthodox' position."[96]

These thinkers were following the example of Paul on Mars Hill in Acts 17 and using the best of contemporary theological and philosophical ideals to explain and defend the apostolic teaching. In this way, early Christian theologians not only critiqued the philosophers but also sought common ground to persuade or explain Christian theology.[97] The philosophers were moving closer to truth, Clement and Lactantius argued, but the prophets uniquely expressed it.[98] Justin puts things more bluntly: "Whatever things were rightly said among all men, are the property of us Christians." He believed all truth to be God's truth, and anything found in creation to be useful for Christians;

his use of the logos doctrine is well known for its resonances with Greek philosophy. The divine logos was communicated partially through the Greek
philosophers and poets, but when Christ appeared, he surpassed all others
and became the "whole rational being."[99] Many of the apologists praised the
philosophers, especially the Platonists, for the ways their rational insights ap-
proximated the truth of Scripture. But while the philosophers may have had
momentary insights, Christian revelation alone provided the best metaphysical framework to encourage human flourishing and promote virtue among its
adherents. It was through the revelation of the true Logos that perfect knowledge was revealed.

The Antiquity of Christianity

Second, the apologists argued for the antiquity of Christian revelation, suggesting that the Scriptures were more ancient, and therefore more authoritative,
than any philosophical text.[100] This argument for antiquity flowed naturally
from their rule of faith, with its assumptions about the doctrine of God and
nature of revelation. The antiquity of Christianity meant that all good theological and philosophical ideas were gifts of the one true Creator. Intellectually,
the Christians, appealing to the Scriptures, "claimed access to the primitive
and true wisdom which both Judaism and Hellenism had fragmented and dis-
torted."[101] The ancient philosophers, of course, found this argument prepos-
terous. Some, such as Celsus, argued that Christians are nothing more than
a divided and confused lot. But, Origen reasons, the appearance of diversity
does not mean there is no unity to Christian doctrine.[102] That would be like
criticizing Socrates for all the different philosophical streams that have flowed
from him.

Historically speaking, these arguments are extremely complex and varied
with different authors arguing for various channels of transmission and borrowing.[103] There is little agreement about how the philosophers arrived at
these conclusions, including various speculations about transmission and general revelation. In his *Apology*, Tertullian reasons, "unless I am utterly mistaken,
there is nothing so old as the truth; and the already proved antiquity of the
divine writings is so far of use to me, that it leads men more easily to take it in
that they are the treasure-source whence all later wisdom has been taken." The
philosophers debate the nature of God, the soul, and various other points that

intersect with Christian theology. There must be some cross-pollination between them and the writings of Moses and the prophets, Tertullian reasons. He continues, "What poet or sophist has not drunk at the fountain of the prophets? Thence, accordingly, the philosophers watered their arid minds, so that it is the things they have from us which bring us into comparison with them."[104] Augustine even speculates that Plato may have encountered Christian revelation.[105] He wonders whether Plato had access to translations, though he later assumes that he heard it orally.

Some Christian apologists also argued that the philosophers' speculations were propaedeutic, or that they anticipated Christian revelation.[106] Minucius Felix says to his interlocutor, "You observe that philosophers dispute of the same things that we are saying, not that we are following up their tracks, but that they, from the divine announcements of the prophets, imitated the shadow of the corrupted truth."[107] Justin thought their writings reflected a measure of the logos given to them that allowed them to come to a semblance of the truth.[108] Theophilus of Antioch, writing to his pagan interlocutor Autolycus, says, "sometimes some of them wakened up in soul, and, that they might be for a witness both to themselves and to all men, spoke things in harmony with the prophets regarding the monarchy of God, and the judgment and such like."[109] All of these arguments for antiquity worked to frame the philosophical writings within a general conception of Christian theology and serve to defend the faith of the church.[110]

Christianity as a Public Good

Third, early Christian apologists argued that the church was a positive good for the world. Above all else, Christians strove to live virtuous lives, and their virtue would be a positive, stabilizing influence. Indeed, outsiders often remarked how loyal and compassionate Christians were to each other. Justin argued that converts to Christianity made better members of the society, better citizens of the empire.[111] Similarly, Aristides claimed that Christians made the best citizens because they had a concern for the well-being of their community and were animated by the virtues of modesty, joy, love, compassion, self-sacrifice, and self-discipline. He cast this vision memorably:

They [Christians] do not worship strange gods, and they go their way in all modesty and cheerfulness. Falsehood is not found among them; and they love one another, and from widows they do not turn away their esteem; and they deliver the orphan from him who treats him harshly. And he, who has, gives to him who has not, without boasting. And when they see a stranger, they take him in to their homes and rejoice over him as a very brother; for they do not call them brethren after the flesh, but brethren after the spirit and in God. And whenever one of their poor passes from the world, each one of them according to his ability gives heed to him and carefully sees to his burial. And if they hear that one of their number is imprisoned or afflicted on account of the name of their Messiah, all of them anxiously minister to his necessity, and if it is possible to redeem him they set him free. And if there is among them any that is poor and needy, and if they have no spare food, they fast two or three days in order to supply to the needy their lack of food. They observe the precepts of their Messiah with much care, living justly and soberly as the Lord their God commanded them. Every morning and every hour they give thanks and praise to God for His loving-kindnesses toward them; and for their food and their drink they offer thanksgiving to Him.[112]

This kind of a vision for society, in which the Christian community provided for their own while living virtuously in the world, made it highly attractive to a world and society that did not share these virtues. This transformation entails that Christians are kind to all people, regardless of social standing. "We are the same to emperors as to our ordinary neighbors," Tertullian writes. Christian compassion thus made a positive contribution to the world, shaped it in constructive ways, and proved a powerful attraction to those who witnessed it. Christians are a positive good for society; they perform all kinds of social services and good works.[113]

The apologetic impulse is just as necessary today as in the early church. We, too, need key figures with the intellectual acumen to engage the prevailing philosophical assumptions around us. We need Christian intellectuals able to discern what is good and true and beautiful within the culture and turn it to apologetic and evangelistic purposes—the kind of Christian intellectuals who can read the signs of the times and embody Christian doctrine and morality in a manner intelligible and persuasive in our own times. The apologetic arguments of the early church offer us some help in this endeavor. We need to work hard to clarify the distinctiveness and merits of Christian doctrine and morality. Certainly, the truth of Christianity has been tested through the centuries and is grounded in a metanarrative that transcends a particular moment. While Christians have not always lived up to the highest standards of Christian ethics, the Christian life is a public good and offers the best path to human flourishing.

CONCLUSION

Seeking cultural sanctification in a world full of gods meant that the church had to learn how to navigate the terrain of paganism and live among people who held radically different theological and moral convictions. The resulting public theology was not conceived in purely social terms. The church recognized the importance of intellectual engagement and interaction with the philosophical climate of the world around them, as witnessed in Caecilius's debate with Octavius recounted at the beginning of this chapter. It is no accident that the first few centuries of the early church were known as the era of the apologists. These figures—such as Justin Martyr, Tertullian, and Origen—were following a precedent laid down in the New Testament. If Romans like Pliny, Celsus, and Porphyry scorned the Christian case and shrewdly defended their sacred traditions, they might have had the dominant institutions and cultural power on their side, but they did not always have the best moral and theological arguments.

Christians today also live in an age for apologetics; that ancient world looks an awful lot like ours. Stories such as that of Minucius Felix and his friends Octavius and Caecilius remind us of the importance of intellectual discourse in a pagan world. Cultural sanctification is not only concerned with the practical but also with the intellectual. When the church was living on the margins of the culture, they aimed to prepare believers for casual conversations that organically raised questions about matters of ultimate concern. The early church cultivated an environment that honored Christian intellectuals and encouraged an apologetic and evangelistic posture embedded in their own time. Through this kind of posture, the church can defend the faith and preserve its treasures amid the toils and trials of the age.

Now more than ever we need Christians who can defend the faith in the public square. Not that every Christian needs to enroll in seminary; rather, that all Christians should be ready for these kinds of intellectual encounters. The emergence of the Christian intellectual points to the enduring function of the pastor as the theological and intellectual guide for the Christian community. Pastors must have more theological training and discipleship to be ready to meet the intellectual challenges that face the church. The intellectual role must be married with religious conviction and aim to protect the community amid the prevailing philosophical winds. This does not mean that the surrounding culture must be rejected. On the contrary, it ought to be, wherever possible, used to communicate the truthfulness of Christianity in doctrine and life.

Besides such intellectual work, we need to imitate the early church in engaging the social structure around us. The church must also demonstrate its faith through social interactions and moral convictions. To that topic we turn next.

PUBLIC LIFE

The Soldier's Crown

Emperor Septimius Severus, an early persecutor of Christianity, died on 4 February 211 and was succeeded by the coemperors Caracalla and Geta. They moved to garner the favor of the Roman army by bestowing upon them a monetary gift called a *donativum*.[1] Such gifts were common when a new emperor assumed power, and they meant to curry the favor of the Roman legions. The new rulers knew that no government could carry on without military support. These gifts were distributed at a ceremony where soldiers were given a small crown of laurel leaves, which signified the blessings and privilege bestowed upon them for their loyalty.

Tertullian, a Christian rhetorician residing in Carthage, North Africa, reported that at one of these ceremonies, a Christian soldier refused to wear the crown. Because of his religious convictions, he held the crown in his hand instead to communicate his honor for the emperor but allegiance to God. Like a dark stain on a beautiful white gown, his uncrowned head stood out among the throng of soldiers. They knew why he refused to wear the crown, and they were not impressed. They mocked him, threatened him with all kinds of insults, and finally reported his indiscretion to the tribune, who questioned his insolence. "Why are you so different in your attire?" the tribune asked.[2] The soldier explained that his religious conviction would not permit him to wear any such symbol of adoration for the emperor. He was willing to serve the empire, but he drew the line at any notion of imperial worship. The other soldiers continued to decry his stance; refusing to wear the emperor's crown was tantamount to rejection of the civil religion—to treason. This disrespect could not be tolerated, so they arrested him and condemned him to prison where he was likely martyred.

This incident was a flashpoint for the Christian community in North Africa. Certainly, the lingering pains of Septimius Severus's persecution still haunted their memories. Fearing a revival of persecution, they questioned the wisdom of the soldier's actions. Tertullian quoted them: "Why does he have to make so much trouble for the rest of us Christians over the trifling matter of dress? Why must he be so inconsiderate and rash and act as if he were anxious to die? Is he the only brave man, the only Christian among all his fellow soldiers?"[3] But if some deemed the Christian soldier's actions selfish because he put other Christians at risk, others thought the crown signified a deeper, religious allegiance to the emperors and so commended his defiance.

This incident captures the challenge facing Christians reentering society after baptism. The dividing lines between the church and the world are not altogether clear, and the early church had no designated manual to help it figure out how to live in the world. These kinds of arguments were essential to the shaping of Christian identity. In its posture of defiance, Christianity "subverted the whole priestly calendar of civic rituals and public festivals on which Roman rule in the provinces rested" and was thus a "revolutionary movement" that undermined the whole Roman way of life.[4] As the soldier's story attests, this could be a complicated and often costly gesture. From the moment the Christian awoke in the Roman Empire, there was a constant onslaught of daily moral decisions that had to be made. For as Tertullian reminded his fellow Christians, after joining the community of faith "every forward step and movement, at every going in and out, when we put on our clothes and shoes, when we bathe, when we sit at table, when we light the lamps, on couch, on seat, in all the ordinary actions of daily life, we trace upon the forehead the sign."[5] The "sign" here was undoubtedly the sign of the cross that marked out the Christians for their doctrinal and moral convictions.[6] Since early Christians could no longer maintain all their old habits and entertainments, they had to begin the slow process of resocializing, of navigating the interactions between Christian identity and earthly citizenship.

This narrative helps us understand the next step in tracing the early church's vision of cultural sanctification. The first entailed shaping a Christian identity through a coordination of catechesis and liturgy, which led to a renegotiation of citizenship under a political dualism that flowed from Christian doctrine and morality. Broadening out from this political theology, they developed a public theology for intellectual life. We now consider how they took that into their social life as well.

Here, too, pagans viewed Christians with negative assumptions and misconceptions. In response, the early Christian vision of cultural sanctification exacted a process of *resocialization*, among considerations of *contingency*, *sanctification*, and *improvisation*. That is, after joining the church, Christians had to struggle through the evolving circumstances of the social world, always trying to manage their cultural absorption or acculturation. All the while, they sought perfection and conformity to the likeness of Christ. This entailed cultivating "a culturally discerning" spiritual life—one that was actively indigenizing within the culture but always sorting out the virtues and vices lodged within it. We will see this specifically in their treatment of occupations, leisure and entertainment, military service, and marriage and family. In all this, the church was not wholly focused on internal sanctification but attentive to the external needs of their world, affirming a compassionate social engagement that attracted outsiders. All these features guided the church in the sanctification and transformation of the culture.

Pagan Views of Christianity

By the end of the second century, Christians were thoroughly entrenched within Roman culture and social life. To begin with, their numbers were growing at a rate quite unsettling to many of their neighbors. At least in North Africa, said Tertullian, Christians had spread out rapidly: "Though we are but of yesterday, we have filled all that is yours, cities, islands, fortified towns, classes of public attendants, the palace, the senate, the forum . . . nearly all the citizens you have in nearly all the cities are Christian."[7] Many Romans agreed, in dismay; they whined, "the State is filled with Christians—they are in the fields, in the citadels, in the islands: they make lamentation, as for some calamity, that both sexes, every age and condition, even high rank, are passing over to the profession of the Christian faith."[8]

Given this growth, Christians and non-Christians carried on regular everyday interactions, in the marketplace and conversations at social gatherings in public places. Pagans "came in contact with the movement in a number of casual ways," Nock says in his classic work on conversion, because "there was little, if any, direct preaching to the masses."[9] The church was not distinguished from the culture by anything in their outward appearance, especially since they were not typically found among the upper crust of society and thus blended in even more with those around them. What did distinguish them was their distinctive doctrine and practice. Christianity came on the scene with "very distinctive roots" and, though fully embedded, was never fully enmeshed in the culture.[10]

Public skepticism toward Christianity also produced gossip and rumors as might be expected among people living in close quarters with each other. Not everyone was attracted to Christianity; there was widespread suspicion, misunderstanding, and ridicule. This led to constant tensions between the pagan and the Christian communities that played out in daily interactions. Refusing to worship pagan gods, Christians were subjected to various forms of interrogation. They were excluded from public places; ultimately, some were tortured and killed for their convictions.[11] This hostility escalated in the times of Decius, Valerian, and Diocletian, as these emperors tried to bring unity to the fractured empire. Christian theologians often discussed how pagans charged them with all kinds of outlandish arguments. They "regard us as a human herd cut off from other people," Tertullian said, and Minucius Felix's pagan interlocutor suggested that Christians were a "shadowy and cunning race, silent in public, but chattering in lonely corners."[12]

Obviously, Christians were making a name for themselves, and the church had to live with the negative consequences. But how did they do so? How did early Christians think through the challenges of living in a world marked by temples to idols on every street and an economic system fueled by idol worship? They had to undertake a process of resocialization, cultivating a cultural discernment in every aspect of their own spiritual lives.

A CULTURALLY DISCERNING SPIRITUAL LIFE

The postconversion challenges facing Christians arose when they reentered society as baptized people and navigated the conflicts raised by their new convictions. This process demanded a culturally discerning spiritual life. In their postconversion resocialization, those who came up out of the waters of baptism had to navigate the pagan world by a new set of convictions. They encountered their neighbors in a new perspective and had to weave new patterns of social engagement so as to live faithfully in light of their theological and moral convictions. And they had to do so in ways that made the Christian life a living testimony to the moral beauty of the gospel.

The culturally discerning spiritual life involved contingency, sanctification, and improvisation. Across ever-changing social conditions, Christians learned to improvise patterns of conviction and tradition as they sought sanctification within the culture. They were not perfect but did display steady confidence in their theological convictions.

The church is never reserved to one people or one political system. The early Christian apologist Aristides, for example, argued that the Christian community formed a new *ethnos*, a new people, distinct from Greeks, Babylonians, Egyptians, and Jews. While these groups might in varying degrees approach the truth, only Christians "have come nearer to truth and genuine knowledge than the rest of the nations."[13] New Testament scholar Wayne Meeks compares Aristides's discussion of conversion to the *ethnos* of Christianity with the experience of immigrants who leave their native land and need to adapt to a new place and a new way of life. He defines the "resocialization" of the reenactment in a new setting of "the primary socialization that occurs normally in the interactions between child and family, the process in which the self receives those components of its structure and those basic values that are contributed by its environment."[14] Just as a child is reared and guided with the morals and the values of its family and then grows to maturity and enters society, so also is the Christian discipled and guided in the distinctive theological and moral assumptions of the church and matures to live Christianly in the world. This resocialization, however, is built upon different theological assumptions and maintains distinctive moral convictions so that those who convert begin following new cultural and moral patterns of the Christian life.

In social sciences, the concept of resocialization is related to the notion of acculturation, "the changes that arise following 'contact' between individuals and groups of different cultural backgrounds."[15] For ancient Christians, this became a dynamic process in which the elements of their Roman identity were filtered through their Christian morality, like separating the wheat from the chaff. Meeks says that "for the vast majority, the Christian life was an amphibian life, life at the same time in the old world that was passing away and in the new world that was coming." Christians were "moving back and forth between the two sets of social practices" in accordance with their moral sensibilities.[16] A key passage that helped shape this kind of movement was Matthew 6:24: "No one can serve two masters, for either he will hate the one and love the other, or he will be devoted to the one and despise the other. You cannot serve God and money."[17] This text addressed much more than taxes; it called for a holistic framework by which the church could undertake the life of cultural discernment. The service of two masters had to be carefully regulated and deciphered, particularly in terms of forming habits, mores, and customs. The early church assumed that devotion to Christ necessitated that their process of cultural absorption be governed by their choice to follow Christ within the culture in a way that was faithful to Christian morality.

The process of Christian acculturation happened at both the personal and institutional levels. On the personal level, like the soldier mentioned in the opening story, Christians were challenged to live moral lives among their neighbors so as to display their good works to others *through social interactions*. For many, this kind of witness manifested Christian virtue in all aspects of life, not least by the kinds of social interactions that Christians refused. Alongside personal interactions, acculturation also happened at the institutional level where the church viewed itself as a family, an organic body manifesting the work of God within creation. That community would be, for example, devoid of any association with paganism. As such, their gatherings, rituals, morals, and culture would be quite distinct from those of any other social or political organization. For this reason, the clergy had to remain committed to the task of organizing and leading the church, because if the "deacons, and presbyters, and bishops" turned their backs and ran, Tertullian writes, "who of the plebs will hope to persuade people."[18]

CULTIVATING A CULTURAL DISCERNMENT

In the earlier chapter on catechesis and the spiritual life, we met the three notions of *contingency, sanctification,* and *improvisation* as characterizing the process of living Christianly in any and every situation. Seeking *sanctification* amid the *contingency* of varying cultural situations involved a struggle of reso-cialization that necessitated the cultivation of cultural discernment. "Discernment" entails the "process of assessing and evaluating, particularly in relation to trying to determine God's will in a particular situation or for one's life direction."[19] Enmeshed in their culture and engaged in the normal patterns of its life, the early church was called to discernment because "Christians' practices were not confined to sacred occasions and sacred locations—shrines, sacrifices, processions—but were integral to the formation of communities with a distinctive self-awareness."[20] How were they to seek holiness in their world?

In the early second-century text called the Didache, we can see the process of cultural discernment in action. The text describes how to welcome newcomers into the community:

> Everyone "who comes in the name of the Lord" is to be welcomed. But then examine him, and you will find out—for you will have insight—what is true and what is false. If the one who comes is merely passing through, assist him as much as you can. But he must not stay with you for more than two or, if necessary, three days. However, if he wishes to settle among you and is a craftsman, let him work for his living. But if he is not a craftsman, decide according to your own judgement how he shall live among you as a Christian, yet without being idle. But if he does not wish to cooperate in this way, then he is trading on Christ. Beware of such people.[21]

Sojourners among the Christian community were welcomed and supported, but that support was limited; those who wished to join the community had to take up an occupation. If not, the community had to discern how to maintain them without fostering idleness.

We find a more detailed account of cultural discernment in Hippolytus's tract *On the Apostolic Tradition*. This text tells us that anyone interested in joining the church had to go through an initial interview to ferret out potential problems in their lives or backgrounds.[22] Newcomers were "questioned concerning the reason that they have come forward to the faith" and "questioned concerning their life and occupation, marriage status, and whether they are slave or free."[23] While many vocations were acceptable, any involving sexual immorality, pagan religious offices, or gladiatorial games had to be abandoned before the candidate could proceed further. Some others, such as teachers or military personnel, might continue their work with some cautioning and qualification. The same kind of sifting is also evident in Tertullian, who tied everything back to the problem of idolatry: "no profession, no trade, which administers either to equipping or forming idols, can be free from the title of idolatry."[24] Christians had to think carefully through every aspect of their lives, examining their vocation to see how it might influence their spirituality; as Greer argues, "theology in the early church was always directly or indirectly concerned with the common life of Christians."[25] The intersections of the common life were precisely where the tensions between the Christian and pagan ethical concerns became manifest.

For contemporary Christians raised in the seeker-sensitive movement, this kind of personal interrogation of potential new members may seem a bit shocking. Early Christians did not immediately welcome just anyone into the church; the church's identity and purity needed to be safeguarded and preserved through a slow, steady, and deliberate process. The early church played the long game and grew slowly. There were no dramatic mass conversions, only a work of church planting that attracted locals through casual contacts and everyday interactions.[26] This was a revolution marked by "gradualism" and proved to be the "ultimate factor" that led to the rise of Christianity, says sociologist Rodney Stark. The "central doctrines of Christianity prompted and sustained attractive, liberating, and effective social relations and organizations,"[27] steadily undermining the Roman patterns of culture. It grew naturally out of the Christians' dual citizenship.[28] The moral of the story is that the "Christian can be neither fully involved in his society nor fully withdrawn from it. Instead, he must keep his sights on the pilgrim's path."[29]

If for Origen the essence of the intellectual life was the pursuit of virtue, the same applies to social life. Together the church worked through the process of sanctification as it sought to be conformed to the likeness of Christ. There was no bifurcation between early Christian liturgical and social life because of their focus on sanctification and ultimately glorification or beatitude. The incident of the soldier and the crown provides a touchpoint for this conversation. Thinking through the soldier's decision, Tertullian asked his reader, "What will discipline do?"[30] That is, Tertullian drew the dividing line between the Christian and the pagan at the same point of "discipline" (*disciplina*) common in all his writings.[31] Discipline was often connected to martyrdom, but it was also used more generally to refer to the daily spiritual pursuit of Christian virtue.[32] In Tertullian's reasoning, discipline involves orienting the will to follow the rules or laws that govern the Christian's spiritual life.[33] God's law provided the framework for daily living so that faith would be formed by gradual stages under "the perfect light of the Christian discipline."[34] Many other early Christian theologians agreed. The dual call to live a disciplined life according to divine law while simultaneously living by the normal patterns of life *within* the culture defined the early Christian understanding of cultural discernment.

CULTURAL DISCERNMENT AND THE SPIRITUAL LIFE

To show how early Christians cultivated that discernment, let's review some specific ways in which they thought through issues related to their occupations, entertainments, military service, and marriage and family. Church leaders were concerned about those who might be joining the faith for the wrong reasons or motives, exploit the community, or exhibit hypocrisy in their behavior. Thus, they asked serious questions about the relationship between the social world and the spiritual life. Contingency and improvisation emerged amid changing circumstances, creating new issues for the church to consider. Their decisions were not always easy or straightforward. They did not reject all entertainments and occupations, but they did strive to ensure that each and every feature of their social lives was oriented toward the true God and reflected true Christian virtue. Though the following survey is only a brief discussion of these points, it should be enough to give us a feel for how they proceeded.

Occupations

In the process of catechesis, the early church showed remarkable concern over occupational life. It wanted to know what new believers did for a living, not to estimate future tithes but out of concern for the persons' spiritual lives. It wanted to distance itself from certain professions on moral grounds.[35] The ancient pagan world being filled with idols, the church found it challenging to disassociate itself from the industry of idolatry. Further, the ancient world was a society run by patronage in which everyone "was bound to someone more powerful above him." The working environment was regulated by "severe and meticulous codes of etiquette," including how clients dressed and interacted with their patrons. The church was thus entering an economic system marked by the "heart-breaking comprehensiveness of . . . systematic exploitation."[36] At the same time, the early church had a positive view of labor, not least because the community needed to provide for its members. So the issue was not the work itself (see Hippolytus's and Tertullian's celebration of Christians' presence across many occupations mentioned above) but the morality participating in their occupations. The early Christian handbook, *On the Apostolic Tradition*, records how aspiring members were queried on this point in their initial interview.

> If any is a pimp or procurer of prostitutes he should desist or he should be rejected. If any is a sculptor or a painter he should be instructed not to make idols; he should desist or he should be rejected. If any is an actor, or makes presentations in the theater, he should desist, or he should be rejected. If somebody teaches children it is better that he desist; if he have no other trade let him be allowed. Likewise a charioteer who competes, or anyone that goes to the races, should desist or be rejected. If anyone is a gladiator, or trains gladiators in fighting, or one who fights with beasts in the games, or a public official engaged in gladiatorial business should desist, or he should be rejected. If any is a priest of idols, or a guardian of idols, he should desist, or he should be rejected.[37]

The text continues discussing these points and others, but clearly church leaders took the matter of occupations very seriously. Just as clearly, not all occupations were equal.

On the Apostolic Tradition assumes a threefold scheme that differentiates between occupations deemed unacceptable on moral grounds, those that were acceptable in a qualified sense, and those that were entirely acceptable. Navigating between these categories required careful discernment. The most obvious concern was idolatry, with many occupations being in some way linked to idol production and distribution. Anything involving sexual immorality and murder was also proscribed. This included most obviously prostitution but also various forms of entertainment, such as an actor who performed shows in the theater or anyone involved in the gladiatorial games, such as a charioteer, gladiator, gladiator trainer, or a public official involved with the games. The nature of the events themselves, along with the idolatry and other acts of immorality attending them, led to depravity. Pagan religions or traditions such as astrology or divination were also proscribed. They were seen, both by their nature and by the social consequences flowing from them, as standing in direct conflict with sound spirituality. All these categories were part of what Martin Hengel calls "the great refusal." [38]

Other jobs were considered acceptable so long as they were reoriented toward Christian virtue. Painters or sculptors, for example, could continue their work, but they had to use their gifts and talents to promote beauty, not idol worship. Along these same lines, the text encouraged teachers to find another profession because the work of the ancient schoolmaster or grammaticus was linked with pagan literature, but if they were unable to do so, they might continue to teach with vigilance. Public officials or military soldiers were also encouraged to leave their posts but could continue so long as they were not involved in gladiator shows or overseeing anyone's death.

Finally, while *On the Apostolic Tradition* says nothing about trades such as farming or commerce, one can assume that the same general guidelines would apply. There were many professions that were acceptable and ordinary. In general, as Hengel puts it, the church had a "positive evaluation of manual labor and the moderate acquisition of possessions."[39] Tertullian, for example, spoke positively of Christians in these occupations.[40] Already in the New Testament, Christians were involved in all kinds of economic activities by which they supported the poor within the church and the church's ministries. Paul was, after all, a tentmaker (Acts 18:3), and other early Christians were clearly involved in the economic life of the ancient world (1 Thess 4:11). As mentioned above, the second-century Didache encourages Christians to welcome everyone "who comes in the name of the Lord" but also insists that anyone who wished to join the church should work to provide for them and the community: "if he [an outsider] wishes to settle among you and is a craftsman, let him work for his living. But if he is not a craftsman, decide according to your own judgment how he shall live among you as a Christian, yet without being idle," lest they exploit the church.[41]

Like the *On the Apostolic Tradition*, Tertullian cautioned Christians to be vigilant about the ways that idolatry was infused into every occupation. The faithful must find a calling that afforded a livelihood without "outstepping the path of discipline" and participating in the production, distribution, or sale of idols. Tertullian also differentiated among occupations on moral grounds. Many occupations associated with idolatry could be put to other uses: "the plasterer knows both how to mend roofs, and lay on stuccoes, and polish a cistern, and trace ogives, and draw in relief on party-walls many other ornaments beside likenesses. The painter, too, the marble mason, the bronze-worker, and every graver whatever, knows expansions of his own art, of course much easier of execution." Tertullian, too, rejected astrologers and magicians and was harder on schoolteachers.[42] He also urged merchants and public officials to remain free of idolatry.

The most notable feature of this whole conversation is the church's determination to decipher what kinds of occupations were possible within the discipline of the Christian spiritual life. It recognized that a Christian's moral and spiritual life could not be divorced from one's work life, that one's occupation demanded a high standard of morality, and that any cultural activity must observe the general moral standards expressed by the divine law. So teaching was not a problem, but teaching idolatry was. Entertainment and government were not a problem, but vices associated with them, such as murder or the lust for power, were. Work in the world had to be divested of the kinds of vices that permeated pagan antiquity, and the church had to recognize its role in this process. In short, conversion to Christianity necessitated a discernment between the kinds of occupations that promoted sin and those that aided a healthy spiritual life.

Employment is a place where theology and morality intersect with real life. This is not just a matter of wealth and poverty but of whether Christians should participate in certain professions, businesses, industries, companies, or anything else that participates in immorality. The early church challenges us to look in the mirror and think about our occupations. If there is anything we can learn, it is the need to be very discerning in our jobs, the virtues and vices associated with them. Not just the people involved but the nature of the work itself and the way it contributes to human flourishing require prayerful reflection. We must start asking hard questions about how we lead companies and enterprises so as to promote authentic Christian virtues. The primary issue in the early church and also for us today is the question of virtue. If the early church has anything to teach us, it is that virtue and the spiritual life are more important than all hopes of financial gains and professional prestige.

Leisure and Entertainment

Romans' occupations did not absorb all their time; they did not come close to our standard eight-hour workday. They enjoyed a healthy amount of free time that could be filled with all kinds of entertainments, not to mention their many holidays and feast days. The Roman calendar was divided between days that allowed and days that prohibited business (*dies fasti* and *dies nefasti*, respectively). The latter involved a mixture of public holidays or public games intended to amuse the people. Occasional days were set aside for shows in the theater or the circus to honor the gods or special days to honor the Caesars. Carcopino reports that in the time of Claudius, the Roman calendar "contained 159 days expressly marked as holidays, of which 93 were devoted to games given at public expense." The precise number of days waxed and waned with each emperor and the state of the empire under his rule. While the Caesars felt the need to protect the empire's borders and maintain the food supplies, they were also compelled to entertain their people.[43] The people of Rome lusted for their entertainments.

The extravagance and self-indulgence of Rome, Kyle Harper argues, all the festivals, races, plays and dramas, and other events in the amphitheater, aimed to stimulate the appetites; moderation required heroic feats of restraint.[44] Religion was "inseparably bound up" with all these entertainments;[45] both animal and human sacrifices to the gods abounded. Roman culture in general was sexually overheated and furiously violent. In this environment, the church struggled to live Christianly. It issued no shortage of exhortations to avoid the games for three principal reasons: the vices pervading these gatherings, the presence of idolatry, and the way these games polluted Christian lives.[46]

First, the church viewed Roman entertainment as filled with vices.[47] In his fiery rhetoric for moral purity, Tertullian lamented being surrounded by a culture infused with such wickedness with no way to separate completely from them. He listed all kinds of festivals, circuses, and combats that were polluted "in respect of their origins, their titles, their equipments, their places of celebrations, their arts and vices." The gladiatorial arena involved violence, rage, and death, while the theater provoked eroticism and the indulgence of immoral appetites. All in all, Roman entertainments were suffused with sexual immorality, gossip, lies, idolatry, debauchery, and murder.[48] Tertullian pressed his prohibition against entertainments to the extreme of forbidding any interaction with or attendance at them, even in moderation.

Cyprian, another North African, shared Tertullian's concerns about public shows. The gladiatorial games, for example, were a place where "blood may gladden the lust of cruel eyes."[49] He lamented, "Man is slaughtered that man may be gratified, and the skill that is best able to kill is an exercise and an art. Crime is not only committed, but it is taught. What can be said more inhuman—what more repulsive?" Cyprian concluded in an exasperated tone about the effect these spectacles had upon those in attendance: "Can he who looks upon such things be healthy-minded or modest? Men imitate the gods whom they adore, and to such miserable beings their crimes become their religion."[50]

Alongside these, Lactantius also painted a dramatic portrait of the Roman lust after death and violence in the arena:

> For he who reckons it a pleasure, that a man, though justly condemned, should be slain in his sight, pollutes his conscience as much as if he should become a spectator and a sharer of a homicide which is secretly committed. And yet they call these sports in which human blood is shed. So far has the feeling of humanity departed from the men, that when they destroy the lives of men, they think that they are amusing themselves with sport, being more guilty than all those whose blood-shedding they esteem a pleasure.[51]

For Lactantius, the spectators, too, participated in the acts of immorality. How could a person who claimed to be just and pious, even by Rome's standards, demand "cruel and inhuman votes for their death, not being satiated with wounds nor contented with bloodshed." If the combatants were wounded or killed too quickly, the crowd cried out for more violence.[52] Lactantius averred that Christians could not participate in the games as a combatant or even attend them lest they give their approval to the killing.

The theater, too, was filled with all kinds of immorality: "lewdness, obscenity, and sensuality often were the thematic core of Roman theatrical productions."[53] To Cyprian, the "old horrors of parricide and incest" pervaded the stage.[54] Clement of Alexandria insisted that spectacles and plays "that are full of scurrility and of abundant gossip" should be forbidden.[55] Felix condemned theatrical entertainments in which "the debauchery is more prolonged: for now a mimic either expounds or shows forth adulteries; now nerveless player, while he feigns lust, suggests it; the same actor disgraces your gods by attributing to them adulteries, sighs, hatreds; the same provokes your tears with pretended sufferings, with vain gestures and expressions."[56] At the same time, the early church objected to "the intimate link between the theater and the wider Roman sex industry; and the sexual exploitation of women and boys in the theater and its immediate environs."[57]

The thread uniting all these responses was an emphasis on promoting virtue. As the apologist Minucius Felix put it, the Christian ought to be distinguished from the pagan by virtue, character, and modesty: "We are all born with one lot; it is only by virtue that we are distinguished."[58] The Christian life demanded the high calling of conformity to the likeness of Christ. Participation in the games, even the very act of attending them, supported violence and exalted idols, whereas Christians should strive for peace with everyone and for the holiness without which no one will see the Lord (Heb 12:14). As Theophilus explained, "with them temperance dwells, self-restraint is practiced, monogamy is observed, chastity is guarded, iniquity exterminated, sin extirpated, righteousness exercised, law administered, worship performed, God acknowledged: truth governs, grace guards, peace screens them; the holy word guides, wisdom teaches, life directs, God reigns."[59]

But not everyone, even among the Christian community, was interested in giving up their entertainments. Tertullian had to rebut several reasons that believers gave for indulging such enjoyments of life.[60] In the first place, some Christians argued for a platonic mind-body dualism under which the enjoyments of the senses had no effect upon the mind or conscience. Others were antinomians: God wanted people to enjoy life and celebrate the blessings of creation. And indeed, Tertullian saw something in such elements of public shows as the "horse, the lion, bodily strength, and musical voice," while the "rocks, stones, marbles, pillars" in the buildings housing the amusements were artistic gifts of God. But these elements had all been misused and abused by creatures who contorted them to the pleasures of their whims and vices.

As with our professional lives, the Christian community today should give some serious thought to our entertainments. This entails monitoring both what comes into our homes and our souls and our commitment of time. There is no rule to apply to every context, but an improvisation framed by virtue is essential here. Evangelicals often threaten justifiable boycotts against offensive productions of media corporations, but every business must make choices about the moral posture of its work and practices. No company, no art, is immune from moral judgments and moral claims, and Christians are called to persistently exercise these so as to live Christianly. Just as Daniel ate the king's food and supported the king's rule but drew the line at the king's edict against prayer, we need to determine where to draw our own lines by exercising critical cultural discernment.

Military Service

Christian participation in the military is complicated and fraught with tensions. There are competing interpretations among those who read the church fathers with either pacifist or nonpacifist leanings.[61] But the fundamental challenges of the first three centuries have not changed; Christians are encouraged to maintain responsible citizenship while at the same time avoiding murder and idolatry in the name of the state. To repeat, the early church believed that God has installed government to wield the sword, but other divine commands call the faithful to value life and reject murder. The presence of Christians in the military raised these questions until the rise of Constantine when attitudes began to shift toward greater sympathy for Christian involvement in military service. This ultimately led to the development of Augustine's just war theory.[62] But in the earliest centuries of the church, when the pagan world thrived, how did the church interact with the military life?

First, while the New Testament tells of soldiers converting to Christianity, there is a significant silence about military service prior to the end of the first century.[63] This silence likely means that there were relatively few Christians serving in the military. But by the turn of the second and into the third century, Christianity was clearly penetrating the military ranks. The opening story about our soldier and his crown says as much. In another place, Tertullian tells a story about soldiers in the second-century army of Marcus Aurelius who, suffering from drought during a military campaign, prayed for rain and saw their prayers answered.[64] Evidently, Christians were serving in the military, and other soldiers were sympathetic to their theological convictions. We can see this indirectly as well in the fears of pagan leaders and intellectuals about the presence of Christians in the military. The pagan intellectual Celsus, for example, thought this might lead to the dissolution of Rome. If everyone became Christian, he fears the emperor would be abandoned, and all things would be left "in the power of the most lawless and savage barbarians."[65] In short, there were serious concerns that Christians would not act to preserve and protect the empire.

Despite these fears, Christians were slowly making inroads into the military ranks, raising important questions about what was required of those serving

Caesar. *On the Apostolic Tradition* takes it as given that there are Christians
serving in the military and offers some mediating positions on the ways that
they can continue in their profession. If any new convert was a member of
the military, he "must not execute men. If he is ordered, he must not carry
it out. Nor must he take a military oath."[66] The moral and theological issues
were already evident: the prohibited behaviors along with idolatry were woven
into military life. Harnack summarizes the overall arguments against military
service in the first three centuries of the church:

> 1) it was a warrior's profession and Christianity on principle rejected war
> and the shedding of blood; 2) the officers, under given circumstances, had
> to pass the sentence of death, and the soldiers in the ranks had to carry out
> everything they were ordered to do; 3) the unconditional oath required
> of the soldier was in conflict with the unconditional obligation to God;
> 4) the cult of the emperor was at its strongest in the army and was hardly
> avoidable for each individual soldier; 5) the officers had to offer sacrifices,
> and the regular soldiers had to take part; 6) the military standards appear to
> be heathen sacra; to reverence them was hence idolatry . . . ; 7) the conduct
> of soldiers in peacetime conflicted with the Christian ethic; 8) the tradi-
> tional rough games and jokes in the army . . . were offensive in themselves
> and were connected in part with the service of idols and the festivals of
> the gods.[67]

In Harnack's summary, theological concerns about human life, unconditional
allegiance to a pagan state, a vision of Christian sanctification and moral
purity, and avoidance of idolatry all drove the early church's struggle with
military service.

Second, the early church had an aversion to killing and consistently condemned any form of murder or homicide. Romans were infatuated with bloodshed, as manifested in the gladiatorial combats and on the battlefield. The
church, armed with the spirituality embodied in the Ten Commandments
and the Sermon on the Mount, condemned this insatiable desire for death.[68]
As the apologist Minucius Felix put it, "To us it is not lawful either to see or to
hear of homicide; and so much do we shrink from human blood, that we do
not use the blood even of eatable animals in our food."[69] On the same subject,
Athenagoras wrote, "But we, deeming that to see a man put to death is much

the same as killing him, have abjured such spectacles."[70] Origen made the same claim: "For He did not deem it in keeping with such laws as His, which were derived from a divine source, to allow the killing of any individual whatever."[71] Many other early Christians make similar arguments.[72]

Second, the church struggled with blending notions of heavenly and earthly citizenship, and these two visions intersected definitively in military service. Christians resisted giving unconditional allegiance to a pagan state, the same state that maintained a posture of skepticism and oppression toward Christianity. Celsus criticized Christians for undermining Roman warfare; in reply, Origen tried to demonstrate the church's allegiance to Rome while simultaneously defending the church's aversion to military service. The church served the state through spiritual, not physical, warfare; he said, "The more pious a man is the more effectively does he assist the emperors—more so than the troops that go out and kill as many."[73] This may sound like avoiding the question, but it follows the church's fixed conviction about divine transcendence and providence. Origen could not discuss warfare without focusing upon the spiritual life that was part of a cosmic struggle involving more than the concerns of any one nation or empire.

For other theologians like Tertullian, military service had the potential to confuse earthly and heavenly citizenship. He asked his readers how Christians should "carry a flag, too, hostile to Christ?" Regarding the oath soldiers took, Tertullian asked whether it was "lawful for a human oath to be super-added to one divine, for a man to come under promise to another master after Christ."[74] It did not matter whether the Christian was serving in peacetime or wartime, for how could a Christian "serve even in peace, without a sword, which the Lord has taken away?"[75] There was no distinction made here between the various roles of the soldier; the challenge for Tertullian was not the military profession itself but the acts of murder associated with it. No one can serve two masters, and those who joined the military would be constantly driven to try.

Third, a vision of Christian sanctification and moral purity, especially in terms of avoiding idolatry, impinged on military service. In his work *On the Crown*, Tertullian listed out all the various immoral offenses that a Christian had to endure to remain in the military. The major violations included murder, torture, and pagan worship, but many other behaviors involved in military activity also transgressed God's law. Tertullian made special provision for those who converted to Christianity after joining the military but still encouraged them to leave the profession because all sorts of challenges would ensue for those trying not to offend God.[76] Origen, too, believed that the basic problem in military service was ethical and contrary to following Christ's teaching. Unlike the Jews who took up arms to fight for the Lord, Christians "no longer take up sword against nation, nor do we learn war any more, having become children of peace, for the sake of Jesus, who is our leader."[77] The church saw the path of Christ to be one that required moral purity and the avoidance of killing and idolatry. This meant hard decisions for Christians about participation in a military that was thoroughly infused with killing for the sake of a pagan nation and pagan gods.

While we live in a different time today, some of the same issues are resurfacing. In what ways does military service require servicemen and servicewomen to support immorality? What moral agenda has shaped the modern military? There is long history of just war theorizing and ongoing debates about the legitimacy of governments, but what happens when the policies of the government do not allow Christians to serve in ways that conform to their sincerely held consciences? The questions facing Christians in military service are not unlike those in the ancient world. Without debating the merits of just war theory, the more specific point is how those who live by Christian morality will be able to endure in contexts that oppress their sincerely held religious beliefs.

Once again, the early church saw no direct Christian command prohibiting military service but undertook serious consideration about the ways that Christians performed within the military. Like other segments of society, they embraced a discerning improvisation guided by Christian doctrine and morality. I honor those who have fought bravely for the freedoms we enjoy, but what happens when we are living in a world where the requirements for military service burden the Christian conscience to the point that it is difficult to serve? There is a long history of political dualism and reflection to help guide the church's approach to military service, but the cultural moment demands that we become vigilant about the limits of service and the Christian's role within the military.

Marriage and the Family

The topic of marriage and family raises a whole host of issues surrounding human sexuality, children, and gender. These topics are so culturally charged that there is little doubt that the early church's views will appear "too stringent" or "foolishly narrow." But the early church was also "deeply concerned that marriages flourish, that children are raised in the faith, that single people are helped to live holy, chaste sexual lives, and that those called to the vocation of virginity are supported by specific church teachings and structures to help them fulfill their call."[78] The challenge to follow the teachings of the Scripture was not adopted without consideration of the religious and social context, and there is no doubt that the early Christian vision of marriage and family was a radical departure from the sexual ethic of the empire. Kyle Harper argued that it was a "paradigm shift" or "quantum leap to a new foundational logic of sexual ethics." The Christian doctrine of sin entered the cultural framework of sexuality and fundamentally reshaped the ancient sexual ethic. The shift was deeply theological in nature and transitioned from Roman society's honor-shame moral paradigm to a theological one that identified specific sexual practices as sin. The "legacy of the church," Harper tells us, "lies in the dissolution of an ancient system where status and social reproduction scripted the terms of sexual morality."[79]

In Roman law, the family was a "microcosm of the Roman *res publica*."[80] The expectation was that the paterfamilias directed the house, but conflicts and tensions characterized family life just as political issues did the Roman republic. In this setting, the most important relationships were those of blood relatives and families, because they ensured the most natural way for people to flourish. The authority of the paterfamilias diminished over the centuries as communities and women were given more dignity and respect. But many marriages also struggled with the challenges of divorce and childlessness, most of the time out of decisions of conscience rather than specific personal issues. There was an emphasis on fidelity, and the contract typically mandated or valorized fidelity, but most of the time, marriage was a legal transaction that was sealed by the signing of a contract.[81] The husband received a dowry as part of the legal arrangement but had to return it in case of divorce. For the Romans, the purpose of marriage was the "promise of producing legitimate children and passing on a patrimony intact to the next generation." Marriage was thus, first and foremost, a contractual agreement tied to their views of citizenship and the flourishing of the republic. Romans thus valued the *function* of marriage, producing children, over the relationship itself. Marriage often happened at an early age for the bride, around twelve to fourteen, while the husband was typically much older. The wife was a partner but submissive to her husband, always encouraged to be a good manager of the household and intimately connected to her husband's public life. Loyalty in marriage was prized and communicated by the virtues of chastity, devotion, loyalty, and purity.[82]

In contrast to this Roman view, Christian views of marriage shifted the focus from family and citizenship to the "joining between a man and a woman," in the process bringing "profound political, economic and social changes in the Roman Empire." The attention to the *persons* involved changed the focus to the marriage itself, which was "a radical notion to Roman thought and law." Since Romans saw marriage as contractual, they offered no serious objections to divorce for any reason, especially infertility. By contrast, early Christian marriage took on a "transcendent spiritual dimension." Christian marriage was a "one flesh union" that was "inseparable, physically and spiritually," which meant divorce was not altogether acceptable.[83] This did not mean that divorce was unavoidable. Justin Martyr described a situation where a pagan woman converted to Christianity and attempted to evangelize her husband. When that was rejected, she eventually divorced him. Her husband did not appreciate her actions and reported her and those instrumental in her conversion to the authorities to be punished and killed.[84]

Christians also challenged basic Roman assumptions about children and the purpose of sex in marriage. The apologist Minucius Felix wrote, "But we maintain our modesty not in appearance, but in our hearts we gladly abide by the bond of a single marriage; in the desire of procreating, we know either one wife, or none at all."[85] Aristides wrote in his *Apology* that Christian women "are pure as virgins, and their daughters are modest; and their men keep themselves from every unlawful union and from all uncleanness, in the hope of a recompense to come in the other world."[86] Tertullian even rejected a second marriage in the case of death and downplayed the importance of having children![87] While he may have pressed this point too far, he wanted to emphasize marriage's purpose as sanctification; having children was the result of a loving marriage, not merely the purpose.[88] Tertullian's point was extreme, especially in a Roman context, but he was refocusing the purpose of marriage in the Christian life and heavenly citizenship. Speaking of the unity and beauty in marriage, Tertullian writes,

> Where the flesh is one, one is the spirit too. Together they pray, together prostrate themselves, together perform their fasts; mutually teaching, mu-

tually exhorting, mutually sustaining. Equally (are they) both (found) in
the Church of God; equally at the banquet of God; equally in straits, in
persecutions, in refreshments. Neither hides (aught) from the other; neither shuns the other; neither is troublesome to the other. The sick is visited,
the indigent relieved, with freedom. Alms (are given) without (danger of
ensuing) torment; sacrifices (attended) without scruple; daily diligence
(discharged) without impediment: (there is) no stealthy signing, no trem-
bling greeting, no mute benediction. Between the two echo psalms and
hymns; and they mutually challenge each other which shall better chant
to their Lord.[89]

Mutual love, harmony, respect, and the stress on sanctification emphasized
the basic joys that could be found in the union with another. There were also
specific duties to be carried out by each partner in the marriage and the regular
expectation of mutual love and affection.

On the Apostolic Tradition gives instructions about married life for catechumens: "If a man has a wife, or a woman has a husband, let them be taught to
be content, the husband with his wife, and the wife with her husband. If there
is a man who does not live with a woman, let him be taught not to fornicate,
but to either take a wife according to the law, or to remain as is."[90] Early on, the
church had to be clear about its views of marriage and laid out clarifications
at the beginning of the catechetical process. No doubt it struggled with these
matters, and some committed all kinds of heinous acts, but these were also
part of the pagan world. As Greer writes, "Christians define their attitude in
opposition to a profligate age, and it is largely the reaction to the times that
explains Christian insistence upon chastity."[91]

Discussing marriage and sexuality entails culturally charged conversations
today, but the early church's commitment to Christian doctrine and practice
while living amid a highly sexually charged environment reminds us that
there is a way to chart a path forward. Sexual ethics cannot be minimized or
sidelined—from the very beginning of the church, this was essential to their
doctrine and practice (Acts 15:20)—but through the slow process of resocialization and discernment, the church continually turned their people back to
the basic commitments of fidelity in marriage and the bond between a man
and woman. The cultural conflicts between contemporary Christian attitudes
toward sexuality and marriage and those outside the church are evident. If

Christians commit themselves to faithful marriages, raising godly children, and loving the church, these things will be a visible testimony to the goodness of Christian faith and morality. At the same time, the church should never tire of doing good and caring for the vulnerable and those who suffer; if we do these good things, they will know us by our love (John 13:35).

This survey of occupations, entertainments, military service, and marriage only scratches the surface of the early church's social witness. Clearly, the modern church faces many of the same challenges. Resocialization and acculturation in an ever-changing secular world remain an ongoing struggle. In the middle of it all, Christians should focus on virtue and sanctification with their eyes on both this world and the next. This echoes the apostolic exhortation: "Beloved, I urge you as sojourners and exiles to abstain from the passions of the flesh, which wage war against your soul. Keep your conduct among the Gentiles honorable, so that when they speak against you as evildoers, they may see your good deeds and glorify God on the day of visitation" (1 Pet 2:11–12). As we keep this dual focus, we must hold fast to Christian doctrine and practice and commit ourselves to demonstrating our faith in public. In time and with the Lord's kindness, the church will season the culture with good things and transform it. Through regular interactions, we must develop an active cultural discernment and regular improvisation to help navigate the social world in faith.

Compassionate Social Engagement

The early church did not simply think in terms of distinctiveness and purity; it also turned outward in active mercy and compassion. The very work of social reform and positive social change amounted to a positive good. Its high standards of purity marked it as a community bent on serving and caring for the least of those inside and outside their community. For us, developing cultural discernment entails thinking about not merely how the church is distinct but also how it serves in the social sphere and encourages virtue to flourish.

The Roman economy around the early church was preindustrial; 80 to 90 percent of the population worked in agriculture. There was virtually no middle class, and poverty was widespread throughout both the cities and the countryside. Thus, while social status could be shaped by gender, ethnicity, family lineage, legal status, occupation, or education, "financial status was often the most influential factor in determining one's place in the social economy."[92] Early Christians thus had to live out their faith in the midst of a social world that was often harsh and difficult for much of the population.

Within this economic and social context, early Christians argued first and foremost that the church contributed a positive good to the culture. They prized the visible social witness of a community of faith living in holiness and love for God and neighbor. The wealthy and learned often mocked these virtues as a weakness. For example, the pagan writer Lucian of Samosata, in his work *The Passing of Peregrinus*, deemed Christian compassion as naively merciful. Peregrinus was a recent convert who had converted under false pretenses; when he ended up in prison and the church came to support him, Lucian found this to be ridiculously stupid.

> These gullible people believe that they are immortal and will go on living. Therefore, they do not fear dying, and many of them are willing to give themselves up to the authorities. In addition, their first leader persuaded them that they become brothers and sisters when they give up their Greek gods and worship him. . . . They have no concern for possessions and treat them as common property. . . . Any imposter could easily join them and become wealthy by capitalizing on their naivete.[93]

Indeed, some did aim to deceive the church and take advantage of Christian generosity and compassion. Ironically, however, the church's compassion was ultimately attractive to the nonscoffers who benefitted from their generosity.

Even Julian, the fourth-century pagan emperor, recognized the intrinsic value of Christian morality. In a letter to the pagan high priest of Galatia, Julian complained that the pagans had not matched the virtues of the Christians: "why do we not observe that it is their benevolence to strangers, their care for the graves of the dead and the pretended holiness of their lives that have done most to increase atheism [or Christianity]?" The pagan community "ought really and truly to practice every one of these virtues. And it is not enough for you alone to practice them, but so must all the priests in Galatia, without exception."[94] What Julian observed in the fourth century represented the culmination of a long struggle between the virtues of the Christian society and those of traditional Rome.

These kinds of practices had the double effect of supporting the community within the church and attracting those from without. As Greer writes,

"The example of Christian community life was probably more persuasive to unbelievers than the proclamation of the Christian message. It is impossible to resist the conclusion that at one level the church grew rapidly more because its common life acted as a magnet attracting people than because the Christians were effective in the public preaching."[95] There is no doubt that the Christian vision of compassion, emanating from within the church out into virtuous living in the larger culture, conveyed to the world around them their animating virtues of hospitality, mercy, and compassion, enacted with prudence.

Christian compassion was first directed toward those inside the church. The church was a family, and the family took care of each other. In his *Ecclesiastical History*, Eusebius described how the church at Rome in the second century had shown compassion to its members and relieved people in all kinds of distress.[96] It "never abandoned the notion that the new humanity could be compatible with the family in the ordinary sense of the word." Its family orientation meant that "Christians often cared for one another, not necessarily for those outside the faith."[97] This applied especially to widows and the most vulnerable in the community. In Roman culture, widows were penalized if they did not remarry within two years, whereas in the church, they were encouraged in the opposite direction.[98] Consequently, the early church often had a high percentage of females and worked hard to care for them as a community.

We can see this in the case of almsgiving. Besides clear examples of this in the New Testament (Acts 2:42–47; 4:32–35), by the middle of the second century, the church was organizing its tithes to help those suffering in the community. Justin Martyr described this as a cross-class unity: "the wealthy come to the aid of the poor, and we are always together. Over all that we receive we bless the Maker of all through His Son Jesus Christ and through the Holy Spirit." During worship, after Scripture reading and the Eucharist, there was a time of almsgiving when "those who prosper, and so wish, contribute what each thinks fit; and what is collected is deposited with the Ruler, who takes care of the orphans and widows, and those who, on account of sickness or any other cause, are in want, and those who are in bonds, and the strangers who are sojourners among us, and in a word [he] is the guardian of all those in need."[99] The idea here was to demonstrate the provision of God for his people and the way that membership within the church served as a means to support and provide for their spiritual and material needs.

While their emphasis on Christian compassion began in the church, "it clearly often extended to the unbelieving neighbor."[100] Giving was a "regular and central part of Christian practice" and could not be contained within the Christian community alone.[101] Note the last clause in Justin Martyr's statement: the alms collected are distributed not just to "the orphans and widows and those who, through sickness or any other cause, are in want" within the church but also to "those who are in bonds and the strangers sojourning among us."[102] The Christian community was notable for caring for its poor and sick, even the pagans.[103] Tertullian describes the social activity of Christians, saying, "they support and bury poor people, to supply the wants of boys and girls destitute of means and parents, and of old persons confined now to the house; such, too, as have suffered shipwreck; and if there happen to be any in the mines, or banished to the islands, or shut up in the prisons, for nothing but their fidelity to the cause of God's Church, they become the nurslings of their confession."[104] In sum, the Christian community offered to all people "a radical message of love and charity, flaunted the idea that even the foolish and uneducated could be wise, that the virtuous simpleton could outargue learned philosophers, that the rich should be generous to the poor, that the holy should care for the sick."[105] The church was a light in the midst of the surrounding darkness, and its vision for human flourishing was ultimately more satisfying and successful than that of any other religious or philosophical system in the ancient world.

CONCLUSION

This chapter began with the story of the soldier who practiced civil disobedience by refusing to wear an imperial crown. This was an instance of the struggle of resocialization facing the early church. Following baptism, Christians returned to society and attempted to reacclimate themselves under a new identity through a process of persistent everyday interaction. Clearly, the early church was concerned with much more than retreating from or confronting their culture; it sought to develop a Christian life oriented toward cultural sanctification. Cultural sanctification was to develop through the coordinated efforts of *contingency, sanctification,* and *improvisation.* New Christians had to make daily choices while cultivating "a culturally discerning spiritual life"—a life that was actively indigenizing in the world around them while navigating between the virtues and vices in every situation. This involved occupational life, leisure and entertainments, military service, and marriage and family.

These were no easy decisions, but the Scriptures provided the basic doctrine and ethics that guided them on their journey. Finally, the church was interested as well in the material needs of others and affirmed a compassionate social engagement that attracted outsiders. All these features guided the church in sanctification and ultimately transformed the culture.

While pagan observers viewed the church as immoral, naive, and generally comprised of the lower classes of society, the church worked through a process of cultural discernment to address issues of moral distinction and separation. Some things never change. The pagan vision of the church is alive and well today; if there was ever a time when the church needed to cultivate cultural discernment, it is now. The early church was not concerned with drawing up a list of dos and don'ts or forcing Christians to remove themselves from society. Instead, it learned the art of thinking carefully through every aspect of life so that doctrine and morality would shape their whole vision. But they did this all under a firm hope in the coming kingdom of God. That final piece of the picture we will examine next.

5

HOPE

The Martyr's Confidence

The cities of Lyons and Vienne were separated by just a few miles along the banks of the Rhone River on the outskirts of the Roman Empire. They were important trading stops for those making their way inland from Marseilles. Lyons was the larger city and hosted the annual gathering of the Gallic tribes who all came to pledge their allegiance to the emperor.[1] To demonstrate that commitment, in August of 177 the tribes joined together with the local Roman citizens to persecute the Christians. The Christians were told not to appear in public and were excluded "from homes, baths, and the market square." This, however, was not sufficient. Soon the local authorities, with the support of the citizens of both cities, arrested a group of Christians and charged them with various crimes such as incest, cannibalism, and refusing to worship the pagan gods. They dragged the Christians through the streets while the crowds screamed at them and physically abused them. They despised them like sworn enemies.

The Christians were led to the main town square and interrogated by a military commander and city officials. When they refused to worship the pagan gods, they were locked up and prepared for a festival of tortures. Not all the Christians were ready to face persecution. Some were "untrained and feeble, incapable of bearing the tension of a great conflict." Some ten of them buckled under pressure and worshiped the pagan gods; they "succumbed to the strain like a baby that dies in childbirth." However, many were faithful and faced their trials with boldness.

The most determined martyr among them was a woman named Blandina. At first, the church was concerned that she might not make a bold confession because of the frailty of her body. But they were wrong. As she was tortured, "Blandina was filled with such strength that the torturers, who worked in shifts from dawn to dusk tormenting Blandina with every possible method, were exhausted and finally gave up. . . . There was nothing left to do to her that hadn't already been done." Those who tortured her "marveled she was still alive with her entire body ripped open and broken in every place. The men acknowledged that even one form of torture should have released her soul, not to mention such terrible ones like the many they applied." Blandina, "like a well-trained athlete, kept growing stronger throughout her confession," and she "was refreshed and experienced rest and relief from her agony by exclaiming, 'I am a Christian! We don't do anything wrong!'" Finally, she was shut up in prison. For several days, she and a young boy named Ponticus were brought to the amphitheater to watch their fellow Christians die. While they watched, the authorities tried to force Blandina and Ponticus to swear by the pagan idols. But they both remained steadfast and refused.

Finally, Ponticus died from his wounds, leaving only Blandina. Through all her trials, she was an "aristocratic mother" who encouraged "her children to faithfulness and sent them ahead of her triumphantly to their King." In her last trial, Blandina was enclosed in a net and tossed before a bull, who attacked her until she died. The Christians said that she did not even feel its attacks "thanks to her heavenly hope, her firm grasp on what she believed, and her spiritual intimacy with Christ." Amid all the brutality of the Romans' torments, the Christians saw the glimmer of hope. They comforted each other with the assurance of Paul that "our present sufferings aren't worth comparing to the glory that will be revealed in us" (Rom 8:18). They knew that life does not end in death, that there is another kingdom coming.

The pagans were so cruel that they would not allow the Christians to bury Blandina and the other martyrs. "Where is their God?" they jeered, "These people chose faithfulness to their religion over their own lives—but what good did it do them?" The pagans had no concern for the future. They ridiculed the Christians' claim to a transcendent, providential God, for their own hope lay in preserving Roman political power. Thus, the Christians had to suffer.

...

This account of martyrdom in the second century comes down to us in the form of a letter written from the churches in Lyons and Vienne to the churches of Asia and Phrygia.[2] It intended to encourage other Christian communities facing similar episodes of persecution to hold on to a firm hope in the return of Christ. Even a good life in the present age was as nothing compared to the beauty of the eternal life awaiting the faithful in the coming kingdom of God. The theological virtue of hope reverberated through every account of persecution. Like an anchor steadying the ship amid a storm, hope tethered them to God while violence raged around them.

Thankfully such sufferings are not our lot, but the church in the West does find itself, once again, struggling with the pagan world. No one knows where this story will go, but we believe we know how it will end. Any good story, as Aristotle taught us, has a beginning, middle and end.[3] Whatever strategy for cultural witness Christians employ, the early church reminds us to always walk in hope. Have no fear; Christ is coming again.

What was the vision of hope that differentiated the early church from the surrounding Roman world? This difference is key to understanding how the church weathered the storm and how its theological perspective proved attractive to outsiders. Christian hope was, and is, defined by two key tenets: the future kingdom of God, and eternal life or beatitude. This last piece of the puzzle fits together the picture of cultural sanctification. Through all the other means and methods, hope motivated early Christians to live the good life in the present. Christ, in reigning now, allows Christians to live through all circumstances in faith, hope, and love. With the fires of the pagan world swirling around them, early Christian martyrs like Blandina could face life and death in hope. As we witness the dissolution of Christendom, the virtue of hope will become more important in the coming years as the West continues to undergo a cultural turn. Hope will be a lighthouse that helps the church navigate through the fog to the safe harbor of the kingdom of God.

COMPETING VISIONS OF HOPE

One essential difference between the Christian and pagan worldview was their visions of the future. In the ancient world, "pagan and Christian inhabitants of the Roman Empire lived in two radically different mental worlds" with profoundly different views of the future. Traditional Romans followed a realized view of hope tied to the political structures and national identity of the empire. The pagans "identified the world of the past, present, and future with the Roman state; their historians spoke of the glory of the Roman Republic, great battles, and heroic deeds."[4] The political successes of the Roman Empire, no doubt, contributed to this mindset, especially in the first few centuries when the empire was at its height. But in all the effusive talk about the glories of Rome, there was no serious reflection upon the afterlife. For the pagan, hope was fixed on what this life had to offer—in Christian eyes, a sad and despondent view of reality to be sure. As Smith writes, "There remains a tragic sense, and a kind of profound futility, in the Homeric assumption that the best a man can hope for is to kill gloriously and die gloriously, so that his name will be recalled in the lyrics chanted by bards when the man himself is no longer around to hear the songs."[5] In Homer, "the dominant image is that there is no life beyond the grave. . . . This superb view of man's condition heightens the poignancy of a hero's life. We are what we do; fame, won in life, is our immortality."[6] There are sacred things and a sacred life, but it is all lived here and now. Thus, "life is—or at least can be—a beautiful and sometimes sublime thing, but its beauty and sublimity are finite and immanent to this world. . . . There is not, and there need not be, anything else. Not for us mortals, at least."[7] The only thing to do is to live your best life now. Yet, such honor and fame were available only to a few.

Nor did the philosophical schools show much more interest in the afterlife. The philosophers "worried more about the beginning of the world than about its possible end."[8] The doctrines of Plato and his immediate successors, often called the Old Academy, believed that the cosmos and matter were eternal. Philosophers such as Speusippus and Xenocrates taught that "the world and the soul were not created at a point in time."[9] The world and matter run in cyclical, not linear, patterns and offer no ultimate telos. Stoics and Epicureans had no use for eschatology either. The great Stoic emperor Marcus Aurelius captured that sentiment well: "Why worry about misfortunes when you know that within a very little time . . . you will be dead; and soon not even your names will be left behind." More succinctly, "fame after life is no better than oblivion."[10] Some philosophers discoursed about an afterlife in Elysium, some discussed communion with the gods, and some "set up a judgment-seat in the realms below,"[11] but these could hardly inspire ordinary people. When pagan intellectuals heard of Christians' views of the future, they mocked them. Celsus and Lucian, for example, laughed at their belief that they would live forever and disparaged the resurrection and eschatology.[12] The pagans, Tertullian lamented, trusted the philosophers and the poets more than God and laughed at the Christians "for proclaiming that God will one day judge the world."[13] The future, for the Romans, was left uncertain and unknown.

Many in our time have come around to the same view—this nation, the material world, these people are everything. The only hope is to build their kingdom here and now. For pagans, the only hope in life and death is radically focused on this world. Success in life means to have political control and conform the political realities to their view of the gods and morality, or to maximize pleasure in pursuit of self-interested satisfaction. Christians must think differently. We love this world, and we work to redeem it inch by inch. But we are also pilgrims who walk in confidence, like the martyrs of Lyons and Vienne, knowing that present things are fleeting. We can never be too enamored with political power or material blessings, or hopeless when they are gone. God reminds us that his story of redemption is bigger than one people group or nation. Hope has a way of enduring the harshest criticisms and galvanizing the community.

THE CHRISTIAN HOPE

The Christian hope taught in the New Testament and early Christianity was radically different. The church, as Tertullian put it, is "a body knit together as such by a common religious profession, by unity of discipline, and by the bond of common hope."[14] In the second chapter, we have already considered doctrine (or "a common religious profession") and morality (or what Tertullian calls "discipline") in this role, but now need to see hope alongside these as the distinctive mark of the Christian community. Early Christians told a different story with a different ending, an ending that breathed with hope for all people, not just the philosophers or aristocracy. Many found this story compelling. True, Christians in the early church, just like today, had their fair share of disagreements over the end times, and we need not get into the weeds of their various views. It is enough to consider the general threads of their doctrine of the future that unified the community and built a bulwark amid the pagan world. Two themes are most important: the narrative of salvation history and the resurrected life.

First, they saw that God has staged a plan of redemption that involved the people of God throughout the Old and New Testaments and that now enveloped the church. That plan, second, would culminate with resurrection and beatitude. Many in the ancient world—as today—found the notion of a resurrection fanciful, even ridiculous; yet it helped the church deal with cultural challenges and sporadic persecution. Christians in the ancient world looked forward to the day when the people of God would proclaim together, "O death, where is your victory? O death, where is your sting?" (1 Cor 15:55–56). Together, these views thread the Scriptures, encouraging the early church to live faithfully in the present world while holding out hope for the next. Hope will do the same for us today.

Hope and Salvation History

Living in the shadow of the mighty Roman Empire, the theologians of the first few centuries "give a central place to the Christian hope."[15] They were interested not merely in communicating some scattered points of doctrine but in a great cosmic story that moved from creation to consummation. This drama of salvation history, with all its moral implications, was a new thing in the Roman world. As Meeks writes, "If anything may be said to be unique in Christianity's contribution to Western ethical sensibilities, it is this dramatic history of everything and all people, centering on the erratic response of God's elect people to God's speaking and acting, and culminating in the calling to account of every creature for what they have done in God's world."[16] A transcendent God who reigns over all and will one day set all the wrongs right and establish a kingdom that will have no end remains a distinctive feature of the church's faith.

We already see this narrative vision in the Scriptures. Passages such as the genealogies of Matthew 1 and Luke 3 assume a coherent ancestral link between the figures of the Old Testament and the person of Christ. These accounts take Christ's messianic role to be the culmination of history. There are other passages, such as Stephen's sermon in Acts 7 or Paul's sermon in Acts 13, that stress the narrative continuity between the events and people of the Old Testament and the coming of Christ. The most decisive passages for telling the complete narrative of salvation history are in the unified narrative of Hebrews 11–12 that recounts the history of salvation through the Old Testament leading up to Christ in Hebrews 11 and then connects it with the work of the church and the coming kingdom of God in Hebrews 12. Through persecution and internal struggles, Hebrews encourages the church to "be grateful for receiving a kingdom that cannot be shaken" and challenges them to "offer to God acceptable worship, with reverence and awe" (Heb 12:28). All these passages assume a salvation-historical shape of the Christian view of reality contrary to the Roman one and the hope of a coming kingdom of God.

The church in the second and third centuries received this narrative vision and continuously communicated it, beginning in catechesis. Whenever the ancient Christians approached the Scriptures, they would "look back to those mighty acts of revelation as well as forward to the future climax which they foreshadowed."[17] In chapter 2, I discussed the narrative shaping of the rule of faith that situates the church within the streams of salvation history. Confessing this rule at baptism was the performative act that not only affirmed the divine narrative but acknowledged one's place in it. When they made this confession and joined the church, new believers were stepping out of the water and onto the land of a new reality. Those joining the church would affirm the two bookends in the rule of faith: belief in "one God, the Father Almighty, Maker of heaven, and earth, and the sea, and all things that are in them," and also belief in the judgment of the reprobate and the hope that the righteous will be surrounded with everlasting glory.[18] The rule of faith thus had a narrative thread that sewed together the beginning and end of things and put Christians in its line.

Catechetical instruction, too, was ordered around a rehearsal of the Christian story. Irenaeus's catechetical text, *On Apostolic Preaching*, follows a universal history of the Scriptures, with eschatology offering up "a grand, continuous conception of salvation-history."[19] The book begins with creation and then moves through several cycles of retelling the history of redemption along several unifying threads. Meeks finds that at least by the time of Irenaeus, "some Christians had come to think of a genuinely universal history," one that "encompassed the story of the world, for it began 'in the beginning,' and followed the history of humanity, from its creation and its fatal, primeval error, through the subsequent dialectic of God's saving or punishing actions and human responses and derelictions, to the climactic act of redemption and the ultimate judgment of all."[20] Such an account arcs above and beyond mere empirical details toward a final telos, the vision of the new heavens and new earth for which the early Christian writers hoped.

In the fifth century, Augustine ordered his *The Catechizing of the Unin-structed* in the same way. His purpose was not merely to transfer knowledge but to shape the life and faith of the hearers, situating them under a doctrine of God and within a history of salvation that moves them toward a greater love for God and others. In Augustine's thinking, it is enough for new believers to be "catechized in the first instance from what is written in the text, *In the beginning God created the heaven and the earth*, on to the present times of the Church." The key was to expound the arc of Scripture as a whole, a single story that moves from the first creation to the new creation.[21] Therein new disciples could find their proper place and identity.[22]

Relating salvation history was commonplace in early Christian apologetic and evangelistic encounters.[23] Theophilus of Antioch, for example, distin-guished the narrative structure of the Old Testament from the Roman con-ception of history. Contrary to the latter, which equated the beginning of time with the founding of Rome, Theophilus aimed for a universal account of his-tory—"not only of the dates after the deluge, but also of those before it, so as to reckon the whole number of all the years, as far as possible; tracing up to the very beginning of the creation of the world, which Moses the servant of God recorded through the Holy Spirit."[24] No doubt the modern world would be skeptical of Theophilus's precise dating, but it is harder to discount the larger vision of a cosmic arc uniting the end and the beginning. While pagans like Celsus feared that a Christian state would spell the dissolution of the Roman world and way of life, Origen's transcendent vision imagined a future Christian kingdom that was already taking root; "indeed it will one day triumph, as its principles take possession of the minds of men more and more every day."[25]

For Christians, says scholar Stephen Smith, "the world is not sufficient unto itself." Rather, "its blessed qualities of beauty and sublimity are reflective of a more transcendent Reality and point beyond themselves to a beautified exis-tence that 'eye hath not seen, nor ear heard, neither have entered into the heart of man.'"[26] The world pointed to a creator who would one day set the wrongs right and bring all things into submission to one divine kingdom. For Irenaeus, in the coming of that kingdom, "neither is the substance nor the essence of the creation annihilated (for faithful and true is He who has established it), but the fashion of the world passes away." Then God's people would flourish in an "incorruptible state" that precludes the possibility of being old.[27] That, he concludes, would be the new heaven and the new earth, in which the new man shall remain continually, always holding fresh converse with God.[28] In short, the early church not only pieced all of this world together into a coherent whole but offered hope in the life to come.

This was important for the humble, sinful, broken, and outcast who looked to Christ for salvation. The fusion of the beginning and the end of history offered a way to make sense of lived experience and gave a purpose for living in light of future events. For those who struggled in life, Veyne writes, under the "historical-metaphysical epic of Creation and Redemption . . . one now knew where one came from and for what one was destined."[29] Christianity's belief in the afterlife gained significant advantage over the pagan worldview for both evangelistic and apologetic arguments. The resonances between the early church and today mean that there is still hope for hope. The Christian hope continues to be a distinctive feature of the Christian faith. The modern world ties all its hopes to redistributions of power and new political configurations. While these acts encourage justice here and now, the church knows that they are not enough. One eye must keep looking up toward the hope of a new kingdom that is to come. The affirmation that this world is not some happy accident should encourage the faithful not to be dismayed or downtrodden by the torrents blowing around us.

Hope and Resurrection

A key feature in the Christian's claim for hope is resurrection and the blessed life that the resurrected faithful will enjoy. While the grand narrative of salvation pictured a cosmic reality, resurrection offered something specific: eternal life with God. We know from the New Testament that some Jewish leaders questioned Jesus about the resurrection, and the apostles often faced disputes about it in Acts, prompting Paul to provide a detailed defense of the doctrine in 1 Corinthians 15.[30] Such skepticism persisted in the second century.

Pagans, recognizing resurrection as a key marker of Christian doctrine, often ridiculed this belief. Origen, for example, described how Celsus "often reproached us about the resurrection." For Celsus, there could be no resurrection because the flesh was disgusting and deplorable: "For what sort of body, after being entirely corrupted, could return to its original nature and that same condition which it has before it was dissolved? As they have nothing to say in reply, they escape to a most outrageous refuge by saying that 'anything is possible to God.' But indeed, neither can God do what is shameful nor does He desire what is contrary to nature."[31] Celsus understood that Christians did not have a "rational view" in which God was "subject to the laws of nature and reason." Instead, Christians believed that God "stood completely above and beyond nature and was therefore capable of doing whatever he willed no matter how much it disrupted the order of the world."[32] Celsus argued the contrary: "God would neither desire nor be able to make it everlasting contrary to reason. For he himself is the reason of everything; therefore he is not able to do anything contrary to reason, or to his own character."[33]

Justin Martyr provides a good example of Christian retorts to such arguments. Christians, he said, simply expected "to receive again our own bodies, though they be dead and cast into the earth, for we maintain that with God nothing is impossible."[34] He admitted that the thought of a resurrection might sound incredible, but "it is better to believe even what is impossible to our own nature and to men, than to be unbelieving like the rest of the world." Citing both Matthew 19:26 and 10:28, Justin insisted that what seems impossible to us is possible with God and that there is no reason to fear those who can take your life when we all should fear God who "is able to cast both soul and body into hell."[35]

In a final interchange before his martyrdom, Justin held fast to the hope of the future life. At some point, he was arrested and dragged before Roman authorities for his criticism of Urbicus, the prefect of Rome, and Crescens, a Cynic philosopher. The trial was conducted by Junius Rusticus, a well-known Stoic philosopher friend of the emperor Marcus Aurelius. The account of his final trial is found in a text known as the *Acts of Justin and His Companions*, which records not only Justin's martyrdom but also that of several of his friends who were arrested with him.[36] During his interrogation, Rusticus asked him, "are you convinced that if I have you whipped and beheaded you'll go up to heaven?" Justin responded, "If I endure these things, then yes, I have hope because of my endurance. I know God's blessing will remain upon everyone who lives a devout life, lasting even through the final judgment by fire." Rusticus then asked, "So you suppose you'll ascend to heaven?" Justin replied, "I don't just suppose it. I am absolutely certain of it." Rusticus warned Justin that if he did not obey him, he would be punished. But Justin answered, "If we are punished, we have the sure promise of salvation."[37] With that, Rusticus ordered Justin and his companions to be led away and executed. His hope liberated him to speak the truth even when it would result in his own suffering. Nonetheless, even as he faced the death sentence, the text emphasizes Justin's unwavering confidence in the hope of salvation. This testimony echoes Justin's opening in his *First Apology*, written to Emperor Antoninus Pius: "you can kill, but not hurt us."[38] His confidence was grounded in hope: this prefect, this city, this empire would not have the final say. Christians place their hope in a coming kingdom and the expectation of the Lord's return, and the resurrection opened the ultimate hope for all those who with Justin are suffering in this life.

Irenaeus also offered a serious defense of the resurrection, this one directed more against the gnostics than the empire. Irenaeus laid out a narrative of salvation culminating in beatitude; it was necessary "that the human person should in the first instance be created; and having been created, should receive growth; and having received growth and having abounded, should recover [from the disease of sin]; and having recovered, should be glorified; and being glorified, should see his Lord." While gnostics denied the hope of the resurrection body, Irenaeus cited Christ's own resurrection as paradigmatic for that of all believers. The whole body must be raised lest the goodness of the material world be rejected. Moreover, the human person, who is the temple for the Spirit, was comprised of body and soul.[39] In Irenaeus's reading, the immortal and incorruptible life was the goal of God's plan for humans from the beginning of creation. The resurrection also made a moral argument, he insisted; divine justice demanded that all people be raised to glorification or judgment.[40] At one point, he framed the hope of resurrection in the form of a prayer: "await the hand of thy Maker which creates everything in due time." He reminded his readers that humanity was the workmanship of God and that the resurrected body was to be consummately beautiful: "His hand fashioned thy substance; He will cover thee over too within and without with pure gold and silver, and He will adorn thee to such a degree, that even 'the King Himself shall have pleasure in thy beauty.'"[41]

Too many early Christian apologists defended the resurrection to give more than a few examples. Citing 1 John 4:2–3, Polycarp condemned anyone who denied the resurrection or the final judgment.[42] Theophilus appealed to nature and saw analogies to the resurrection in the changing seasons, growth of seeds, and the cycles of the moon.[43] Athenagoras provided one of the earliest detailed theological and philosophical defenses of the doctrine. First, God had the power to raise disintegrated bodies. Second, the very purpose of creation, the nature of humanity, and the justice of God all demanded that the dead be raised.[44] Those who reject the resurrection, Athenagoras continued, did not really understand Christians' theological and philosophical arguments. Those who denied the resurrection "ought to regard the origin of the human race as dependent upon no cause at all—a position that is only too easy to refute—or else, if they attribute the origin of all beings to God, they ought to examine the ground on which this dogma is based." If this be true, then it follows that the resurrection was entirely credible, and given God's majesty and wisdom, "it is just as easy for Him to know what has gone into dissolution as to know beforehand what has not yet come to pass."[45] Some today will not find this or his other arguments persuasive, but some in the ancient world did. The simple hope of the resurrection, bolstered by such apologetic arguments, was particularly persuasive when the church pointed to the "perpetual and inseparable companionship" and "exultant contemplation of our Benefactor" that would be enjoyed in the resurrection.[46]

This was the ultimate benefit of resurrection, the blessed life with God: "God is the one who is yet to be seen, and the beholding of God is productive of immortality, but immortality renders one near unto God."[47] From the very beginning, the creation of humanity in the "likeness to God," said Irenaeus, was the "foundational principle of human existence."[48] In the divine economy, the human person "is created from the outset to progress along a given *oikonomia* of development and growth, such that in due time, 'the Son might yield up his work to the Father' and the handiwork might at last become 'a perfect work of God.'"[49] Thus the "immortal and incorruptible life appears as the goal of God's plan for humanity from its very creation."[50] From the human side, the righteous after resurrection were rewarded with "incorruption and fellowship with God,"[51] an "immortality and vitality that includes the body and its natural environment as well as the 'inner' faculties."[52] Sinners would also receive back the same bodies that they now have in order to undergo punishment, a point Justin reiterated often.[53]

This eschatological apologetic remained an important feature of the church's defense of the faith up to the time of Augustine. The closing paragraphs of the *City of God*, written against pagans lamenting the fall of Rome, end with beatitude. Speaking of the Sabbath rest that all the faithful will enjoy in the final eschatological state, Augustine wrote that this eternal "eighth day" was "consecrated by the resurrection of Christ, and prefiguring the eternal repose not only of the spirit, but also of the body," will be a state where the faithful "shall rest and see, see and love, love and praise." Such is "what shall be in the end without end. For what other end do we propose to ourselves than to attain to the kingdom of which there is no end?"[54] No doubt the expectation of resurrection was "an attraction for many who found life heavy and unjust and who looked for conditions under which its inequalities would be set right."[55] This hope, culminating the grand narrative that pointed the faithful to the eternal realities of the gospel, recurs again and again throughout the writings of the early church. The momentary persecutions and cultural rejection they experienced paled in comparison to the beautiful hope of eternal life with God.

Augustine's final scene of beatitude brought to fullness the love of God and the love of neighbor that were the ultimate purpose, the destination, of salvation history. Theologically, love is the end of the Christian life; biblically, it is the same. Whatever one says about the Scriptures, Augustine insisted to those instructing new believers, teach it in such a way that those "to whom you are discoursing on hearing may believe, on believing may hope and, on hoping may love."[56] "The paradox of the Christian life," says one interpreter of Augustine, "is that the evils we suffer in our earthly pilgrimage must be taken with absolute seriousness, but so must the destiny that awaits us in the city of God. There are no victories or defeats in the present that really matter. All that counts is the final victory for the saints in the age to come."[57]

In sum, amid all the torments and tortures to which early Christians were subjected, their theologians "give a central place to the Christian hope."[58] With all its energy focused on the present life and building an immediate earthly kingdom, the Roman mindset could not contend with such hope. Christians offered the pagan populace something much better. The same is true today. Certainly, some today will find the idea of resurrection and beatitude foolish. But those who place all their hopes in political wrangling and the perfection of earthly achievements will eventually be disappointed. Just as many in the ancient world found hope compelling, if we live in hope, so will many today. For this reason and in the face of those who might laugh at the notion, let us offer hope. Offer it often and always. Hope should sing out from our lives and echo from our pulpits. We should never grow weary of offering hope. Never let the trials and frustrations of earthly struggles sway us from offering hope. Those who reject God and mock hope know not what they do, and the Christian hope always stands ready to welcome them home.

APOLOGETICS AND THE HOPE OF THE SPIRITUAL LIFE

But how did this vision of the future shape early Christian spiritual lives? First, hope in the coming kingdom motivated Christians to live virtuously in the present. Christians sought to live now as they will then when they are glorified and enjoy the blessings of the kingdom. Even now, the indwelling of the Spirit offers a portion of the blessedness that is to come, and this is experienced only in the gathering of the Christian community.[59] Hope in the coming kingdom also gave them confidence to face any situation of suffering and death. If you already know how the movie ends, you do not fear when the main characters suffer; you know they will escape. Second, the emphasis on hope was also important in their defense of the faith. When they faced difficult apologetic contests, the church appealed to divine transcendence and warned all people about God's justice and judgment. These were probably not popular appeals, but the early church only felt they were following the teaching of the apostles. Predictions of judgment had the twofold effect of warning their fellow citizens, while at the same time providing motivation for the faithful to live virtuously.

The Christian hope, however, is not merely about the future but also the present. Early Christians understood that the Scriptures call them to a higher moral standard, not just for the sake of fulfilling some command but also because they lived in expectation of a coming judgment and eternal reign of God. There was no shortage of Christian exhortation to live holy lives here and now because Christ was coming again. After all, all moral claims require a narrative substructure; as Alasdair MacIntyre argues, "generally to adopt a stance on the virtues will be to adopt a stance on the narrative character of human life."[60] Similarly, Wayne Meeks observes that "a particular narrative, consistent in its broad outline though wondrously variable in detail, has been at the heart of the Christian moral vision."[61] The conviction that God reigns as Ruler and Judge over all motivated early Christians to live virtuously, in accordance with the law of God. "We know of no ruler more kingly or more just than He [the Word of God]," said Justin.[62]

Such exhortations pervade early Christian writings. One of the earliest Christian sermons, a short homily called 2 Clement, urged Christians to "love one another, that we may all come to the kingdom of God." Later, the same text encourages the faithful, saying, "Let us have faith brothers and sisters!

We are competing in the contest of the living God, and are being trained in the present life in order that we may be crowned in the life to come."[63] Like 2 Clement, Justin assured the emperor that "more than all other men are we your helpers and allies in promoting peace, seeing that we hold this view, that it is alike impossible for the wicked, the covetous, the conspirator, and for the virtuous, to escape the notice of God, and that each man goes to everlasting punishment or salvation according to the value of his actions." If all people knew and believed in an impending judgment, it would shape the way that they thought about their lives and the world. People would restrain themselves and adorn themselves with virtue in order to "obtain the good gifts of God, and escape the punishments." Those who wished to avoid punishment from Roman authorities simply tried to avoid detection, said Justin, but no one could hide from the eye of God, so those who confess God to be all-knowing would "live decently on account of the penalties threatened, as even you yourselves will admit."[64] Ironically, Justin wondered, perhaps the emperor actually feared that all men would become righteous, leaving him with no one to punish. Origen, responding to the pagan Celsus, describes how Christians train their fellow citizens in the godly life and warn them about the coming judgment. He writes that Christians "educate the citizens and teach them to be devoted to God, the guardian of their city; and they take those who have lived good lives in the most insignificant cities up to a divine and heavenly city." To these who have been faithful to God and dwell within the heavenly city, Origen adds, it will be said of them (citing the words of Ps 82:1, 7), "you were faithful in a very insignificant city; come also to the great city where 'God stands in the congregation of the gods and judges between the gods in the midst,' and numbers you even with them, if you no longer 'die like a man' and do not 'fall like one of the princes.'"[65]

The faithful strove to be holy as God is holy precisely because they hoped, one day, to dwell with God in the final kingdom. As detailed in the Epistle to Diognetus in the opening chapter, the church understood a different ending to the story of salvation from the Roman narrative because "Christians live as strangers amidst perishable things, while waiting for the imperishable in heaven."[66] Christians remembered the wisdom of Job 12:23: "He makes nations great, and he destroys them, he enlarges nations, and leads them away." Kingdoms will come and go, and nations rise and fall, but the hope of the Lord's return is the unchanging conviction that guides the faith of the church. There is an end to the Christian story beyond rejection, oppression, and death, because Christ will come again in glory to judge the living and the dead and establish a kingdom that will have no end.

The hope of Christ's return and the resurrected life also served apologetic and evangelistic aims in the early church. Christians proclaimed that Christ would return in judgment for the sinner and blessing for the faithful.[67] From one vantage point, this can make the early Christian vision of God a "sternly just distributor of rewards and punishments,"[68] but the church was never shy about pointing toward the final judgment. They took their cues from the apostles who often defended the return of Christ and the separation of the righteous and the reprobate. Discussions of judgment are difficult on many levels and not often a welcomed topic of conversation over Sunday-afternoon tea. But for the early church, this was the natural implication of their doctrine of God, and they regularly emphasized the impending divine judgment. God would not leave those who reject him unpunished, or hesitate to bestow upon the faithful untold blessings. The Romans were not concerned about the future judgment, as historian Ramsey MacMullen writes: "Punishment in *after*life received hardly a mention in non-Christian debate. That may have been partly because of disbelief in resurrection of the flesh, but no doubt more because of the general disbelief in immortality of any sort at all."[69] Christians disturbed this disbelief when they continually reminded their pagan neighbors that there was an end in which Christ would come again in glory to judge the living and the dead.

The announcement of the Lord's return served an edifying end in the early church as well. Christians, above all people, strove to live peacefully and virtuously knowing that "everyone goes to eternal punishment or salvation in accordance with the character of his acts."[70] The Athenian Christian philosopher Athenagoras stressed "the moral importance for Christians of their hope for resurrection and a future life." These entailed "the prospect of judgement for humanity" while at the same time affirming the "value of human existence."[71] Justin persistently warned his readers about the judgment to come.[72] If everyone took that prospect seriously, "no one would choose wickedness even for a little while, knowing that he goes to the everlasting punishment of fire; but would by all means restrain himself, and order his path with virtue, that he might receive the good gifts of God, and avoid the punishments."[73] For Justin, this conviction was a key distinguishing mark of the faith.[74]

Justin even warned the emperor, and with him all Romans, saying, "if you also, like thoughtless people, prefer the custom [of persecuting Christians] to truth, do what you have power to do." But, Justin adds, the Scriptures show that even the emperor has no more ability to thwart the plans of God than the power "brigands have in a desert." Justin sensed that the emperor and other political authorities were rightly concerned about the rumors of Christians seeking an earthly kingdom, but he assured them that Christians were looking for something quite different—a divine kingdom where God reigns. The thoughts of Christians were "not fixed on the present," Justin writes, so they "are not concerned when men cut us off; since also death is a debt which must at all events be paid." He closed his *First Apology*, saying, "we forewarn you, that you will not escape the coming judgment of God," and if injustice continues, he adds, the people of God will cry out, "What is pleasing to God, let that be done."[75]

Like Justin, other early Christians issued warnings of impending judgment and rewards. Aristides, for example, writes that Christians rejoice when a faithful member of the church dies, because they are only "being transferred from one place to another." However, when a "sinner dies, they weep bitterly over him, because they know he is sure to be punished."[76] An apologetic emphasis on the coming judgment is a key feature in 2 Clement:

> Let not any one of you say that this our flesh is not judged nor raised again. Consider this: in what were ye saved, in what did ye recover your sight, if not in this flesh? We ought, therefore, to guard our flesh as the temple of God; for in the same manner as ye were called in the flesh, in the flesh also shall ye come. There is one Christ, our Lord who saved us, who being at the first spirit, was made flesh, and thus called us. So also shall we in this flesh receive the reward. Let us, therefore, love one another, that we may all come to the kingdom of God.

But if God has saved his people and those whom he has saved have been given "sight," they were now to demonstrate this faith through works in the body, so when they stood before God, they could give an account for their works. The abiding emphasis on a future judgment was always tied to the consequences of actions performed in the body.

Perhaps some might debate this approach or its precise wording, but the language of the early church resonates with hope. In the end, Justin realized that this might not be enough, that persuading those who reject the faith was not as easy as writing a few chapters and offering some reasoned defense of Christianity. It is still debated whether the emperor ever saw Justin's *Apology*.

Perhaps not. But in any case, the text communicates a certain posture toward the emperor and the state based on the abiding conviction that Jesus Christ will come again in glory to judge the living and the dead and establish a kingdom that will have no end. While Justin prayed that the emperor Antoninus Pius, or whoever else read this text, would find the Christian arguments persuasive, he also recognized that the coming kingdom of God did not depend upon the whims of the emperor.

Through all their activities and trials, ancient Christian writings often cycle back to discuss hope. In their debates about how to navigate their cultural moment, Christian hope, like a track running under their feet, led them forward, step by step. Christians look for the coming kingdom of God with hope, and in this hope, they live.

CONCLUSION

This discussion of hope guides our argument of cultural sanctification home. We have seen that early Christian identity was fashioned through doctrine, ethics, and liturgy and framed by a narrative of salvation history. This structure culminated in the hope of the coming kingdom of God, a fitting conclusion for the ultimate work of God. As the church defined a dual citizenship and made important arguments for social and intellectual engagement, the Christian hope tied all these pieces together. The early church expected that the nations would war, and political chaos return, but eventually Christ would come again and set things right.

This vision of hope subverted the ancient order that located hope in the political and social structures of the Roman Empire. Over against the empire's supposed glorious unending sway, the Christian vision of hope cast a larger narrative of salvation that moves from creation to the new heavens and earth, subordinating Rome within it. The Christian metanarrative consumed the Roman alternative and offered to the world something they had not had before: hope in the life of the world to come. This life included resurrection and beatitude where the faithful enjoy all the blessings and privileges of life with God. If many in the ancient world found the notion of resurrection ludicrous, it helped sustain the faithful through many moments of oppression and persecution. It can do so again today.

The church also emphasized that Christ's return would bring judgment for those who rejected God, and blessings for the faithful. The reality that

Christ would come to judge the living and the dead motivated the faithful to live virtuously in the present and encouraged them to defend the faith with confidence. On the other side of this life lay the resurrected life with judgment for the reprobate and joy of beatitude for the church. The church managed to survive and even thrive in the ancient world because the offer of beatitude was ultimately more satisfying and hopeful than what could be found through philosophical inquiry, bodily satisfaction, or political engagement. Through the twists and turns of cultural and political changes, the steady expectation of Christ's return and the future kingdom of God held them fast. This final exhortation to hope should also continue to encourage the church today to face whatever comes along.

CONCLUSION

MONTE CASSINO

The train ride south of Rome to the town of Cassino was not too long. I sat at the window watching the Italian countryside pass by, heading toward the famous monastery of Saint Benedict. The abbey is perched atop Mount Cassino, rising out of the Latin valley to an imposing height. The original monastery was built in 529 but was lost when sacked by the Lombards in the eighth century. Others have been built in its place since then, with many of these iterations sacked and rebuilt in turn. Most recently, the abbey was destroyed during World War II, when the Germans were suspected of using it as a strategic military position to slow the Allies as they pushed their way north to liberate Rome. The current monastery is still active with a small community of monks continuing to follow the rule of Saint Benedict.

We exited the train at Cassino and met a taxi driver who agreed to give me and my companion a ride to the monastery at the top of the mountain. We jumped in, and the driver began zigzagging his way up the side of the mountain past dense forest and an old Polish cemetery with soldiers lost during the World War II battle. The driver deposited us at the entrance of a white stone building. Its enormous doors stood open like large metal arms welcoming us into the monastery. The word *pax*, or peace, was imprinted in the stone wall above the door, signaling the ambiance of the monastery inside.

It was a warm and sunny spring day, with a fierce wind swirling around the monastery grounds. There were very few visitors, and I slowly meandered my way around the abbey admiring the buildings. I passed the garden with the dark sculpture of Benedict commemorating his final moments with his fellow monks holding him up as he departed this world. I walked through the museum and the gift shop and then made my way to the edge of a wall where I could look out and see for miles across the sprawling valley.

Finally, I walked up the central stairs to the main sanctuary and stepped inside. I will never forget that moment. The thick stone walls cut out all the noise, and in an instant, I was engulfed by a thick cloud of silence. I took a seat in the back and began admiring the cavernous church. The sanctuary was dark; the only lights came from the flickering candles on altars scattered around the room. There was no service going on and no one else around to disturb our quiet contemplation. It is difficult to convey the overwhelming silence I experienced in that moment. You could hear the air move. The world outside with all its hustle and bustle seemed a thousand miles away. I sat in prayer and contemplation for what felt like hours, even though it was probably only minutes, and considered what it might have been like for Benedict to find this place and establish a monastery so far removed from the world below.

As the silence wore on, it was easy to see why Benedict would choose this place to build a retreat from a world with a gathering of followers committed to the disciplined spiritual life. Several years earlier, while living in Subiaco, Benedict had composed one of the most important sets of monastic regulations. It is unparalleled as such rules go and has guided the lives of many monastic communities throughout Christian history. There is so much about his rule that I appreciate, especially the emphasis on virtue and humility. Sitting in silence and praying in Benedict's abbey also reminded me of the blessings of spiritual retreat. Some measured asceticism is always good for the soul.

But the story of monasticism, especially as it developed in the third century, has more to do with the rejection of a cultural Christianity than a pagan culture. "From the third century," Henry Chadwick writes, "the question was being put with steadily increasing pressure whether the Church could occupy a position of influence in high society without losing something of its moral power and independence."[1] Benedict lived post-Constantine, after the fall of that pagan empire against which early Christianity struggled. Monasticism raises serious questions about believers' struggle with cultural power and has certainly posed an alternative answer in various forms and communities through the history of Christianity. But the church in the West no longer enjoys a cultural hegemony, and the cultural expressions of Christianity are waning. The Christian community has lost influence and power, because a secularism (or modern paganism) is regnant in the West.

After what felt like a lifetime, I slowly rose and quietly walked out of the church; the bright lights of the outside world blinded me as I opened the door. I descended the steps, walked out of the monastery, and caught another taxi down the mountain to reenter the buzzing Italian world below. The noises and commotion of the city life shocked me back into reality. At that moment, the serenity of the mountaintop and the sanctuary seemed so attractive in comparison to the burden of living in a secular world. But I also thought about so many others in the early history of Christianity who did not live in a Christendom but embedded themselves within a pagan culture and seasoned it with their lives.

In the closing lines of his celebrated work *After Virtue*, Alasdair MacIntyre holds up Benedict as a potential model for cultural engagement: "We are not waiting for a Godot, but for another—doubtless very different—St. Benedict."[2] This line has caused quite a stir and not a little bit of criticism from all sides. The real challenge, as philosopher Jack Caputo points out, is that "MacIntyre does not make a single step forward, which is what repetition demands, but makes an elegant, erudite recollective slide backward."[3] MacIntyre leaves the reader to propose ways forward through the morass of the "emotive" culture he diagnoses, and Benedict is certainly not the only historical example to consider. The world in which we find ourselves is not the Dark Ages with all its struggles to maintain Christendom, nor should everyone follow Benedict into his monastery.

We are entering a world that is post-Christendom, and reminiscent of an ancient pagan world with all the trappings that entails. I am no prophet and do not presume to know where this story goes, but I do know that if there is any path forward, turning to Christians who have walked these roads before is a good thing. The life and writings of Polycarp, Justin Martyr, Blandina, Irenaeus, Tertullian, Origen, and many others who strove to live faithfully in the ancient world offer a vision of engagement as an embedded process actively seeking cultural sanctification.

This book has stuck close to the early Christians who lived and served before the Constantinian age of the fourth century. Occasionally, later figures such as Augustine make their way into this conversation because they were dealing with the lingering vestiges of paganism. The opening chapter argued that the West is becoming secular at a pace that seems unlikely to slow; perhaps we are even further down that road than some want to admit. Charles Taylor defines ours as a "secular age" in search of a moral good that it does not often find in Christianity.[4] Likewise, Carl Trueman, building upon the work of Taylor, argues this age is defined by an "expressive individualism," where "each of us finds our meaning by giving expression to our feelings and desires."[5] In its ongoing search for identity, there appears to be little interest in listening to the church's voice within the culture, and the church is rapidly being pushed to the margins. In this light, our situation is reminiscent of pagan antiquity in which Christianity was born. Now, T. S. Eliot and Steven Smith argue, it is a "modern paganism" that defines the contemporary West.

If this is our problematic situation, there remains a heated debate over the way forward. In the face of a rising modern paganism, some are calling for a retreat from culture, à la Benedict, while others want to charge forward in confrontation and take up arms in a warrior posture. As I mentioned in the introduction, there may be some occasions, through cultural discernment, that Christians need to recuse themselves from certain institutions or activities or stand boldly when confronted with various forms of immorality. But while there may be moments for these extremes, they should not set our abiding posture. Instead, we should embrace a vision of cultural sanctification that helped the church survive and even thrive in the first few centuries while living among their fellow pagan citizens.

Cultural Sanctification

Cultural sanctification, as defined in this book, sees Christians as embedded within their culture but seeking sanctification so as to promote virtue and reject vice in their personal lives, in the church and in the activities and institutions of the surrounding world. As Andrew Walls suggests, the history of missiology shows the church always synthesizing its indigenizing and pilgrim principles. When Christians encounter a culture, they settle down within its social and political structures. But in maneuvering through this new world, they have always reminded each other that they live as sojourners focused on the life of the world to come.

Some important factors certainly differentiate our world from that of early Christianity. Christians today are not working with a clean slate. We had cultural power in the past and did not always use it wisely or in accordance with Christian virtue. We need to admit that. We should also lament the loss of cultural mores and institutions that no longer bear a Christian mark. But these things should not discourage us from the approach to cultural engagement proposed here. There is also a long history of the church making important contributions to Western civilization, including educational and political institutions, and we can continue to draw upon those good things and embed ourselves within the culture as we seek to transform it. There is also a significant difference between the political structures of imperial rule and a basic democratic republic. Thus, Christians today have a greater political voice than did our ancient counterparts, and we need to use that voice wisely. I hope that the vision of cultural sanctification spelled out in this book offers a helpful framework to that end.

Fostering this approach to cultural engagement begins with a sincere conviction about our identity as Christians. In the first few centuries, that identity was fashioned through the regular practices of catechesis and liturgy. The contours of Christian doctrine and morality comprised the curriculum of discipleship, and both are essential. We cannot lose one for the other. Alongside catechesis, liturgy shaped the patterns of a community that often ran counter to the habits and virtues of the surrounding world. The rhythms of the church were defined by the liturgical calendar and a process of prebaptismal catechesis that proceeded slowly. This required patience, for new believers had to be reoriented from many of the assumptions in their old Roman identities and toward a Christian narrative of salvation history.

The church's contemporary conversation gets sidetracked at just this point. A pragmatic focus on *how* to respond to the urgencies of the moment often neglects the importance of prior identity formation through discipleship in Christian doctrine and morality. In other words, catechesis is not an escape from or irrelevant to cultural engagement; it forms the roots from which cultural engagement will grow. In our times, the church needs to take time to reacquaint itself with its own faith and beliefs as we consider how to engage the forces around us. There is no set form for this process; we need to trust the creativity of pastors, ministers, and lay leaders to shape models of discipleship that will be effective in different ways and in different places. But whatever form it takes, there is no substitute for discipleship in the doctrine and morality of the faith or the liturgical patterns of life that cultivate community and distinguish the life of the church.

Upon this foundation, the church developed both a political and a public theology. Early Christians did not feel called to remain within their own hallowed walls but to live as citizens embedded in this world. As the Epistle to Diognetus argued, Christians in the pagan world did not choose between fight or flight but instead desired to demonstrate "the remarkable and admittedly unusual character of their own citizenship."[6] Cultural sanctification entails that Christians embody good citizenship from a threefold set of assumptions: a firm conviction in divine transcendence and providence, a belief that God granted political authority to some leaders, and an active citizenship that held to a political dualism. Contrary to their fellow Romans who closely associated the divine and the state, the church insisted that God is transcendent. Consequently, there was only "one public history" that embraced both the acts of God and humans governed by God's providential care over this creation.[7] They did not reject their responsibilities to civil government, nor did they wish to absorb the culture uncritically, but they maintained their conviction of God's transcendent rule even in the face of being marginalized, persecuted, and occasionally martyred. The church believed that God had providentially appointed rulers for whatever purpose God desired, and that those purposes were maintaining peace and security, promoting justice, defending religious liberty, and encouraging virtue. They brought up these norms when civic leaders subverted or violated them.

As active citizens, early Christians always worked to honor political authorities and prayed for them fervently. They also paid their taxes and supported the work of the government as conscience allowed. Finally, at every turn, they defended religious liberty and worked to promote virtue. Together, these features of political theology promoted a process of cultural sanctification that worked to redeem the creation and, little by little, see the political sphere embrace Christian virtue. To cite the words of the Epistle to Diognetus, the church was the "soul" of the culture and had to embrace its calling to live Christianly in the world, whatever the obstacles.[8] Under the ancient imperial regime, the early church lacked the means to contribute to the political sphere as is possible in modern liberal democracy. Therefore, Christians today should not take for granted their opportunities to participate in the political world and promote virtue. While Christendom may crumble, all is not lost; Christians still have a basic political vision that guided the church across the rough terrain of earlier ages.

The process of cultural sanctification also calls the church to consider its public theology—its vision of engaging the broader world beyond the state. Through constant organic interaction between Christians and non-Christians, the early church embraced the high calling to live virtuously in all aspects of their lives. Since pagan intellectuals relentlessly mocked Christianity as a threat to their way of life, Christians were under no illusions that their arguments would simply be accepted. Yet amid such hostility, both conservative and creative sets of Christian intellectuals connected their lives and clerical duties in response to these critiques. These pioneer pastor-theologians defended the church to give it room to worship and serve. Origen is a key example here, but alongside him were a host of others who married the sacerdotal and the intellectual worlds to help the people of God respond to challenges from without. Origen's perspective on theological education is encouraging. He offered a vision that was stratified to educate people of any intellectual level and prepare them to serve the church. At the same time, he was never shy about engaging philosophy with the proper theological method. He knew that the intellectual life demanded Christians to read the pagans for the sake of evangelism, apologetics, and dogmatic construction in ways that might persuade the populace. Through it all, Origen insisted that virtue is the ultimate purpose of the intellectual life. Any other purpose distracts from the primary goal of Christian thinking. Ministers and institutions that want to survive in a pagan world should consider this model and recover a formative vision that combines theological education with catechetical formation. This includes education of both lay people and leaders in a way that engages the prevailing philosophical arguments of our day.

In this intellectual enterprise, the ancient Christian thinkers used several strategies of persuasion. They defended the uniqueness of Christianity and contended that Christian doctrine and morality are ultimately more intellectually satisfying than the pagan alternatives. They argued for the antiquity of Christianity and at every turn insisted that Christianity promoted the public good. This engagement created space for Christians to live and serve within the world around them. While they hoped to persuade, and occasionally did so, they were never shy about defending the faith in the public square. But their response was also commensurate with their lives, dedicated to the pursuit of virtue. In our intellectual arguments, we must walk this line between rhetoric and virtue and make persuasive arguments, but never in ways that undermine our call to *embody* virtue.

The church was interested in promoting the virtues of its social as well as intellectual life. They were attentive both to the public display of their morality and to the way Christian morality could be preserved within a pagan world. They knew that their religious identity should reshape their inherited views of public life; that is, once believers joined the Christian community, they had to begin the process of *resocialization*, reimagining their norms and values. The process of resocialization always oscillates between the contingency of current circumstances and the objective of sanctification, so the church had to learn to manage their process of cultural absorption, or acculturation. This produced the art of ethical improvisation within the Christian tradition. Holding to Christian virtue as revealed in the Scriptures, they learned the habits of living within any and every cultural situation. This does not mean that they always made the best decisions, but they aspired to let wisdom guide them and walk in hope. This defined a culturally discerning spiritual life—a life indigenized within the culture but learning to navigate between its virtues and vices. In other words, early Christians had to discern how to live according to the biblical commands of morality amid changing and often hostile circumstances, learning patterns of life that remain faithful to Scripture. We can follow this process of cultural discernment in early Christians' discussions of their occupational lives, leisure and entertainments, military service, and marriage and family. This operation was not wholly focused on internal holiness but also on external activities that encouraged a compassionate social engagement, both supporting the church's ministry and attracting outsiders. Altogether, this blend of holiness and activism offered the world a religion that was a positive good for the culture.

The culminating piece of cultural sanctification was Christian hope. Christians now as then cannot approach the immediate challenges before us and forget the basic conviction that Christ will come again in glory to judge the living and the dead and establish a kingdom that will have no end. The Romans offered little in the way of hope. But early Christians worshiped, worked, served, lived, and died under this enduring hope. That hope was a key distinction between them and the ancient world. The same is true today and must be remembered in the throes of political and cultural struggles when we can get distracted or despair. With the early church, we must embrace hope above all things and long for the coming kingdom of God and the resurrected life that awaits the faithful. In the end, hope should assist the church in cultural sanctification, motivating us to live the good life in the present world. Christ is reigning now, so when tempests seem to shake our foundations, let us stand in hope.

There is much the contemporary church can learn from the ancient one. The ancients, to be sure, were not perfect; there were plenty of saints and sinners to go around. But the church survived and even thrived in times like our own, and God was faithful through it all. Yet our own world is different, too, without such lions as Justin, Polycarp, Irenaeus, Tertullian, Blandina, Origen, and Augustine, not to mention the apostles themselves. We have to do our own good work of exhorting the faithful to holiness and defending the faith before a pagan world. This will require both basic theological and moral formation and serious cultural discernment. No doubt the demise of Christendom is a fearful time, and fear is a paralyzing emotion. But a most common injunction in the Bible is "fear not; take courage." In the words of the Epistle to Diognetus, Christians must remember "the important position to which God has appointed them, and it is not right for them to decline it."[9] We can face this cultural moment with hope, even when the clouds look ominous, for we can remind each other that we are, as the inscription in the Lateran Baptistery says, "consecrated to another city, whom the Spirit brings forth from the fertile waters."[10]

Notes

Introduction

1. Hugo Brandenburg, *Ancient Churches of Rome from the Fourth to the Seventh Century: The Dawn of Christian Architecture in the West* (Turnhout: Brepols, 2005), 20–21.

2. Brandenburg, *Ancient Churches of Rome*, 20.

3. Richard Krautheimer, *Three Christian Capitals: Topography and Politics* (Berkeley: University of California Press, 1983), 12.

4. Robert Wilken discusses the importance of the Lateran complex in Constantine's religious vision. See Robert Louis Wilken, *Liberty in the Things of God: The Christian Origins of Religious Freedom* (New Haven: Yale University Press, 2019), 25–26.

5. Maureen Miller, *The Bishop's Palace: Architecture and Authority in Medieval Italy* (Ithaca, NY: Cornell University Press, 2000).

6. Raymond Davis, ed., *The Book of Pontiffs* (Liber Pontificalis), 3rd ed. (Liverpool: Liverpool University Press, 2001), 38. A long tradition links Constantine's baptism with this baptistery, and the images around the room tell the story of his life and conquests. Eusebius of Caesarea, however, reports that he was baptized further east by Eusebius of Nicomedia just before his death (Eusebius, *Vit. Const.* 4.61–62). Still the image of Constantine and the connections to his reign were enough for Sixtus to renovate it in honor of the famous emperor.

7. David Tyler Thayer, "The Lateran Baptistery: Memory, Space, and Baptism" (master's thesis, University of Tennessee, 2012), 26.

8. *Book of Pontiffs*, 38.

9. Brandenburg, *Ancient Churches of Rome*, 47.

10. Everett Ferguson, *Baptism in the Early Church: History, Theology, and Liturgy in the First Five Centuries* (Grand Rapids: Eerdmans, 2009), 769.

11. There are many studies, but for a few examples, see Philip Jenkins, *The Next Christendom: The Coming of Global Christianity*, 3rd ed. (New York: Oxford University Press, 2011), and Stephen Bullivant, *Nonverts: The Making of Ex-Christian America* (New York: Oxford University Press, 2022).

12. Charles Taylor, *A Secular Age* (Cambridge: Belknap, 2007), 1, 3, 171.

13. Carl R. Trueman, *The Rise and Triumph of the Modern Self: Cultural Amnesia, Expressive Individualism, and the Road to Sexual Revolution* (Wheaton, IL: Crossway, 2020), 46. Trueman builds upon Taylor's use of "expressive individualism." See Taylor, *Secular Age*, 474–75.

14. Trueman, *Rise and Triumph*, 406.

15. Ferdinand Mount, *Full Circle: How the Classical World Came Back to Us* (New York: Simon & Schuster, 2010), 1. There are many other books with similar arguments. Take, for example, Melissa Lane, *Eco-Republic: What the Ancients Can Teach Us about Ethics, Virtue, and Sustainable Living* (Princeton: Princeton University Press, 2012). Lane argues that the "modern project so defined is built on certain flawed assumptions" and turns to the ancient Greeks to help rethink personal virtue, character, and the relation between an individual and society. See Lane, *Eco-Republic*, 23. Or consider Natalie Haynes, *The Ancient Guide to the Modern Life* (London: Profile Books, 2012), 254, who shows how "classics is everything we used to be and much of what we are now."

16. Mount, *Full Circle*, 2–3.

17. Mount, *Full Circle*, 168. Others, such as Alasdair MacIntyre, have made similar observations. MacIntyre's celebrated work *After Virtue* points to Nietzsche and argues that the moral condition of the modern secular world is in "a state of grave disorder," and assumes that the orienting moral guide of the West is *emotivism*, where all moral choices are merely a matter of preference. There is no coherent morality upon which society can be ordered, and theology is marginalized, so any and every form of spirituality and morality can proliferate. Instead, there is only diversity with no way to adjudicate between appropriate renderings of morality. See Alasdair MacIntyre, *After Virtue*, 2nd ed. (Notre Dame: University of Notre Dame Press, 1984), 256.

18. Mount, *Full Circle*, 163, 241.

19. In the end, Mount pulls back just a bit. In his estimation, the return to the classical world is a "classical-lite" that emphasizes a "sensuous, this worldly way of living without the gravitas that underpinned it." Mount, *Full Circle*, 374.

20. T. S. Eliot, "The Idea of a Christian Society," in *Christianity and Culture* (New York: Harvest, 1948), 10.

21. Eliot, "Idea of a Christian Society," 18.

22. Steven D. Smith, *Pagans and Christians in the City: Culture Wars from the Tiber to the Potomac* (Grand Rapids: Eerdmans, 2018), 14.

23. Robin Lane Fox, *Pagans and Christians: In the Mediterranean World from the Second Century A.D. to the Conversion of Constantine* (Harmondsworth: Penguin, 1988), 27.

24. Fox, *Pagans and Christians*, 30–31.

25. Smith, *Pagans and Christians*, 14. Others have made similar observations, such as Peter Gay, *The Enlightenment: The Rise of Modern Paganism* (New York: Norton, 1995).

26. John Behr, *Irenaeus of Lyons: Identifying Christianity* (Oxford: Oxford University Press, 2015), 1.

27. Michael J. Kruger, *Christianity at the Crossroads: How the Second Century Shaped the Future of the Church* (Downers Grove, IL: InterVarsity Press, 2018), 230.

28. John D. Wilsey, *American Exceptionalism and Civil Religion: Reassessing the History of an Idea* (Downers Grove, IL: InterVarsity Press, 2015), 222–24.

29. Michael Green, *Evangelism in the Early Church*, rev. ed. (Grand Rapids: Eerdmans, 2003), 13.

30. Gerald L. Sittser, *Resilient Faith: How the Early Christian "Third Way" Changed the World* (Grand Rapids: Brazos, 2019), 15.

31. Rod Dreher, *The Benedict Option: A Strategy for Christians in a Post-Christian Nation* (New York: Sentinel, 2017), 12.

32. Robert Louis Wilken, *Christians as the Romans Saw Them*, 2nd ed. (New Haven: Yale University Press, 2003), 201.

33. John Bolt, "Abraham Kuyper or Saint Benedict? The Challenge of Christian Cultural Discipleship Today: A Review Essay," *Calvin Theological Journal* 54 (2019): 147–64, 149.

34. MacIntyre, *After Virtue*, 12; Trueman, *Rise and Triumph*, 85–88.

35. MacIntyre, *After Virtue*, 12, 244–45.

36. Jonathan Wilson, *Living Faithfully in a Fragmented World: From* After Virtue *to a New Monasticism* (Eugene, OR: Cascade, 2010), x, 25.

37. Dreher, *Benedict Option*, 2, 7, 18.

38. Robert Louis Wilken, "Christianity Face to Face with Islam," *First Things*, January 2009, https://www.firstthings.com/article/2009/01/christianity-face-to-face-with-islam.

39. Stephen Wolfe, *The Case for Christian Nationalism* (Moscow, ID: Canon, 2022), 287–88.

40. Thomas Crean and Alan Fimister, *Integralism: A Manual of Political Philosophy* (Heusenstamm: Editiones Scholasticae, 2020); Wolfe, *Case for Christian Nationalism*.

41. Bullivant, *Nonverts*, 209–15.

42. Bullivant, *Nonverts*, 209–15.

43. Paul Williams, *Exiles on Mission: How Christians Can Thrive in a Post-Christian World* (Grand Rapids: Baker, 2020), 6, 22–23.

44. See, for example, William Edgar, *Created and Creating: A Biblical Theology of Culture* (Downers Grove, IL: InterVarsity Press, 2016); Andy Crouch, *Culture Making: Recovering Our Creative Calling* (Downers Grove, IL: InterVarsity Press, 2008); Greg Forster, *Joy for the World: How Christianity Lost Its Cultural Influence and Can Begin Rebuilding It* (Wheaton, IL: Crossway, 2014); David Crump, *I Pledge Allegiance: A Believer's Guide to Kingdom Citizenship in Twenty-First-Century America* (Grand Rapids: Eerdmans, 2018); and David VanDrunen, *Politics after Christendom: Political Theology in a Fractured World* (Grand Rapids: Zondervan Academic, 2020).

45. Hunter, *To Change the World*, 280.

46. Forster, *Joy for the World*.

47. VanDrunen, *Politics after Christendom*, 18.

48. Williams, *Exiles on Mission*, 45.

49. I borrow this phrase from Vince Bantu, who uses it to describe the historic approaches of missiology in the ancient church in his recent book: *A Multitude of All Peoples: Engaging Ancient Christianity's Global Identity* (Downers Grove, IL: InterVarsity Press, 2020). I see the same kind of missional attitudes and approaches in early Christianity.

50. Bantu, *Multitude of All Peoples*, 229.

51. Andrew F. Walls, *The Missionary Movement in Christian History: Studies in the Transmission of Faith* (Maryknoll, NY: Orbis Books, 1996), 7.

52. Walls, *Missionary Movement*, 8.

53. Rowan A. Greer, *Broken Lights and Mended Lives: Theology and Common Life in the Early Church* (University Park: Pennsylvania State University Press, 1991), 211.

54. Bantu, *Multitude of All Peoples*, 229.

55. Sittser, *Resilient Faith*, 6.

56. Wayne A. Meeks, *The Origins of Christian Morality: The First Two Centuries* (New Haven: Yale University Press, 1993), 50.

57. For example, see Hunter, *To Change the World*, 284–85; Smith, *Pagans and Christians*, 127.

58. Clayton N. Jefford, "Introduction," in *The Epistle to Diognetus (with the Fragments of Quadratus): Introduction, Text, and Commentary* (Oxford: Oxford University Press, 2013), 28. See also Diogn. 1.1.

59. Jefford, "Introduction," 53.

60. Diogn. 5.1–17.

61. Diogn. 6.1–10.

62. Bullivant, *Nonverts*.

63. Jenkins, *Next Christendom*.

64. C. S. Lewis, introduction to *On the Incarnation: Saint Athanasius*, Popular Patristics Series (Yonkers: St. Vladimir's Seminary Press, 2012), 13.

CHAPTER 1

1. Hippolytus, *Trad. ap.* 17. Translations from Hippolytus, *On the Apostolic Tradition*, introduction and commentary by Alistair Stewart-Sykes (Crestwood, NY: St. Vladimir's Seminary Press, 2001).

2. Hippolytus, *Trad. ap.* 21.

3. Charles Norris Cochrane, *Christianity and Classical Culture: A Study of Thought and Action from Augustus to Augustine* (New York: Oxford University Press, 1957), vi.

4. Clifford Geertz, "Ethos, World-View, and the Analysis of Sacred Symbols," *Antioch Review* 17 (1957): 622–23.

5. Robert Louis Wilken, *The Spirit of Early Christian Thought: Seeking the Face of God* (New Haven: Yale University Press, 2003), xiii.

6. Lewis R. Rambo, *Understanding Religious Conversion* (New Haven: Yale University Press, 1993), 165–70.

7. Everett Ferguson, "Catechesis and Initiation," in *The Early Church at Work*

and Worship: Catechesis, Baptism, Eschatology, and Martyrdom (Eugene, OR: Cascade, 2014), 2:19.

8. Alan Kreider, *The Patient Ferment of the Early Church: The Improbable Rise of Christianity in the Roman Empire* (Grand Rapids: Baker, 2016), 2–3.

9. A. D. Nock, *Conversion: The Old and the New in Religion from Alexander the Great to Augustine of Hippo* (Oxford: Oxford University Press, 1933), 7, 16.

10. Rambo, *Understanding Religious Conversion*, 168.

11. Martin Goodman, *Mission and Conversion: Proselytizing in the Religious History of the Roman Empire* (Oxford: Clarendon, 1994), 105.

12. Kreider, *Patient Ferment*, 70.

13. Nock, *Conversion*, 77, 135.

14. Origen, *Cels.* 3.59.

15. Nock, *Conversion*, 121.

16. Wayne A. Meeks, *The Origins of Christian Morality: The First Two Centuries* (New Haven: Yale University Press, 1993), 28.

17. Nock, *Conversion*, 16.

18. Meeks, *Origins of Christian Morality*, 25.

19. Nock, *Conversion*, 167, 179. See also discussion of the philosophical schools in Nock, *Conversion*, 167–79.

20. Pliny, *Letters* 10.96–97.

21. Pliny, *Letters* 10.96–97.

22. Tertullian discusses the correspondence between Pliny and Trajan and criticizes it as illogical. Either the Christians have committed crimes and should be sought out, or they are not guilty and should be free to worship. See Tertullian, *Apol.* 2.

23. Nock, *Conversion*, 210.

24. For the narrative of Justin's conversion, see Justin, *Dial.* 1–9.

25. Justin, *2 Apol.* 12.

26. Justin, *Dial.* 7.

27. Justin, *Dial.* 8. Other apologists, such as Aristides, describe the important role the Scriptures played in their conversions. Aristides studied the Scriptures and concluded that these writings alone have the knowledge of "things which are to come." See Aristides, *Apol.* 16.

28. Tobias Georges, "The Role of Philosophy and Education in Apologists' Conversion to Christianity: The Case of Justin and Tatian," in *Conversion and Initiation in Antiquity: Shifting Identities—Creating Change*, ed. Birgitte Secher Bøgh (Frankfurt am Main: Lang, 2014), 284–85.

29. Justin, *1 Apol.* 14.

30. Meeks, *Origins of Christian Morality*, 18.

31. David W. Bebbington, *Evangelicalism in Modern Britain: A History from the 1730s to the 1980s* (New York: Routledge, 1989), 2–17.

32. For a discussion of the moral and theological training of the new catechumen, see Paul F. Bradshaw, *Early Christian Worship: A Basic Introduction to Ideas and Practice* (Collegeville, MN: Liturgical Press, 2000), 26.

33. Clinton E. Arnold, "Early Church Catechesis and New Christian's Classes in Contemporary Evangelicalism," *Journal of the Evangelical Theological Society* 47 (2004): 39–54.

34. Kreider, *Patient Ferment*, 2.

35. Irenaeus, *Epid.* 2.

36. Irenaeus, *Epid.* 2.

37. See also 1 Tim 3:16, Phil 2:5–11, and Col 1:12–20.

38. For a discussion of the sources of revelation in the early church, see Stephen O. Presley, "Scripture and Tradition," in *Historical Theology for the Church*, ed. Jason G. Duesing and Nathan A. Finn (Nashville: Broadman & Holman, 2021), 71–88.

39. J. N. D. Kelly, *Early Christian Doctrines* (New York: HarperCollins, 1978), 37.

40. Bengt Hagglund, "Die Bedeutung der 'regula fidei' als Grundlage theologischer Aussagen," *Studia Theologica* 12 (1958): 1–44.

41. Irenaeus, *Epid.* 3, 6.

42. Irenaeus, *Epid.* 3.

43. Carl R. Trueman, *The Rise and Triumph of the Modern Self: Cultural Amnesia, Expressive Individualism, and the Road to Sexual Revolution* (Wheaton, IL: Crossway, 2020), 387.

44. Jens Zimmermann, *Incarnational Humanism: A Philosophy of Culture for the Church in the World* (Downers Grove, IL: InterVarsity Press, 2012), 30.

45. Tertullian, *Prax.* 2.

46. Origen, *Princ.* preface 2.

47. Paul M. Blowers, "The Regula Fidei and the Narrative Character of Early Christian Faith," *Pro Ecclesia* 6 (2007): 202.

48. Christoph Markschies, *Gnosis: An Introduction*, trans. John Bowden (London: T&T Clark, 2003), 16–17.

49. Irenaeus, *Haer.* 1.10.1.

50. Tertullian, *Prax.* 2.

51. Origen, *Princ.* preface 2.

52. Irenaeus, *Epid.* 2.

53. Kreider, *Patient Ferment*, 2.

54. For a discussion of key texts, see Alistair Stewart(-Sykes), *On the Two Ways: Life or Death, Light or Darkness; Foundational Texts in the Tradition* (Yonkers: St. Vladimir's Seminary Press, 2011). Several texts discuss the two ways tradition: Didache, Epistle of Barnabas, Irenaeus, and Teaching of the Twelve Apostles. There may be some connection back to the description of the church as "the Way" in Acts, but scholars debate this connection.

55. Other possible biblical allusions to these phrases and especially the contrast between life and death: Prov 6:23; 16:17; Heb 13:7.

56. Did. 1.

57. Stewart(-Sykes), *On the Two Ways*, 20.

58. Did. 1.

59. Did. 2–3. In these commands, it is possible to see what the later tradition will identify as the four cardinal virtues: prudence, justice, fortitude, and temperance. Christians were not necessarily thinking in these categories, but as Scripture guided their moral reflections, they gravitated toward contemplation of the virtues. Prudence, for example, is the mother of all virtues and describes the "realization of the good" in a person who is acting upon reality. Among other things, prudence emphasizes humility, purity, boldness, straightforwardness, candor, and simplicity of character. See Josef Pieper, *The Four Cardinal Virtues: Prudence, Justice, Fortitude, Temperance* (Notre Dame: University of Notre Dame Press, 1966), 22.

60. Irenaeus, *Epid.* 1.

61. Barn. 19.

62. I could lay alongside the discussions of the two ways many other exhortations that support these moral commands. See, for example, Aristides, *Apol.* 15.3–7; 1 Clem. 13; Minucius Felix, *Oct.* 38.

63. Meeks, *Origins of Christian Morality*, 103.

64. New Testament vice lists include Matt 15:19 (Mark 7:21–22); Rom 1:29–31; 13:1; 1 Cor 5:10–11; 6:9–10; 2 Cor 12:20–21; Gal 5:19–21; Eph 4:31; 5:3–5; Col 3:5–8; 1 Tim 1:9–10; 2 Tim 3:2–5; Titus 3:3; 1 Pet 2:1; 4:3.

65. Did. 5.

66. Did. 5.

67. Barn. 20.

68. Irenaeus, *Epid.* 1.

69. Robert Louis Wilken, *Christians as the Romans Saw Them*, 2nd ed. (New Haven: Yale University Press, 2003), 120.

70. Everett Ferguson, *From Christ to the Pre-Reformation*, vol. 1 of *Church History: The Rise and Growth of the Church in Its Cultural, Intellectual, and Political Context*, 2nd ed. (Grand Rapids: Zondervan, 2013), 61. Ferguson writes, "Even the writings most acceptable to orthodox Christians—e.g. those from Clement, Ignatius, Polycarp—have been criticized as representing a severe falling away from apostolic Christianity.... The usual charge is that the Apostolic Fathers retreated from the robust doctrines of grace and faith enunciated by Paul and took refuge in moralism and legalism."

71. Eric Osborn, *Ethical Patterns in Early Christian Thought* (Cambridge: Cambridge University Press, 1976), 5, 215, 218.

72. Samuel Wells, *Improvisation: The Drama of Christian Ethics* (London: SPCK, 2004), 45.

73. Frances Young, *The Art of Performance: Towards a Theology of Holy Scripture* (London: Darton, Longman, & Todd, 1990), 160.

74. Wells, *Improvisation*, 12, 46.

75. Tertullian, *Idol.* 24.

76. Brett Scott Provance, *Pocket Dictionary of Liturgy and Worship* (Downers Grove, IL: InterVarsity Press, 2010), 79.

77. James K. A. Smith, *Desiring the Kingdom: Worship, Worldview, and Cultural Formation* (Grand Rapids: Baker Academic, 2009), 25, 40.

78. Charles Taylor, *A Secular Age* (Cambridge: Belknap, 2007), 171, 172.

79. Trueman, *Rise and Triumph*, 37.

80. Wilken, *Christians as the Romans Saw Them*, 32, 73.

81. Acts 1:14, 42; 6:4; Rom 12:12; Col 4:2. Possible allusions to specific times of prayer: Acts 10:9; 12:5–12; 16:25.

82. Gerald L. Sittser, *Resilient Faith: How the Early Christian "Third Way" Changed the World* (Grand Rapids: Brazos, 2019), 125.

83. Justin, *1 Apol.* 67.

84. Wilken, *Spirit of Early Christian Thought*, 29.

85. Andrew McGowan, *Ancient Christian Worship: Early Church Practices in Social, Historical, and Theological Perspective* (Grand Rapids: Baker Academic, 2014), 1.

86. Justin, *1 Apol.* 67.

87. Meeks, *Origins of Christian Morality*, 96.

88. Wells, *Improvisation*, 61.

89. Tertullian, *Bapt.* 19.

90. Alistair Stewart-Sykes, *Tertullian, Cyprian, and Origen on the Lord's Prayer* (Yonkers: St. Vladimir's Seminary Press, 2004).

91. Did. 8; Bradshaw, *Early Christian Worship*, 77.

92. Agnes Cunningham, SSCM, *Prayer: Personal and Liturgical, Message of the Fathers* (Wilmington, DE: Glazier, 1985), 25.

93. Robert Louis Wilken, *The First Thousand Years: A Global History of Christianity* (New Haven: Yale University Press, 2012), 2.

CHAPTER 2

1. Mart. Pol. 3.

2. Mart. Pol. 8.

3. Mart. Pol. 9.

4. Mart. Pol. 9.

5. Mart. Pol. 10.

6. Mart. Pol. 12.

7. Mart. Pol. 14.

8. Paul Williams, *Exiles on Mission: How Christians Can Thrive in a Post-Christian World* (Grand Rapids: Baker, 2020), 22.

9. Augustine, *Conf.* 10.6.

10. J. N. D. Kelly, *Early Christian Doctrines* (New York: HarperCollins, 1978), 87.

11. Robert Louis Wilken, *Christians as the Romans Saw Them*, 2nd ed. (New Haven: Yale University Press, 2003), 59.

12. Steven D. Smith, *Pagans and Christians in the City: Culture Wars from the Tiber to the Potomac* (Grand Rapids: Eerdmans, 2018), iii.

13. Carl R. Trueman, *The Rise and Triumph of the Modern Self: Cultural Amnesia, Expressive Individualism, and the Road to Sexual Revolution* (Wheaton, IL: Crossway, 2020), 388.

14. Oliver O'Donovan, *The Desire of the Nations* (Cambridge: Cambridge University Press, 1996), 2.

15. Charles Norris Cochrane, *Christianity and Classical Culture: A Study of Thought and Action from Augustus to Augustine* (New York: Oxford University Press, 1957), 456.

16. O'Donovan, *Desire of the Nations*, 2.

17. Kelly, *Early Christian Doctrines*, 87.

18. For example, see, Justin, *1 Apol.* 9.3; 13.14; 14.1; 25.2; 61.11; Theophilus, *Autol.* 1.5; Aristides, *Apol.* 15.3.

19. Kelly, *Early Christian Doctrines*, 85.

20. Smith, *Pagans and Christians*, 111.

21. It appears that the letter was delayed due to persecution. See 1 Clem. 1.1; 7.1. The letter also references the persecutions of Peter and Paul under Nero and alludes to earlier times when the church was facing persecution.

22. Unity is clearly a key theme; the language of *harmonia* or "concord" is used fourteen times in the letter.

23. Irenaeus, *Epid.* 6.

24. Irenaeus, *Haer.* 2.1.2.

25. See Anthony Briggman, *God and Christ in Irenaeus* (Oxford: Oxford University Press, 2019), 74.

26. Lashier, *Irenaeus and the Trinity*, 81–82.

27. Diogn. 7.

28. Kelly, *Early Christian Doctrines*, 83.

29. Diogn. 3.

30. Herm. Vis. 1.1. See also 1 Clem. 59.

31. Origen, *Cels.* 8.70.

32. Paul Veyne, *When Our World Became Christian* (Malden, MA: Polity, 2010), 20.

33. Trueman, *Rise and Triumph*, 80–81.

34. Mart. Pol. 10.

35. Even the book of Acts closes with Paul under house arrest and preparing to face political authorities in Rome.

36. Lester L. Field Jr., *Liberty, Dominion, Two Swords: On the Origins of Western Political Theology, 180–398* (Notre Dame: University of Notre Dame Press, 1995), 46.

37. Irenaeus, *Haer.* 5.24.2.

38. Athenagoras, *Leg.* 5.

39. Tertullian, *Apol.* 32.

40. 1 Clem. 61.

41. Barn. 19.

42. See Tertullian, *Apol.* 5.3; Irenaeus *Haer.* 5.24.3.

43. Origen, *Comm. Rom.* 9.28.2.

44. Origen, *Comm. Rom.* 9.28.2.

45. Origen, *Comm. Rom.* 9.28.2.

46. Irenaeus, *Haer.* 5.24.3.

47. Origen, *Comm. Rom.* 9.26.

48. Hugo Rahner, *Church and State in Early Christianity* (San Francisco: Ignatius, 1992), 46.

49. Rahner, *Church and State,* 3–4.

50. Tertullian, *Apol.* 24.

51. Hippolytus, *Comm. Dan.* 3.23.1–2.

52. Justin, *2 Apol.* 2.

53. For a translation of "The Martyrdom of Saints Justin, Chariton, Charito, Euelpistos, Hierax, Paion, Liberian and Their Comrades," see Bryan M. Litfin, *Early Christian Martyr Stories: An Evangelical Introduction with New Translations* (Grand Rapids: Baker Academic, 2014), 66–69. There are several versions of this text of varying length. Scholars typically accept the shortest one as the original. See Litfin, *Early Christian Martyr Stories,* 66.

54. Rahner, *Church and State,* 3.

55. Tertullian, *Cor.* 13.

56. Tertullian, *Idol.* 15, 17.

57. Rahner, *Church and State,* xvii.

58. Alan Kreider, *The Patient Ferment of the Early Church: The Improbable Rise of Christianity in the Roman Empire* (Grand Rapids: Baker, 2016), 43.

59. Augustine, *Civ.* 14.28; 19.17; 19.26.

60. Smith, *Pagans and Christians,* 128.

61. Rahner, *Church and State,* xvii.

62. Origen, *Cels.* 8.2.

63. Tacitus, *Ann.* 15.44.

64. Smith, *Pagans and Christians,* 142, 145.

65. Wilken, *Christians as the Romans Saw Them,* 124–25. This also explain why Christians were often called the "third race" as a derogatory term. Tertullian tells us it was not uncommon to hear the phrase "away with the third race" yelled at Christians at the circus games. As a third race, they were neither Greek nor Jewish, implying that they were separated and isolated from any known group. Christians had no place in society, no social standing or social capital.

66. Tertullian, *Apol.* 28–33.

67. Origen, *Cels.* 8.67, 70.

68. Theophilus, *Autol.* 1.2.

69. Origen, *Comm. Rom.* 9.27.

70. 1 Clem. 60–61.

71. Pol. *Phil.* 12.

72. Theophilus, *Autol.* 1.11.

73. Hippolytus, *Comm. Dan.* 3.24.6–9.

74. Hippolytus, *Comm. Dan.* 3.22.1.

75. Justin, *1 Apol.* 17.

76. Theophilus, *Autol.* 1.2.

77. Tertullian, *Apol.* 30–32.

78. Rahner, *Church and State*, 15–16.

79. Origen, *Cels.* 8.74.

80. Matt 22:21; Justin, *1 Apol.* 17.

81. Tertullian, *Apol.* 42.

82. Origen, *Comm. Rom.* 9.29.

83. Tertullian, *Apol.* 24.

84. Origen, *Cels.* 8.63–70.

85. Tacitus, *Ann.* 15.44.

CHAPTER 3

1. Minucius Felix, *Oct.* 1–2.

2. Minucius Felix, *Oct.* 13.

3. Minucius Felix, *Oct.* 38.

4. Minucius Felix, *Oct.* 38.

5. Some question the legitimacy of this dialogue and the polemical nature. Though it is difficult to confirm, I am inclined toward a sympathetic reading and assume that he is relating a real conversation or at least a composite or ideal conversation based upon others that he had or witnessed. Either way, the dialogue shows that the early church valued civic discourse and intellectual engagement.

6. Christoph Markschies, *Christian Theology and Its Institutions in the Early Roman Empire: Prolegomena to a History of Early Christian Theology* (Waco, TX: Baylor University Press, 2015), 55. He cites the definitive study by Barbara Aland, "Christentum, Bildung und römische Oberschicht: Zum 'Octavius' des Minucius Felix," in *Platonismus und Christentum: Festschrift für Heinrich Dörrie*, ed. H.-D. Blume and F. Mann, Jahrbuch für Antike und Christentum Ergänzungsband 10 (Münster: Aschendorff, 1983), 18n45.

7. Origen, *Cels.* preface 1.

8. Mark A. Noll, *The Scandal of the Evangelical Mind* (Grand Rapids: Eerdmans, 1995), 3.

9. Mark A. Noll, *Jesus Christ and the Life of the Mind* (Grand Rapids: Eerdmans, 2011), 151.

10. Tertullian, *Apol.* 1.

11. Robert Louis Wilken, *Christians as the Romans Saw Them*, 2nd ed. (New Haven: Yale University Press, 2003), 22.

12. Justin, *2 Apol.* 3.

13. Origen, *Cels.* 1.12.

14. Origen, *Cels.* 1.2.

15. Origen, *Cels.* 1.2; see 1 Cor 2:4.

16. Origen, *Cels.* 1.2.

17. Origen, *Cels.* 3.44.

18. Origen, *Cels.* 3.55.

19. There are many references, but for a sampling see Origen, *Cels.* 1.9, 27, 62; 3.44, 55, 59; 4.33; 6.14.

20. Origen, *Cels.* 3.59.

21. Origen, *Cels.* 1.17, 27.

22. Origen, *Cels.* 3.52.

23. Peter Brown, *Power and Persuasion in Late Antiquity: Towards a Christian Empire* (Madison: University of Wisconsin Press, 1992), 5.

24. Origen, *Cels.* 3.75.

25. Origen, *Cels.* 3.75.

26. Robert Louis Wilken, *The Spirit of Early Christian Thought: Seeking the Face of God* (New Haven: Yale University Press, 2003), xiv.

27. It is worth nothing that Rebaque's categories here are taken from Marxist Antonio Gramsci's work *Prison Notebooks*, where he makes these distinctions among the intellectual class. The only difference here is that the Christians are the organic intellectuals working to preserve the tradition that was handed down through catechesis.

28. Fernando Rivas Rebaque, "Justin Martyr as an Organic Christian Intellectual in Rome," in *Christian Teachers in Second-Century Rome: Schools and Students in the Ancient City*, ed. H. Gregory Snyder (Leiden: Brill, 2020), 134.

29. Rebaque, "Justin Martyr," 135.

30. Rebaque, "Justin Martyr," 134. Rebaque derives these categories from Antonio Gramsci, *Gli intellettuali el'organizzazzione della cultura*, 8th ed. (Torino: Giulio Einaudi Editore, 1969).

31. Rebaque, "Justin Martyr," 135. Rebaque recognizes that between these intellectual poles of organic and traditional, there are various kinds of freelance philosophers who are independent and only loosely connected with any particular religious or social group.

32. Annewies van den Hoek, "The 'Catechetical' School of Early Christian Alexandria and Its Philonic Heritage," *Harvard Theological Review* 90 (1997): 76.

33. Wilken, *Christians as the Romans Saw Them*, 101.

34. Justin recounts his conversion in the opening chapters of his *Dialogue with Trypho*. See Justin, *Dial.* 1–8.

35. L. William Countryman, "The Intellectual Role of the Early Catholic Episcopate," *Church History* 48 (1979): 262.

36. Countryman, "Intellectual Role," 261–62.

37. Countryman, "Intellectual Role," 263, 266.

38. Origen, *Cels.* 6.34.

39. Countryman, "Intellectual Role," 267.

40. His contribution is forever tainted by the reception of his thought and condemnation at the sixth ecumenical council. That council was politically complex, and the council was more focused on condemning the reception of his thought in later figures. See Donald Fairbairn and Ryan M. Reeves, *The Story of Creeds and Confessions: Tracing the Development of the Christian Faith* (Grand Rapids: Baker Academic, 2019), 147–49.

41. Peter W. Martens, *Origen and Scripture: The Contours of the Exegetical Life* (Oxford: Oxford University Press, 2012), 25.

42. Martens, *Origen and Scripture*, 33.

43. Origen, *Cels.* 3.49.

44. Eusebius, *Hist. eccl.* 6.3.3; 6.18.

45. Eusebius, *Hist. eccl.* 6.18.3.

46. Gregory, *Orat. paneg.* 78–80.

47. Gregory, *Orat. paneg.* 83–86.

48. Adolf von Harnack, *Mission and Expansion of Christianity in the First Three Centuries*, trans. James Moffatt (New York: Putnam's Sons, 1905), 2:183–239.

49. Gregory, *Orat. paneg.* 182.

50. Origen, *Philoc.* 13.4

51. Origen, *Cels.* 3.58.

52. Origen, *Cels.* 4.1.

53. David Satran, *In the Image of Origen: Eros, Virtue, and Constraint in the Early Christian Academy* (Oakland: University of California Press, 2018), 56.

54. Origen, *Cels.* 6.7.

55. Origen, *Cels.* 6.8; Plato, *Ep.* 344b.

56. Gregory, *Orat. paneg.* 7, 14.

57. See discussion of the rule of faith in chapter 2.

58. John Behr, "Introduction," in *Origen: On First Principles; A Reader's Edition* (Oxford: Oxford University Press, 2019), xlvii.

59. Origen, *Philoc.* 13.1, 2.

60. Frances Young, *Biblical Exegesis and the Formation of Christian Culture* (Cambridge: Cambridge University Press, 1997), 50, 51, 54.

61. Young, *Biblical Exegesis*, 70. Others stress the dominance of the "oppositional" attitude of early Christian apologists in the second and third centuries. See Mark Edwards, Martin Goodman, and Simon Price, eds., "Introduction: Apologetics in the Roman World," in *Apologetics in the Roman Empire: Pagans, Jews, and Christians* (Oxford: Oxford University Press, 1999), 6.

62. Young, *Biblical Exegesis*, 292.

63. Origen, *Cels.* 3.75.

64. Gregory, *Orat. paneg.* 13.

65. Gregory, *Orat. paneg.* 14.

66. Gregory, *Orat. paneg.* 14.

67. Gregory, *Orat. paneg.* 14.

68. Origen, *Ep. Greg.* 1.

69. Origen, *Cels.* 4.1.

70. Gregory, *Orat. paneg.* 13.

71. Gregory, *Orat. paneg.* 9–15.

72. Gregory, *Orat. paneg.* 9.

73. Origen, *Cels.* 8.17.

74. Carl Vernon Harris, *Origen of Alexandria's Interpretation of the Teacher's Function in the Early Christian Hierarchy and Community* (New York: American, 1966), 196.

75. Origen, *Hom. Ps.* 3.6. This is a homily on Ps 36.

76. Minucius Felix, *Oct.* 38.

77. Cyprian, *Pat.* 3.

78. Alan Kreider, *The Patient Ferment of the Early Church: The Improbable Rise of Christianity in the Roman Empire* (Grand Rapids: Baker, 2016), 13–14.

79. Presley, "Origen on Preaching," in *A Legacy of Preaching: Apostles of the Revivalists*, ed. Benjamin K. Forrest et al. (Grand Rapids: Zondervan, 2018), 81–94.

80. Gregory, *Orat. paneg.* 12.

81. Satran, *In the Image of Origen*, 93.

82. Wilken, *Christians as the Romans Saw Them*, 126, 154.

83. Eusebius, *Hist. eccl.* 6.18.2; 6.19.6.

84. Martens, *Origen and Scripture*, 37. Epiphanius would make a similar charge that Origen mingled Greek philosophy with Christianity, but from the opposite perspective (*Pan.* 64.72).

85. Martens, *Origen and Scripture*, 39.

86. For example, Daniel Aleshire describes the current transitions happening in theological education and argues that in the coming years, theological education will need to become more focused on formation and cultivate spiritual and moral integrity. See Daniel O. Aleshire, *Beyond Profession: The Next Future of Theological Education* (Grand Rapids: Eerdmans, 2021).

87. G. R. Boys-Stones, *Post-Hellenistic Philosophy: A Study of Its Development from the Stoics to Origen* (New York: Oxford University Press, 2001).

88. Boys-Stones, *Post-Hellenistic Philosophy*, 154.

89. Larry W. Hurtado, *Destroyer of the Gods: Early Christian Distinctiveness in the Roman World* (Waco, TX: Baylor University Press, 2016), 9. See Hurtado's discussion in the appendix for a fuller explanation (191–96).

90. Hurtado, *Destroyer of the Gods*, 9, 193.

91. Tertullian, *Apol.* 19, 46, 47.

92. Justin, *Dial.* 8.

93. Origen, *Ep. Greg.* 3.

94. Tertullian, *Praescr.* 6.

95. Origen, *Comm. cant.* 3.4.

96. Boys-Stones, *Post-Hellenistic Philosophy*, 158.

97. E. Glenn Hinson, *The Evangelization of the Roman Empire: Identity and Adaptability* (Macon, GA: Mercer University Press, 1981), 61–63.

98. Clement of Alexandria, *Protr.* 5.8; Lactantius, *Inst.* 4.5.

99. Justin, *2 Apol.* 10, 13; *Dial.* 7.2. See also Lactantius, *Inst.* 4.6.

100. Justin, *1 Apol.* 45, 59–60. See also Theophilus, *Autol.* 3.20–30 and Lactantius, *Inst.* 4.5.

101. Young, *Biblical Exegesis*, 69.

102. Origen, *Cels.* 3.13. Origen supposes that Celsus has confused Christians with gnostics or some other sect that has deviated from the church's teaching.

103. Boys-Stones, *Post-Hellenistic Philosophy*, 202.

104. Tertullian, *Apol.* 47.

105. Augustine, *Civ.* 8.11; *Doctr. chr.* 2.43.

106. Boys-Stones, *Post-Hellenistic Philosophy*, 192.

107. Minucius Felix, *Oct.* 34.5.

108. Justin, *2 Apol.* 10.2; *1 Apol.* 44.8–10; 46.3.

109. Theophilus, *Autol.* 2.8.

110. Boys-Stones, *Post-Hellenistic Philosophy*, 200–201.

111. Wayne A. Meeks, *The Origins of Christian Morality: The First Two Centuries* (New Haven: Yale University Press, 1993), 20–21.

112. Aristides, *Apol.* 15.

113. Tertullian, *Apol.* 36, 39.

CHAPTER 4

1. This story is recorded in Tertullian, *The Crown* (*Cor.*), which was composed in the early third century.

2. Tertullian, *Cor.* 1.

3. Tertullian, *Cor.* 1.4.

4. Keith Hopkins, *A World Full of Gods: The Strange Triumph of Christianity* (New York: Plume, 2001), 76.

5. Tertullian, *Cor.* 3. The sign of the cross was a common way of symbolically marking out the Christian, and Tertullian presents one of the earliest references. See Bruce W. Longenecker, *The Cross before Constantine: The Early Life of a Christian Symbol* (Minneapolis: Fortress, 2015); Robin M. Jensen, *The Cross: History, Art, and Controversy* (Cambridge: Harvard University Press, 2017), 36; Ildar Garipzanov, *Graphic Signs of Authority in Late Antiquity and the Early Middle Ages* (Oxford: Oxford University Press, 2018), 81–82.

6. See discussion of the symbol of the cross in Justin Martyr, *1 Apol.* 55, 60; Irenaeus, *Epid.* 34.

7. Tertullian *Apol.* 36.4, 8. In another place, Theophilus of Antioch tells us that "the whole world is filled with inhabitants" (*Autol.* 2.32).

8. Tertullian, *Apol.* 1.

9. A. D. Nock, *Conversion: The Old and the New in Religion from Alexander the Great to Augustine of Hippo* (Oxford: Oxford University Press, 1933), 212.

10. Robin Lane Fox, *Pagans and Christians: In the Mediterranean World from the*

Second Century A.D. to the Conversion of Constantine (Harmondsworth: Penguin, 1988), 22.

11. Alan L. Hayes, "Christian Ministry in Three Cities of the Western Empire (160–258 C.E.)," in *Community Formation in the Early Church and in the Church Today*, ed. Richard N. Longenecker (Peabody, MA: Hendrickson, 2002), 131–32.

12. Tertullian, *Apol.* 31; Minucius Felix, *Oct.* 8.

13. Aristides, *Apol.* 15.

14. Wayne A. Meeks, *The Origins of Christian Morality: The First Two Centuries* (New Haven: Yale University Press, 1993), 12.

15. David L. Sam, "Acculturation: Conceptual Background and Core Components," in *The Cambridge Handbook of Acculturation Psychology Account*, ed. John W. Berry and David L. Sam (Cambridge: Cambridge University Press, 2005), 11.

16. Meeks, *Origins of Christian Morality*, 109.

17. See, for example, Clement of Alexandria, *Strom.* 3.26.2; 3.81.2; 4.30.4; 7.71.6; Irenaeus, *Haer.* 3.8.1; Tertullian, *Cor.* 1.1; 12.4–5; *Idol.* 12.2; 19.2; *Spect.* 26.4.

18. Tertullian, *Fug.* 11.

19. Donald K. McKim, *The Westminster Dictionary of Theological Terms*, 2nd ed. (Louisville: Westminster John Knox, 2014), 89.

20. Meeks, *Origins of Christian Morality*, 110.

21. Did. 12.1–5.

22. The Didache also mentions these kinds of initial interviews. See Did. 12.

23. Hippolytus, *Trad. ap.* 15.1–3.

24. Tertullian, *Idol.* 11.

25. Rowan A. Greer, *Broken Lights and Mended Lives: Theology and Common Life in the Early Church* (University Park: Pennsylvania State University Press, 1991), vii.

26. E. Glenn Hinson, *The Evangelization of the Roman Empire: Identity and Adaptability* (Macon, GA: Mercer University Press, 1981), 49.

27. Rodney Stark, *The Rise of Christianity: How the Obscure, Marginal Jesus Movement Became the Dominant Religious Force in the Western World in a Few Centuries* (New York: HarperOne, 1996), 211.

28. Hopkins, *World Full of Gods*, 77.

29. Greer, *Broken Lights*, 205.

30. Tertullian, *Cor.* 2.

31. David E. Wilhite, "The Spirit of Prophecy," in *Tertullian and Paul*, vol. 1, ed. Todd D. Still and David E. Wilhite (New York: T&T Clark, 2013), 66.

32. Tertullian, *Exh. cast.* 10.4–6; *Virg.* 1.5–6; *Mon.* 1.5; 2.1–2; *Jejun.* 1.2; 17.1; *Pud.* 1.20. See also *Or.* 6.2–3; *Marc.* 5.8.12.

33. Tertullian, *Cor.* 4.

34. Tertullian, *Marc.* 4.17.

35. Robert M. Grant, *Early Christianity and Society* (London: Collins, 1978), 85. For a list of professions, see Jerome Carcopino, *Daily Life in Ancient Rome,* 2nd ed. (New Haven, Yale University Press, 2003), 178–80.

36. Carcopino, *Daily Life,* 171–72, 174.

37. Hippolytus, *Trad. ap.* 16.

38. Martin Hengel, *Property and Riches in the Early Church* (Minneapolis: Fortress, 1974), 61.

39. Hengel, *Property and Riches,* 60.

40. Tertullian, *Apol.* 43.

41. Did. 12.

42. Tertullian, *Idol.* 8, 10.

43. Carcopino, *Daily Life,* 183–84, 202–3, 205.

44. Kyle Harper, *From Shame to Sin: The Christian Transformation of Sexual Morality in Late Antiquity* (Cambridge: Harvard University Press, 2013), 53.

45. Carcopino, *Daily Life,* 206.

46. Christopher A. Hall, *Living Wisely with the Church Fathers* (Downers Grove, IL: InterVarsity Press, 2017), 195, 199.

47. Theophilus, *Autol.* 3.15; Athenagoras, *Leg.* 35.

48. Tertullian, *Spect.* 13, 15–19.

49. Cyprian, *Don.* 7.

50. Cyprian, *Don.* 7–8.

51. Lactantius, *Inst.* 6.28.

52. Lactantius, *Inst.* 6.28.

53. Hall, *Living Wisely,* 205.

54. Cyprian, *Don.* 8.

55. Clement of Alexandria, *Paed.* 11.

56. Minucius Felix, *Oct.* 37.

57. Hall, *Living Wisely,* 205.

58. Minucius Felix, *Oct.* 37.

59. Theophilus, *Autol.* 15.

60. Tertullian, *Spect.* 1.

61. John Helgeland, "Christians and Military Service, A.D. 173–337," *Church History* 43 (1974): 149–200.

62. Adolf von Harnack, *Militia Christi: The Christian Religion and the Military in the First Three Centuries* (Philadelphia: Fortress, 1981), 104.

63. Tertullian, *Apol.* 42.

64. Tertullian, *Apol.* 5. See also Eusebius, *Hist. eccl.* 5.5.

65. Origen, *Cels.* 8.68.

66. Hippolytus, *Trad. ap.* 16.

67. Harnack, *Militia Christi*, 65. See also Ronald J. Sider, *The Early Church on Killing: A Comprehensive Sourcebook on War, Abortion, and Capital Punishment* (Grand Rapids: Baker Academic, 2012), 168.

68. Sider, *Early Church on Killing*, 171–73. Sider also cites the way Christ fulfilled the messianic prophecies of coming peace (73–75).

69. Minucius Felix, *Oct.* 30.

70. Athenagoras, *Leg.* 35.

71. Origen, *Cels.* 3.7.

72. Tertullian, *Spect.* 2; Tertullian, *Pat.* 3; Tertullian, *Pud.* 12; Cyprian, *Don.* 6–7; Cyprian, *Pat.* 14; Cyprian, *Letters* 55–56; Archelaus, *Disp.* 2; Arnobius, *Adv. nat.* 1.6; Lactantius, *Inst.* 1.18; 3.18; 5.8–10; 6.6, 20.

73. Origen, *Cels.* 8.73.

74. Tertullian, *Cor.* 11.

75. Tertullian, *Idol.* 19.

76. Tertullian, *Cor.* 11.

77. Origen, *Cels.* 5.33.

78. Hall, *Living Wisely*, 129, 131.

79. Harper, *From Shame to Sin*, 7, 8.

80. Geoffrey Nathan, *The Family in Late Antiquity: The Rise of Christianity and the Endurance of Tradition* (New York: Routledge, 2000), 15.

81. Carcopino, *Daily Life*, 77, 85, 89–90, 95–97.

82. Nathan, *Family in Late Antiquity*, 19, 39.

83. Nathan, *Family in Late Antiquity*, 39, 41, 53.

84. Justin, *2 Apol.* 1.

85. Minucius Felix, *Oct.* 31.

86. Aristides, *Apol.* 15.

87. Tertullian, *Ux.* 1.5; *Exh. cast.* 9.

88. Nathan, *Family in Late Antiquity*, 45.

89. Tertullian, *Ux.* 8.

90. Hippolytus, *Trad. ap.* 15.

91. Greer, *Broken Lights*, 106.

92. Steven J. Friesen, "Injustice or God's Will: Early Christian Explanations of Poverty," in *Wealth and Poverty in Early Church and Society,* ed. Susan R. Holman (Grand Rapids: Baker Academic, 2008), 17, 19–20.

93. Lucian, *Peregr.* 13.

94. Julian the Apostate, *Letters* 3.2–235.

95. Greer, *Broken Lights,* 123.

96. Eusebius, *Hist. eccl.* 4.23.10.

97. Greer, *Broken Lights,* 117, 120.

98. Fox, *Pagans and Christians,* 309.

99. Justin, *1 Apol.* 67.

100. Greer, *Broken Lights,* 120.

101. Meeks, *Origins of Christian Morality,* 108.

102. Justin, *1 Apol.* 67.

103. Edward Gibbon, *History of the Decline and Fall of the Roman Empire* (New York: Fred DeFau, 1906), 2:322–25. See also Rodney Stark, *The Triumph of Christianity: How the Jesus Movement Became the World's Largest Religion* (New York: HarperOne, 2011), 112–19.

104. Tertullian, *Apol.* 39.

105. Hopkins, *World Full of Gods,* 78.

CHAPTER 5

1. This opening section draws on Bryan M. Litfin, *Early Christian Martyr Stories: An Evangelical Introduction with New Translations* (Grand Rapids: Baker Academic, 2014), 71–85.

2. The early church historian Eusebius preserved their letter for us. See Eusebius, *Hist. eccl.* 5.1.1–63.

3. Aristotle, *Poet.* 5.1.

4. Ernst Breisach, *Historiography: Ancient, Medieval, and Modern* (Chicago: University of Chicago Press, 2007), 77.

5. Steven D. Smith, *Pagans and Christians in the City: Culture Wars from the Tiber to the Potomac* (Grand Rapids: Eerdmans, 2018), 185.

6. Robin Lane Fox, *The Classical World: An Epic History from Homer to Hadrian* (New York: Basic Books, 2006), 47.

7. Smith, *Pagans and Christians,* 189–90; 1 Cor 2:9.

8. Robin Lane Fox, *Pagans and Christians: In the Mediterranean World from the Second Century A.D. to the Conversion of Constantine* (Harmondsworth: Penguin, 1988), 265.

9. John Dillon, *The Middle Platonists: 80 B.C. to A.D. 220* (Ithaca, NY: Cornell University Press, 1996), 132.

10. Marcus Aurelius, *Med.* 2.15; 4.21.

11. Tertullian, *Apol.* 47.

12. Origen, *Cels.* 2.5; 6.34; 7.32–33; Lucian, *Peregr.* 13.

13. Tertullian, *Apol.* 47.

14. Tertullian, *Apol.* 39.

15. Brian E. Daley, *The Hope of the Early Church: A Handbook of Patristic Eschatology* (Grand Rapids: Baker Academic, 2010), 20.

16. Wayne A. Meeks, *The Origins of Christian Morality: The First Two Centuries* (New Haven: Yale University Press, 1993), 210.

17. J. N. D. Kelly, *Early Christian Doctrines* (New York: HarperCollins, 1978), 461.

18. Irenaeus, *Haer.* 1.10.1.

19. Daley, *Hope of the Early Church*, 29. See also Stephen O. Presley, "Biblical Theology and the Unity of Scripture in Irenaeus of Lyons," *Criswell Theological Review* 16 (2019): 3–24.

20. Meeks, *Origins of Christian Morality*, 191.

21. Augustine, *Catech.* 3.

22. The second half of the *City of God* provides the full narrative.

23. There are certainly patristic writers that emphasize a realized form of eschatology, but in the second century, the kingdom of God is a future reality for which the community is hoping. See Everett Ferguson, "The Kingdom of God in Early Patristic Literature," in *The Early Church at Work and Worship* (Eugene, OR: Cascade, 2014), 2:186.

24. Theophilus, *Autol.* 2.10–32; 3.23–29

25. Origen, *Cels.* 8.68.

26. Smith, *Pagans and Christians*, 189–90; 1 Cor 2:9.

27. Irenaeus, *Haer.* 5.36.1; 1 Cor 7:31.

28. Irenaeus, *Haer.* 5.36.1. He cites Isa 66:22.

29. Paul Veyne, *When Our World Became Christian* (Malden, MA: Polity, 2010), 29.

30. Matt 22:23; Acts 4:1–2, 33; 17:31–32; 23:6–8.

31. Origen, *Cels.* 5.14; 8.49.

32. Robert Louis Wilken, *Christians as the Romans Saw Them*, 2nd ed. (New Haven: Yale University Press, 2003), 104.

33. Origen, *Cels.* 5.14.

34. Justin, *1 Apol.* 18; Matt 19:26.

35. Justin, *1 Apol.* 19.

36. *The Acts of Justin and His Companions* is also known as "The Martyrdom of Saints Justin, Chariton, Charito, Euelpistos, Hierax, Paion, Liberian and Their Comrades." See Litfin, *Early Christian Martyr Stories*, 66–69.

37. *The Acts of Justin and His Companions.*

38. Justin, *1 Apol.* 2.

39. Irenaeus, *Haer.* 4.38.3; 5.1–15.

40. Daley, *Hope of the Early Church*, 29–30.

41. Irenaeus, *Haer.* 4.39.2; Ps 45:11.

42. Pol. *Phil.* 7.

43. Theophilus, *Autol.* 1.13.

44. Daley, *Hope of the Early Church*, 23.

45. Athenagoras, *Res.* 2.

46. Athenagoras, *Res.* 25. See also Athenagoras, *Leg.* 31.

47. Irenaeus, *Haer.* 4.38.3.

48. Matthew C. Steenberg, *Of God and Man: Theology as Anthropology from Irenaeus to Athanasius* (New York: T&T Clark, 2009), 43.

49. Steenberg, *Of God and Man*, 42. See Irenaeus, *Haer.* 4.39.2.

50. Daley, *Hope of the Early Church*, 29.

51. Justin, *1 Apol.* 10.

52. Daley, *Hope of the Early Church*, 22.

53. Justin, *1 Apol.* 12, 17, 28, 52, 57; *2 Apol.* 1, 7; *Dial.* 45.

54. Augustine, *Civ.* 22.30.

55. A. D. Nock, *Conversion: The Old and the New in Religion from Alexander the Great to Augustine of Hippo* (Oxford: Oxford University Press, 1933), 246.

56. Augustine, *Catech.* 4.

57. Rowan A. Greer, *Broken Lights and Mended Lives: Theology and Common Life in the Early Church* (University Park: Pennsylvania State University Press, 1991), 205.

58. Daley, *Hope of the Early Church*, 20.

59. Daley, *Hope of the Early Church*, 29. See Irenaeus, *Haer.* 5.8.1.

60. Alasdair MacIntyre, *After Virtue*, 2nd ed. (Notre Dame: University of Notre Dame Press, 1984), 144.

61. Meeks, *Origins of Christian Morality*, 189.

62. Justin, *1 Apol.* 12.

63. 2 Clem. 9.6; 20.2.

64. Justin, *1 Apol.* 12.

65. Origen, *Cels.* 8.74.

66. Diogn. 6.

67. See Meeks, *Origins of Christian Morality*, 175–80.

68. Kelly, *Early Christian Doctrines*, 460.

69. Ramsay MacMullen, *Christianizing the Roman Empire: A.D. 100–400* (New Haven: Yale University Press, 1984), 18.

70. Justin, *1 Apol.* 12.

71. Daley, *Hope of the Early Church*, 23.

72. See Justin, *1 Apol.* 12, 17, 28, 52, 57; *2 Apol.* 1, 7; *Dial.* 45.

73. Justin, *1 Apol.* 12.

74. Justin, *2 Apol.* 1; *1 Apol.* 14.

75. Justin, *1 Apol.* 11, 12, 68.

76. Aristides, *Apol.* 15.

CONCLUSION

1. Henry Chadwick, *The Early Church* (New York: Dorset, 1967), 175.

2. Alasdair MacIntyre, *After Virtue*, 2nd ed. (Notre Dame: University of Notre Dame Press, 1984), 244–45.

3. John D. Caputo, *Radical Hermeneutics: Repetition, Deconstruction, and the Hermeneutic Project* (Bloomington: Indiana University Press, 1987), 243.

4. Charles Taylor, *A Secular Age* (Cambridge: Belknap, 2007), 1–4.

5. Carl R. Trueman, *The Rise and Triumph of the Modern Self: Cultural Amnesia, Expressive Individualism, and the Road to Sexual Revolution* (Wheaton, IL: Crossway, 2020), 46. Trueman builds upon the work of Charles Taylor, who describes the nature of expressive individualism. See Taylor, *Secular Age*, 473.

6. Diogn. 6.

7. Oliver O'Donovan, *The Desire of the Nations* (Cambridge: Cambridge University Press, 1996), 2.

8. Diogn. 6.

9. Diogn. 6.

10. Everett Ferguson, *Baptism in the Early Church: History, Theology, and Liturgy in the First Five Centuries* (Grand Rapids: Eerdmans, 2009), 769.

Bibliography

Aland, Barbara. "Christentum, Bildung und römische Oberschicht: Zum 'Octavius' des Minucius Felix." Pages 11–30 in *Platonismus und Christentum: Festschrift für Heinrich Dörrie*. Edited by H.-D. Blume and F. Mann. Jahrbuch für Antike und Christentum Ergänzungsband 10. Münster: Aschendorff, 1983.

Aleshire, Daniel O. *Beyond Profession: The Next Future of Theological Education*. Grand Rapids: Eerdmans, 2021.

Arnold, Clinton E. "Early Church Catechesis and New Christian's Classes in Contemporary Evangelicalism." *Journal of the Evangelical Theological Society* 47 (2004): 39–54.

Bantu, Vince. *A Multitude of All Peoples: Engaging Ancient Christianity's Global Identity*. Downers Grove, IL: InterVarsity Press, 2020.

Bebbington, David W. *Evangelicalism in Modern Britain: A History from the 1730s to the 1980s*. New York: Routledge, 1989.

Behr, John. "Introduction." Pages xiii–lxxix in *Origen: On First Principles; A Reader's Edition*. Oxford: Oxford University Press, 2019.

———. *Irenaeus of Lyons: Identifying Christianity*. Oxford: Oxford University Press, 2015.

Blowers, Paul M. "The Regula Fidei and the Narrative Character of Early Christian Faith." *Pro Ecclesia* 6 (2007): 199–228.

Bolt, John. "Abraham Kuyper or Saint Benedict? The Challenge of Christian Cultural Discipleship Today: A Review Essay." *Calvin Theological Journal* 54 (2019): 147–64.

Boys-Stones, G. R. *Post-Hellenistic Philosophy: A Study of Its Development from the Stoics to Origen.* New York: Oxford University Press, 2001.

Bradshaw, Paul F. *Early Christian Worship: A Basic Introduction to Ideas and Practice.* Collegeville, MN: Liturgical Press, 2000.

Brandenburg, Hugo. *Ancient Churches of Rome from the Fourth to the Seventh Century: The Dawn of Christian Architecture in the West.* Turnhout: Brepols, 2005.

Breisach, Ernst. *Historiography: Ancient, Medieval, and Modern.* Chicago: University of Chicago Press, 2007.

Briggman, Anthony. *God and Christ in Irenaeus.* Oxford: Oxford University Press, 2019.

Brown, Peter. *Power and Persuasion in Late Antiquity: Towards a Christian Empire.* Madison: University of Wisconsin Press, 1992.

Bullivant, Stephen. *Nonverts: The Making of Ex-Christian America.* New York: Oxford University Press, 2022.

Caputo, John D. *Radical Hermeneutics: Repetition, Deconstruction, and the Hermeneutic Project.* Bloomington: Indiana University Press, 1987.

Chadwick, Henry. *The Early Church.* New York: Dorset, 1967.

Cochrane, Charles Norris. *Christianity and Classical Culture: A Study of Thought and Action from Augustus to Augustine.* New York: Oxford University Press, 1957.

Countryman, L. William. "The Intellectual Role of the Early Catholic Episcopate," *Church History* 48 (1979): 261–68.

Crean, Thomas, and Alan Fimister. *Integralism: A Manual of Political Philosophy.* Heusenstamm: Editiones Scholasticae, 2020.

Crouch, Andy. *Culture Making: Recovering Our Creative Calling.* Downers Grove, IL: InterVarsity Press, 2008.

Crump, David. *I Pledge Allegiance: A Believer's Guide to Kingdom Citizenship in Twenty-First-Century America.* Grand Rapids: Eerdmans, 2018.

Daley, Brian E. *The Hope of the Early Church: A Handbook of Patristic Eschatology.* Grand Rapids: Baker Academic, 2010.

Davis, Raymond, ed. *The Book of Pontiffs* (Liber Pontificalis). 3rd ed. Liverpool: Liverpool University Press, 2001.

Dillon, John. *The Middle Platonists: 80 B.C. to A.D. 220.* Ithaca, NY: Cornell University Press, 1996.

Dreher, Rod. *The Benedict Option: A Strategy for Christians in a Post-Christian Nation*. New York: Sentinel, 2017.

Edgar, William. *Created and Creating: A Biblical Theology of Culture*. Downers Grove, IL: InterVarsity Press, 2016.

Edwards, Mark, Martin Goodman, and Simon Price, eds. "Introduction: Apologetics in the Roman World." Pages 1–13 in *Apologetics in the Roman Empire: Pagans, Jews, and Christians*. Oxford: Oxford University Press, 1999.

Eliot, T. S. "The Idea of a Christian Society." Pages 1–78 in *Christianity and Culture*. New York: Harvest, 1948.

Fairbairn, Donald, and Ryan M. Reeves. *The Story of Creeds and Confessions: Tracing the Development of the Christian Faith*. Grand Rapids: Baker Academic, 2019.

Ferguson, Everett. *Baptism in the Early Church: History, Theology, and Liturgy in the First Five Centuries*. Grand Rapids: Eerdmans, 2009.

———. "Catechesis and Initiation." Pages 18–51 in vol. 2 of *The Early Church at Work and Worship: Catechesis, Baptism, Eschatology, and Martyrdom*. Eugene, OR: Cascade, 2014.

———. *From Christ to the Pre-Reformation*. Vol. 1 of *Church History: The Rise and Growth of the Church in Its Cultural, Intellectual, and Political Context*. 2nd ed. Grand Rapids: Zondervan, 2013.

———. "The Kingdom of God in Early Patristic Literature." Pages 176–99 in vol. 2 of *The Early Church at Work and Worship*. Eugene, OR: Cascade, 2014.

Field, Lester L., Jr. *Liberty, Dominion, Two Swords: On the Origins of Western Political Theology, 180–398*. Notre Dame: University of Notre Dame Press, 1995.

Forster, Greg. *Joy for the World: How Christianity Lost Its Cultural Influence and Can Begin Rebuilding It*. Wheaton, IL: Crossway, 2014.

Fox, Robin Lane. *The Classical World: An Epic History from Homer to Hadrian*. New York: Basic Books, 2006.

———. *Pagans and Christians: In the Mediterranean World from the Second Century A.D. to the Conversion of Constantine*. Harmondsworth: Penguin, 1988.

Garipzanov, Ildar. *Graphic Signs of Authority in Late Antiquity and the Early Middle Ages*. Oxford: Oxford University Press, 2018.

Gay, Peter. *The Enlightenment: The Rise of Modern Paganism*. New York: Norton, 1995.

Geertz, Clifford. "Ethos, World-View, and the Analysis of Sacred Symbols." *Antioch Review* 17 (1957): 622–37.

Georges, Tobias. "The Role of Philosophy and Education in Apologists' Conversion to Christianity: The Case of Justin and Tatian." Pages 271–85 in *Conversion and Initiation in Antiquity: Shifting Identities—Creating Change.* Edited by Birgitte Secher Bøgh. Frankfurt am Main: Lang, 2014.

Gibbon, Edward. *History of the Decline and Fall of the Roman Empire.* Vol. 2. New York: Fred DeFau, 1906.

Goodman, Martin. *Mission and Conversion: Proselytizing in the Religious History of the Roman Empire.* Oxford: Clarendon, 1994.

Gramsci, Antonio. *Gli intellettuali el'organizzazzione della cultura.* 8th ed. Torino: Giulio Einaudi Editore, 1969.

Green, Michael. *Evangelism in the Early Church.* Rev. ed. Grand Rapids: Eerdmans, 2003.

Greer, Rowan A. *Broken Lights and Mended Lives: Theology and Common Life in the Early Church.* University Park: Pennsylvania State University Press, 1991.

Hagglund, Bengt. "Die Bedeutung der 'regula fidei' als Grundlage theologischer Aussagen." *Studia Theologica* 12 (1958): 1–44.

Harnack, Adolf von. *Mission and Expansion of Christianity in the First Three Centuries.* Translated by James Moffatt. Vol. 2. New York: Putnam's Sons, 1905.

Harris, Carl Vernon. *Origen of Alexandria's Interpretation of the Teacher's Function in the Early Christian Hierarchy and Community.* New York: American, 1966.

Hayes, Alan L. "Christian Ministry in Three Cities of the Western Empire (160–258 C.E.)." Pages 129–56 in *Community Formation in the Early Church and in the Church Today.* Edited by Richard N. Longenecker. Peabody, MA: Hendrickson, 2002.

Haynes, Natalie. *The Ancient Guide to the Modern Life.* London: Profile Books, 2012.

Hinson, E. Glenn. *The Evangelization of the Roman Empire: Identity and Adaptability.* Macon, GA: Mercer University Press, 1981.

Hippolytus. *On the Apostolic Tradition.* Introduction and commentary by Alistair Stewart-Sykes. Crestwood, NY: St. Vladimir's Seminary Press, 2001.

Hoek, Annewies van den. "The 'Catechetical' School of Early Christian Alexandria and Its Philonic Heritage." *Harvard Theological Review* 90 (1997): 59–87.

Hopkins, Keith. *A World Full of Gods: The Strange Triumph of Christianity.* New York: Plume, 2001.

Hurtado, Larry W. *Destroyer of the Gods: Early Christian Distinctiveness in the Roman World.* Waco, TX: Baylor University Press, 2016.

Jefford, Clayton N. "Introduction." Pages 1–126 in *The Epistle to Diognetus (with the Fragments of Quadratus): Introduction, Text, and Commentary.* Oxford: Oxford University Press, 2013.

Jenkins, Philip. *The Next Christendom: The Coming of Global Christianity.* 3rd ed. New York: Oxford University Press, 2011.

Jensen, Robin M. *The Cross: History, Art, and Controversy.* Cambridge: Harvard University Press, 2017.

Kelly, J. N. D. *Early Christian Doctrines.* New York: HarperCollins, 1978.

Krautheimer, Richard. *Three Christian Capitals: Topography and Politics.* Berkeley: University of California Press, 1983.

Kreider, Alan. *The Patient Ferment of the Early Church: The Improbable Rise of Christianity in the Roman Empire.* Grand Rapids: Baker, 2016.

Kruger, Michael J. *Christianity at the Crossroads: How the Second Century Shaped the Future of the Church.* Downers Grove, IL: InterVarsity Press, 2018.

Lane, Melissa. *Eco-Republic: What the Ancients Can Teach Us about Ethics, Virtue, and Sustainable Living.* Princeton: Princeton University Press, 2012.

Lashier, Jackson. *Irenaeus and the Trinity.* Leiden: Brill, 2014.

Lewis, C. S. Introduction to *On the Incarnation: Saint Athanasius.* Popular Patristics Series. Yonkers: St. Vladimir's Seminary Press, 2012.

Litfin, Bryan M. *Early Christian Martyr Stories: An Evangelical Introduction with New Translations.* Grand Rapids: Baker Academic, 2014.

Longenecker, Bruce W. *The Cross before Constantine: The Early Life of a Christian Symbol.* Minneapolis: Fortress, 2015.

MacIntyre, Alasdair. *After Virtue.* 2nd ed. Notre Dame: University of Notre Dame Press, 1984.

MacMullen, Ramsay. *Christianizing the Roman Empire: A.D. 100–400.* New Haven: Yale University Press, 1984.

Markschies, Christoph. *Christian Theology and Its Institutions in the Early Roman Empire: Prolegomena to a History of Early Christian Theology.* Waco, TX: Baylor University Press, 2015.

———. *Gnosis: An Introduction.* Translated by John Bowden. London: T&T Clark, 2003.

Martens, Peter W. *Origen and Scripture: The Contours of the Exegetical Life.* Oxford: Oxford University Press, 2012.

McKim, Donald K. *The Westminster Dictionary of Theological Terms.* 2nd ed. Louisville: Westminster John Knox, 2014.

Meeks, Wayne A. *The Origins of Christian Morality: The First Two Centuries*. New Haven: Yale University Press, 1993.

Miller, Maureen. *The Bishop's Palace: Architecture and Authority in Medieval Italy*. Ithaca, NY: Cornell University Press, 2000.

Mount, Ferdinand. *Full Circle: How the Classical World Came Back to Us*. New York: Simon & Schuster, 2010.

Nock, A. D. *Conversion: The Old and the New in Religion from Alexander the Great to Augustine of Hippo*. Oxford: Oxford University Press, 1933.

Noll, Mark A. *Jesus Christ and the Life of the Mind*. Grand Rapids: Eerdmans, 2011.

———. *The Scandal of the Evangelical Mind*. Grand Rapids: Eerdmans, 1995.

O'Donovan, Oliver. *The Desire of the Nations*. Cambridge: Cambridge University Press, 1996.

Osborn, Eric. *Ethical Patterns in Early Christian Thought*. Cambridge: Cambridge University Press, 1976.

Pieper, Josef. *The Four Cardinal Virtues: Prudence, Justice, Fortitude, Temperance*. Notre Dame: University of Notre Dame Press, 1966.

Presley, Stephen O. "Biblical Theology and the Unity of Scripture in Irenaeus of Lyons." *Criswell Theological Review* 16 (2019): 3–24.

———. "Scripture and Tradition." Pages 71–88 in *Historical Theology for the Church*. Edited by Jason G. Duesing and Nathan A. Finn. Nashville: Broadman & Holman, 2021.

Provance, Brett Scott. *Pocket Dictionary of Liturgy and Worship*. Downers Grove, IL: InterVarsity Press, 2010.

Rahner, Hugo. *Church and State in Early Christianity*. San Francisco: Ignatius, 1992.

Rambo, Lewis R. *Understanding Religious Conversion*. New Haven: Yale University Press, 1993.

Rebaque, Fernando Rivas. "Justin Martyr as an Organic Christian Intellectual in Rome." Pages 134–57 in *Christian Teachers in Second-Century Rome: Schools and Students in the Ancient City*. Edited by H. Gregory Snyder. Leiden: Brill, 2020.

Sam, David L. "Acculturation: Conceptual Background and Core Components." Pages 11–26 in *The Cambridge Handbook of Acculturation Psychology Account*. Edited by John W. Berry and David L. Sam. Cambridge: Cambridge University Press, 2005.

Satran, David. *In the Image of Origen: Eros, Virtue, and Constraint in the Early Christian Academy*. Oakland: University of California Press, 2018.

Sittser, Gerald L. *Resilient Faith: How the Early Christian "Third Way" Changed the World*. Grand Rapids: Brazos, 2019.

Smith, James K. A. *Desiring the Kingdom: Worship, Worldview, and Cultural Formation*. Grand Rapids: Baker Academic, 2009.

Smith, Steven D. *Pagans and Christians in the City: Culture Wars from the Tiber to the Potomac*. Grand Rapids: Eerdmans, 2018.

Stark, Rodney. *The Rise of Christianity: How the Obscure, Marginal Jesus Movement Became the Dominant Religious Force in the Western World in a Few Centuries*. New York: HarperOne, 1996.

Steenberg, Matthew C. *Of God and Man: Theology as Anthropology from Irenaeus to Athanasius*. New York: T&T Clark, 2009.

Stewart(-Sykes), Alistair. *On the Two Ways: Life or Death, Light or Darkness; Foundational Texts in the Tradition*. Yonkers: St. Vladimir's Seminary Press, 2011.

Taylor, Charles. *A Secular Age*. Cambridge: Belknap, 2007.

Thayer, David Tyler. "The Lateran Baptistery: Memory, Space, and Baptism." Master's thesis, University of Tennessee, 2012.

Trueman, Carl R. *The Rise and Triumph of the Modern Self: Cultural Amnesia, Expressive Individualism, and the Road to Sexual Revolution*. Wheaton, IL: Crossway, 2020.

VanDrunen, David. *Politics after Christendom: Political Theology in a Fractured World*. Grand Rapids: Zondervan Academic, 2020.

Veyne, Paul. *When Our World Became Christian*. Malden, MA: Polity, 2010.

Walls, Andrew F. *The Missionary Movement in Christian History: Studies in the Transmission of Faith*. Maryknoll, NY: Orbis Books, 1996.

Wells, Samuel. *Improvisation: The Drama of Christian Ethics*. London: SPCK, 2004.

Wilhite, David E. "The Spirit of Prophecy." Pages 45–71 in vol. 1 of *Tertullian and Paul*. Edited by Todd D. Still and David E. Wilhite. New York: T&T Clark, 2013.

Wilken, Robert Louis. "Christianity Face to Face with Islam." *First Things*, January 2009. https://www.firstthings.com/article/2009/01/christianity-face-to-face-with-islam.

———. *Christians as the Romans Saw Them*. 2nd ed. New Haven: Yale University Press, 2003.

———. *Liberty in the Things of God: The Christian Origins of Religious Freedom*. New Haven: Yale University Press, 2019.

————. *The Spirit of Early Christian Thought: Seeking the Face of God*. New Haven: Yale University Press, 2003.

Williams, Paul. *Exiles on Mission: How Christians Can Thrive in a Post-Christian World*. Grand Rapids: Baker, 2020.

Wilsey, John D. *American Exceptionalism and Civil Religion: Reassessing the History of an Idea*. Downers Grove, IL: InterVarsity Press, 2015.

Wilson, Jonathan. *Living Faithfully in a Fragmented World: From* After Virtue *to a New Monasticism*. Eugene, OR: Cascade, 2010.

Wolfe, Stephen. *The Case for Christian Nationalism*. Moscow, ID: Canon, 2022.

Young, Frances. *The Art of Performance: Towards a Theology of Holy Scripture*. London: Darton, Longman, & Todd, 1990.

————. *Biblical Exegesis and the Formation of Christian Culture*. Cambridge: Cambridge University Press, 1997.

Zimmermann, Jens. *Incarnational Humanism: A Philosophy of Culture for the Church in the World*. Downers Grove, IL: InterVarsity Press, 2012.

Index of Names and Subjects

Index of Scripture
and Other Ancient Sources